Lecture Notes in Computer Science 16424

Founding Editors

Gerhard Goos
Juris Hartmanis

Series Editors

Elisa Bertino, *Purdue University, West Lafayette, IN, USA*
Wen Gao, *Peking University, Beijing, China*
Bernhard Steffen, *TU Dortmund University, Dortmund, Germany*
Moti Yung, *Columbia University, New York, NY, USA*

The series Lecture Notes in Computer Science (LNCS), including its subseries Lecture Notes in Artificial Intelligence (LNAI) and Lecture Notes in Bioinformatics (LNBI), has established itself as a medium for the publication of new developments in Computer Science research, teaching, and education.

The series enjoys close cooperation with the international research community, publishing the proceedings of many prestigious conferences and collaborating with important societies.

Proposals

A conference or workshop applying for publication in LNCS should have an international program committee, a coherent subject scope limited to related computer science topics, and an appropriate plan for reviewing the submitted papers. To submit a proposal to LNCS please contact lncs@springer.com.

Publishing Service

LNCS offers a full publishing service, including typesetting of papers, making most content available in PDF, HTML, print, and ePub formats. Authors can embed videos in their content, or add electronic supplementary material to be made available in our digital library (SpringerLink).

Open Access

Conference organisers may opt for gold open access of all content in proceedings volumes. Alternatively individual author teams may select gold open access for their proceedings papers. Please contact lncs@springer.com to enquire about terms.

Societies, Communities

LNCS cooperates with prestigious computer science societies and communities, publishing the proceedings of flagship conferences across all major fields. Among the events and associations are ECCV (European Conference on Computer Vision), IACR (International Association for Cryptologic Research), MICCAI (Medical Image Computing and Computer Assisted Intervention Society), the China Computer Federation (CCF), DASFAA (International Conference on Database Systems for Advanced Applications), PRICAI (Pacific Rim International Conference on Artificial Intelligence), IFIP (International Federation for Information Processing), ETAPS (International Joint Conferences on Theory and Practice of Software), ECML PKDD (European Conf. on Machine Learning and Principles and Practice of Knowledge Discovery in Databases), and IAPR (International Association for Pattern Recognition).

Indexing and Distribution

LNCS submits the content and bibliographic metadata of proceedings volumes to the major abstracting and indexing services, including the Conference Proceedings Citation Index (CPCI, part of Clarivate Analytics' Web of Science), DBLP, Scopus, the EI Engineering (Compendex, Inspec), the ACM Digital Library, and Google Scholar. In addition to the indexing services listed above, Springer Nature content is available worldwide through key university and industry library subscription access, and through major distributors such as Amazon and Google Books.

Sublines

The **Formal Methods** subline (https://link.springer.com/series/15554) was established in cooperation with the Formal Methods Europe association, publishing proceedings and tutorials associated with high-quality events. The Advanced Research in Computing and Software Science (**ARCoSS**) subline was established in cooperation with the European Association for Theoretical Computer Science (EATCS) and the International Joint Conferences on Theory and Practice of Software (ETAPS), and it publishes proceedings of high-quality events in theoretical computer science and foundations of programming.

Special Collections

LNCS includes contributed edited works such as **Festschrifts**, dedicated to individuals who have made excellent contributions to the field of computer science, **State-of-the-Art Surveys**, and **Tutorials**. Please contact lncs@springer.com for further details about any of these volume types.

Transactions

We publish the LNCS Transactions in Large-Scale Data- and Knowledge-Centered Systems and the LNCS Transactions in Petri Nets and Other Models of Concurrency (ToPNoC). Please contact lncs@springer.com for further details.

SharedIt

Springer Nature can make shareable links to online PDFs of published proceedings papers available to authors. This encourages reading by users who otherwise don't have subscription access (for example, via a university library). These shareable links can be communicated via social channels, on institutional repositories, on author websites, or on scholarly collaborative networks.

Overleaf

The LaTeX2e Proceedings Templates are available in the scientific authoring platform Overleaf.

Other Benefits of Publishing

By default, conference **organisers and authors are not charged** for publishing in LNCS. Organisers and participants get **free online access** to the SpringerLink-published papers for 4 weeks during and following the conference. LNCS offers readers transparent reviewing data about all published volumes. Authors retain copyright to their papers and **authors can self-archive** their submitted papers. For more information on publishing service and conditions, please contact lncs@springer.com.

Publishing Policies

We require volume editors (conference organisers), authors of proceedings papers, and reviewers engaged to evaluate papers submitted to conferences to follow our publishing policies and respective codes of conduct (https://www.springernature.com/gp/policies/book-publishing-policies).

LNCS Editors

Elisa Bertino (Purdue University), Wen Gao (Peking University), Bernhard Steffen (TU Dortmund), and Moti Yung (Google and Columbia University).

LNAI (Lecture Notes in Artificial Intelligence)

This subseries (https://link.springer.com/series/1244) was established in 1988 as a topical subseries of LNCS devoted to artificial intelligence. The editors are Wolfgang Wahlster (DFKI, Berlin), Randy Goebel (University of Alberta, Edmonton), and Zhi-Hua Zhou (Nanjing University).

LNBI (Lecture Notes in Bioinformatics)

This subseries (https://link.springer.com/series/5381) was established in 2003 as a topical subseries of LNCS devoted to bioinformatics and computational systems biology. The editors are Sorin Istrail (Brown University), Pavel Pevzner (University of California, San Diego) and Michael Waterman (University of Southern California).

Selma Boumerdassi · Nour El-Houda Yellas ·
Éric Renault

Editors

Machine Learning for Networking

8th International Conference, MLN 2025
Paris, France, December 2–4, 2025
Revised Selected Papers

 Springer

Editors
Selma Boumerdassi
Université Paris 8
Saint-Denis, France

Nour El-Houda Yellas
Télécom SudParis
Évry-Courcouronnes, France

Éric Renault
ESIEE Paris—Gustave Eiffel University
Noisy-le-Grand, France

ISSN 0302-9743　　　　ISSN 1611-3349 (electronic)
Lecture Notes in Computer Science
ISBN 978-3-032-18493-1　　ISBN 978-3-032-18494-8 (eBook)
https://doi.org/10.1007/978-3-032-18494-8

Preface

The rapid development of new network infrastructures and services has led to the generation of huge amounts of data, and machine learning now appears to be the best solution to process these data and make the right decisions for network management. The International Conference on Machine Learning for Networking (MLN) aims to provide a top forum for researchers and practitioners to present and discuss new trends in machine learning, deep learning, pattern recognition, and optimization for network architectures and services. This year, MLN 2025 was hosted by INRIA Paris, France, and jointly organized by ESIEE Paris, Télécom SudParis, Laboratoire d'Informatique Gaspar Monge (LIGM), and Université Paris 8 Vincennes—Saint-Denis.

The call for papers resulted in a total of 30 submissions from all around the world: Canada, France, Morocco, Nigeria, Pakistan, South Africa, Sweden, and Tunisia. All submissions were assigned to at least three members of the technical program committee for review in a double-blind process. The program committee decided to accept 14 papers. One invited paper was also presented.

The paper *Slotted Reinforcement Learning-based radio resource allocation in sliced 5G networks* by Gauthier Meffe, Philippe Owezarski, and Pascal Berthou (Université de Toulouse, France) was awarded the prize for the best paper.

Six keynotes completed the program: *Challenges towards in-network learning: algorithms and systems* by Stefano Secci (Conservatoire National des Arts et Métiers, France), *Closed Loop Automation System for B5G and 6G networks* by Nour El-Houda Yellas (Télécom SudParis, France), *Artificial Intelligence for Digital Twin in Wireless Systems* by Mohsen Guizani (Mohamed Bin Zayed University of Artificial Intelligence, Abu Dhabi, UAE), *Optimizing UAV-Based Applications through the Convergence of IoT, ITS, and AI* by Saadi Boudjit (University of Rouen Normandy, France), *Graph Neural Networks for Scalable Network Optimization* by Yassine Hadjadj Aoul (University of Rennes, France) and *CupCarbon Klaines: A Platform to Design Agentic AI for Next Generation Smart Cities* by Ahcene Bounceur (University of Sharjah, UAE).

We would like to thank all who contributed to the success of this conference, in particular the members of the Program Committee and the reviewers for carefully reviewing the contributions and selecting a high-quality program. Our special thanks go to the members of the Organizing Committee for their great help.

We hope that all participants enjoyed this successful conference.

Selma Boumerdassi
Nour El-Houda Yellas
General Chairs

Éric Renault
TPC Chair

Organization

General Chairs

Selma Boumerdassi — Université Paris 8 Vincennes—Saint-Denis, France

Nour El-Houda Yellas — Télécom SudParis, France

Technical Program Chair

Éric Renault — ESIEE Paris—Université Gustave Eiffel, France

Technical Program Committee

Aïssa Belmeguenai	Université de Skikda, Algeria
Aravinthan Gopalasingham	Nokia Bell Labs, France
Cherkaoui Leghris	Hassan II University, Morocco
Chih-Yu Wang	Academia Sinica, Taiwan
Chongjun Ouyang	Queen Mary University of London, UK
Christophe Maudoux	CNAM, France
Dolantina Hyka	Mediterranea University of Albania, Albania
Eirini Eleni Tsiropoulou	Arizona State University, USA
Elva Leka	Polytechnic University of Tirana, Albania
Éric Renault	ESIEE Paris—Université Gustave Eiffel, France
Fred Aklamanu	Google, France
Hacène Fouchal	University of Reims Champagne-Ardenne, France
Hamid Anvari	University of Alberta, Canada
Hella Kaffel Ben Ayed	Université de Tunis El Manar, Tunisia
Jean-François Bercher	ESIEE Paris, France
Lina Zhu	Xidian University, China
Luca Davoli	University of Parma, Italy
Luis Lamani	Polytechnic University of Tirana, Albania
Maha Sliti	Sup'Com, University of Carthage, Tunisia
Manh Cuong Nguyen	ESIEE Paris, France
Miranda Harizaj	Polytechnic University of Tirana, Albania
Morgane Joly	Université de Caen Normandie, France
Mounir Tahar Abbes	University of Chlef, Algeria

Naïla Bouchemal	ECE, France
Nardjes Bouchemal	Mila University Center, Algeria
Nour El-Houda Yellas	Télécom SudParis, France
Paul Mühlethaler	INRIA, France
Pengwenlong Gu	CNAM, France
Rohit Singh	EchoStar Corp, USA
Rosario G. Garroppo	University of Pisa, Italy
Selma Boumerdassi	Université Paris 8, France
Toan-Van Nguyen	San Diego State University, USA
Van Khang Nguyen	Hue University, Vietnam
Van Long Tran	Hue University, Vietnam
Viet Hai Ha	Hue University, Vietnam
Yeong Min	Jang Kookmin University, South Korea
Yuyi Mao	Macau University of Science and Technology, China
Yuzhi Yang	Khalifa University, United Arab Emirates

Publicity Chair

Pengwenlong Gu	CNAM, France

Sponsoring Institutions

ESIEE Paris, France
Télécom SudParis, France
Université Gustave Eiffel, France
Université Paris 8 Vincennes—Saint-Denis, France

Steering Committee

Selma Boumerdassi	Université Paris 8 Vincennes—Saint-Denis, France
Paul Mühlethaler	INRIA, France
Éric Renault	ESIEE Paris—Université Gustave Eiffel, France

Contents

Slotted Reinforcement Learning-Based Radio Resource Allocation in Sliced 5G Networks

Gauthier Meffe[1], Philippe Owezarski[1(⊠)], and Pascal Berthou[2]

[1] LAAS-CNRS, Université de Toulouse, CNRS, LAAS, Toulouse, France
`owe@laas.fr`
[2] LAAS-CNRS, Université de Toulouse, CNRS, UPS, Toulouse, France
`berthou@laas.fr`

Abstract. 5G networks are designed for providing several different services as high speed Internet, low latency and M2M (Machine to Machine) communications. For enforcing such guaranteed services, slicing techniques are of essential importance to ensure isolation between resources allocated to each of these services, especially at the level of RAN (Radio Access Networks) and its time/frequency matrix. Given the scarcity of radio resources, this paper aims at proposing efficient radio resource allocation algorithms and mechanisms for 5G networks, avoiding resource wastes and enforcing slices isolation. The proposed solution highlights a new way of using reinforcement learning, and more specifically the Double DQN (Deep Q-Network) algorithm, based on a slotted approach for 5G resource allocations. The slotted use of Double DQN evaluation exhibits its benefits in terms of allocation performance and low latency.

Keywords: 5G · Radio Resource Allocation · Slotted Reinforcement Learning · DDQN

1 Introduction

5G networks are designed for providing several different services as high speed Internet, low latency and M2M (Machine to Machine) communications. For enforcing such guaranteed services, slicing techniques are of essential importance to ensure isolation between resources allocated to each of these services, especially at the level of RAN (Radio Access Networks) and its time/frequency matrix. Given the scarcity of radio resources, it is important to avoid any resource waste, as well as interferences.

This paper then aims at designing efficient radio resource allocation algorithms and mechanisms for 5G networks. This problem has been already significantly addressed, especially leveraging optimization techniques from the operational research domain, as integer or constraints programming. Indeed, allocating user requests in the time/frequency matrix is a typical optimization problem known as the knapsack problem [1]. Such optimization techniques leverage

© The Author(s), under exclusive license to Springer Nature Switzerland AG 2026
S. Boumerdassi et al. (Eds.): MLN 2025, LNCS 16424, pp. 1–16, 2026.
https://doi.org/10.1007/978-3-032-18494-8_1

solvers that implement integer or constraints programming techniques. However, it takes hours, sometimes days for these solvers to provide the optimal results, and often they even do not converge. Such latency is of course incompatible with the mobile network management constraints. To avoid this latency issue, heuristics are proposed, but they then lose the optimality of the provided allocation scheme.

This placement of blocks in a matrix problem has recently been addressed using machine learning approaches, and especially reinforcement learning (RL) [2–4]. RL is a branch of machine learning that allows an agent to learn on the optimal decision to make based on sequential trials and errors made, receiving feedbacks (on a rewards form) on the performed actions in a given environment. One significant difference between the approaches leveraging optimization techniques from the operational research domain as MILP (Mixed Integer Linear Programming) or CP (Constraints Programming) and the ones based on reinforcement technique lies in the global allocation principle for the first, and the sequential allocation principle for the second. Indeed, MILP or CP know all resources to be allocated to user requests at the beginning and allocate them all in one time. This allocation result has been proved to be optimal. At the opposite, RL-based approaches allocate resources to users one by one, without considering what the next resource block is. RL-based resource allocation is then obviously suboptimal compared to MILP or CP-based allocation results. Existing heuristics addressing efficient resource allocation also leverage sequential resource blocks allocation principle. Their placement efficiency is then unfortunately suboptimal, but they provide results in a very short time compatible with low latencies requested by some users. Among the heuristics (leveraging sequential resource blocks allocation), the skyline algorithm has been proved to be optimal [1]. This paper then deals with improving the RL-based approach by slotting resource allocations principle. The approach then proposes to allocate several resource blocks corresponding to several user requests at the same time, instead of running several sequential allocation processes. Computing the allocation of several user requests in one time permits a better placement of resource blocks, what is impossible with a sequential approach that is blind of the requirements of the following resource blocks to be allocated. The objective is then to perform better than the best heuristic in terms of resource allocation results, while still enforcing the low latency requirements.

The rest of the paper is structured as follows: Sect. 2 details the time/frequency resource allocation problem in the new framework of 5G networks. Section 3 presents the state of researches on the generic knapsack problem. Section 4 is devoted to introducing the selected RL technique with regard to the allocation objectives and constraints. After having selecting the Double DQN (Deep Q-Network) as a promising RL technique for 5G ressource allocation, Sect. 5 describes the related Double DQN-based allocation agent design and implementation, presents its evaluation methodology, and analyzes and discusses the obtained results. Finally, Sect. 6 summarizes the contributions of the paper.

2 5G Radio Resources and Problem Description

This section covers the important 5G terminologies required for the exhibition of the RAN slicing problem. Mainly, the 5G radio resources structure is presented. Then, the RAN slicing enforcement problem is explained as well as the required allocations strategies.

2.1 5G Background

In 5G system, the physical layer is more flexible with respect to the previous generations. Recall that radio resources in 4G are uniformly distributed over a time-frequency grid, i.e. the later is decomposed into resource blocks (RB) of 1 ms over 12 sub-carriers spaced by 15 kHz.

In order to fulfill the variety of services requirements, increase the network reliability and adapt to frequency range, 5G introduces different radio frames numerologies for sub-6 GHz, and above-6 GHz bands. In this article, we focus on the sub-6 GHz bands. The same developed approaches can be easily applied for bands above-6 GHz. Table 1 exhibits the different numerologies for sub-6 GHz bands. Each given numerology μ^1 defines the time-frequency resource size in one Transmission Time interval (TTI), TTI=1ms. That is, a numerology μ refers to the sub-carrier spacing (SCS) in frequency domain and the slot duration in time domain. For instance, as depicted in Fig. 1, for $\mu = 1$ the radio resource size is fixed to 0.5 ms over 12 sub-carriers spaced by 30 KHz. In general, the SCS scales by $2^\mu * 15kHz$ and the slot duration decreases with higher numerology (μ). Such flexibility is essentially introduced as to achieve the diverse services requirements. For example, it is preferable to transmit latency sensitive services in shorter time interval with larger sub-carrier spacing, e.g. $\mu = 3$.

Table 1. 5G Radio frames numerologies for sub-6 GHz bands

μ	SCS (kHz)	Slot duration (ms)
0	15	1
1	30	0.5
2	60	0.25

In order to support the coexistence of the multiple numerologies on same carrier, the resources are structured in the so-called tiles [5]. The tile is the smallest subset of frequency and time resources allocated to a particular slice/service with same numerology μ. Hence, for sub-6 GHz three tiles structures are tailored as shown in Fig. 1. For instance, the tile structure for $\mu = 0$ is 1 ms over 12

---

[1] 3GPP, TR 38.802, TR 38.804: Study on new radio access technology Physical layer aspects, Study on new radio access technology Radio interface protocol aspects. https://www.3gpp.org/.

subcarriers spaced by 15 KHz. Further, multiplexing over time and frequency is required for the transmission of the different numerologies, e.g. over time, 3GPP imposes symbol alignment between tiles to insure orthogonality.

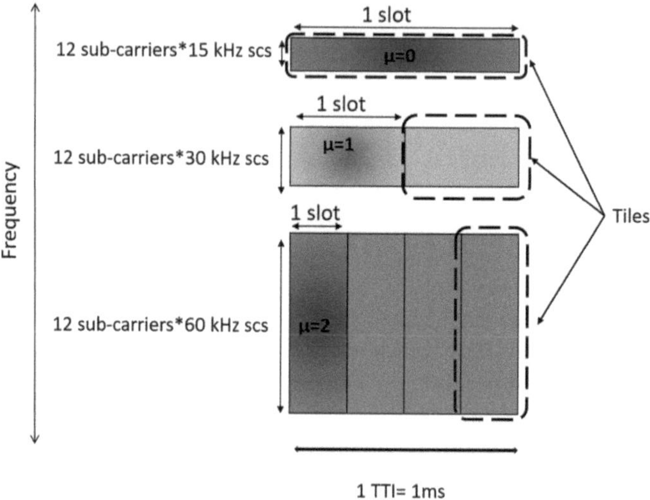

Fig. 1. Sub-6 GHz numerologies

2.2 Problem Formulation

The RAN slicing enforcement algorithms should then allocate resources in a way that maximizes the adjacency of the unallocated portion of resources, instead of having sparse unallocated resources in the time-frequency grid. This objective is illustrated in Fig. 2. Two time-frequency resource grids are schematized as to explain the difference between an optimal (b) and sub-optimal (a) resource allocation for 4 slice requests in 5G context. Each of the 4 slices demands a different amount of resources what induces specific sizes and shapes of requested user blocks to be allocated in the matrix (corresponding to the different 5G numerologies). Even-though both allocations (a) and (b) satisfy the four slice requests during the allocation window T, it is clear that the allocation strategy in (a) is sub-optimal compared to (b). In fact, the resource allocation strategies as in (a) might lead to inefficient resource utilization. 5G proposes a variety of user blocks structures, and some allocation strategies induce a small sparse unallocated resources over the resource grid, as represented in Fig. 2(a). Those small leaved resources are considered as wasted as they do not fit any possible user demand. Only the small continuous unallocated portion of resources can then be reused in an efficient manner, as different user requested block structures could fit in this portion. Thus, it enables the scalability requirement and increases the resource utilization efficiency.

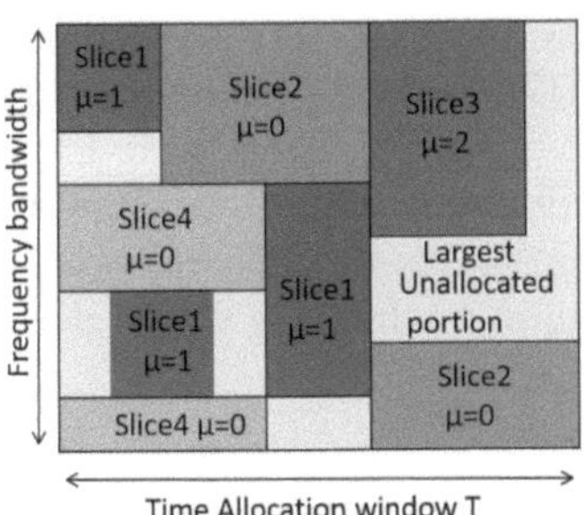

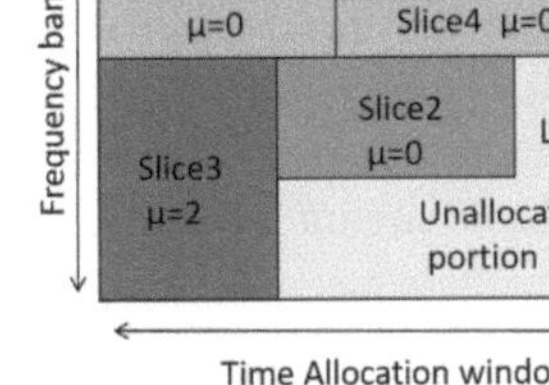

(a) Sub-optimal allocation (small continuous unallocated area)

(b) Optimal allocation (large continuous unallocated area)

Fig. 2. Optimal and sub-optimal resource allocation

3 Related Work

Recently, researches have converged to enforce the RAN slicing from a resource allocation aspect. To overcome the static resources segmentation limitations, shared allocation strategies are proposed [6–8]. Most of the RAN slicing enforcement approaches leverage optimization techniques from the operational research domain, providing optimal resource allocation, but at the expense of unacceptable latency. For instance, Han et al. [8], Yang et al. [9] propose the use of Genetic algorithm to optimize resource management between heterogeneous slices with maximized long-term network utility. By introducing resources virtualization, Chang et al. [10] formulate the problem as a knapsack problem [11]. An algorithm is proposed to maximize the number of accepted slices with an efficient 5G resource partitioning. Papa et al. [12] solve the problem using a Lyapunov optimisation approach. Ojaghi et al. [13] propose a RAN slicing mechanism that uses the Mixed Integer Programming (MIP), and to cope with computation time, they propose a faster heuristic (SlicedRAN), unfortunately then losing the optimality aspect. Hossain and Ansari [14] deal with the slicing issue using Mixed Integer Non Linear programming (MINLP). All these previous works based on optimization techniques cannot be used in operational networks because of their huge latency. Indeed, solvers for computing all these optimization models takes hours or days to reach the optimal solution. And sometimes, they even do not converge, and then, never reach the optimal solution. The related heuristics aiming at solving the latency issue then do not provide the expected optimal solution in terms of resources placement.

Given these optimization model limits, some alternative works propose to use machine learning techniques and more specifically Reinforcement Learning (RL). Then, Zambianco and Verticale [15] also aim at optimizing the use of resources by limiting inter-slices interferences. For that, the issue is solved using Deep Reinforcement Neural networks (DRN). The solution, even if it does not reach the optimal solution, appears to be efficient comparatively to existing heuristics, and provides low latency compared to optimization models. Khodapanah et al. [16], Boutiba et al. [4], Tian et al. [3], Abiko et al. [17], Li et al. [18], Kumar et al. [19], Sun et al. [20], Deng et al. [21], Sciancalepore et al. [22], Amonarriz-Pagola et al. [23] adopt a similar approach based on reinforcement learning. However, they all use a sequential allocation principle with the assumed corresponding allocation efficiency issues. The rest of the paper aims at exhibiting that a slotted version of DRL is meant to improve DRL efficiency.

4   Reinforcement Algorithm

As indicated previously, a new trend for 5G resource allocation starts to investigate machine learning approaches in order to gain flexibility. RL is a machine learning method that allows an agent to learn how to make decisions by interacting with an environment. The agent aims at maximizing a cumulative reward by learning what action to trigger in various cases. It leverages on Action-Value Function (Q-value). The Q-value is an estimate of the future cumulative reward that the agent can expect by triggering a specific action in a given state (Fig. 3).

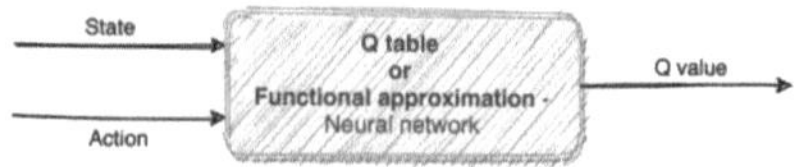

Fig. 3. Action-value function

Given the targeted 5G radio resource allocation problem, Q-Learning is of interest. Q-Learning is a RL algorithm that learns the value of actions independently from the policy followed by the agent. The agent updates its Q-value estimates according to rewards received and its future estimations. Deep Q-Network (DQN) [24] is an extension of Q-learning that uses deep neural networks to approximate the Q function. It aims at combining the perceptual capabilities of deep learning with the decision-making abilities of reinforcement learning. This approach has demonstrated excellent performances on complex tasks especially related to game playing that often have to solve similar problems as the one related to 5G resource allocation [2,11]. The deep neural network in a DQN takes the states of the environment as an input and produces Q-values for all actions as outputs. The agent is free afterwards to select the action that maximizes the Q-value as well as the reward. The architecture is depicted on Fig. 4. Deep Q-Network (DQN) is a powerful method that combines reinforcement learning and deep neural networks for solving complex problems. Using mechanisms as experiments replay and neural networks, DQN successfully stabilizes and improves learning results, allowing the agent to learn efficient policies for various and dynamic environments.

Double Deep Q-Network (Double DQN or DDQN) [25] is a variant that improves the standard DQN algorithm aiming at correcting an overestimate of action values Q that can arise with reinforcement learning. Recently, an improved version of DDQN has been designed: the Dueling Double Deep Q Network (D3QN) [3]. It then can consider resource allocation at both the base station and the network slices. The contribution of this paper being to propose the slotted approach for DRL, and demonstrate its benefits for 5G resource allocation, considering all details of the 5G technology, especially the very complex ones of the physical layer, does not bring significantly useful information. In addition, to simplify the demonstration of the slotted-DRL approach gain, it is sufficient to consider the Double DQN algorithm working only with the sliced network level information.

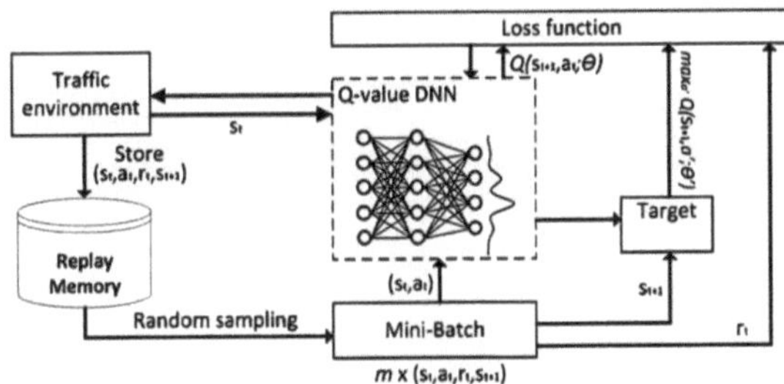

Fig. 4. Deep neural network architecture for DQN

5 Evaluation

This evaluation section aims at demonstrating the benefits of the slotted approach for DRL-based resource allocation. The Double DQN algorithm has been selected as the DRL algorithm, as it appears as a promising solution for providing efficient/optimal allocation results, in real-time. This section evaluates the efficiency of the slotted Double DQN algorithm for allocating efficiently the list of resource blocks requested by users in the full time/frequency matrix of the 5G network. These results will also be compared with the ones obtained with the skyline algorithm, i.e. the optimal algorithm leveraging sequential resource block allocations.

5.1 Evaluation Environment and Methodology

This evaluation is based on a simulation of the time/frequency matrix where each cell corresponds to a resource that can be allocated to a user. Each user has specific requirements in terms of bandwidth and latency. User requests are then represented as bricks of different sizes that Double DQN has to optimally fit in the full time/frequency matrix, i.e. avoiding having small groups of unallocated cells in the matrix that are then very difficult to allocate for future requests.

Many key functions have been developed for handling this environment:

- **Environment initialization**: The initial time/frequency matrix is generated with null values for simulating fully unallocated resources.
- **user blocks placement**: Each user request is represented by a resource block to be allocated. This allocation is made by a placement algorithm based on Slotted Double DQN.
- **Rewards computing**: Rewards are computed based on the number of user requests placed in the matrix. If some blocks are not allocated the reward is decreased.
- Etc.

For all the computings, a platform consisting of a computers cluster has been used.[2] It consists of several servers, including Nvidia GPUs, specifically designed for intensive computings. These GPU are compatible with CUDA, a parallel computing architecture that increases the performances of deep learning algorithms. Using this computing platform is made possible thanks to programming environments as TensorFlow and PyTorch, that are optimized for taking advantage of GPU capabilities. TensorFlow has been specifically integrated with CUDA, what makes the computing of deep learning algorithms more efficient and faster.

5.2   Resource Allocation Efficiency

Evaluation scenario and placement performance metrics
In order not to complexify the visual representation of results, this paper presents an evaluation on a small scenario. On this running example, the time/frequency matrix is limited to a size of 4×4 ressource blocks (RB). The list of user requests is randomly generated. Each user request is represented by a resource block of various sizes going from 1×1 to 4×4. Figure 5 illustrates this by showing 4 out of 16 possible block structures. The yellow block corresponds to the smallest possible resource block in 5G at the time of this study, i.e. 15 kHz x 0,25 ms. The green block corresponds to a user request having soft latency constraints. The blue block correspond to the request of a user needing more throughput with short latency. Finally, the red block represents the request of a user needing high throughput without strong latency requests. Previous works as the ones in [3,4] used a more complex model of the physical resources of RAN. In this paper we argue that a simple model just considering time, frequency and latency is sufficient for exhibiting the benefits of the slotted version of Double DQN compared to other DRL or heuristic algorithms.

---

[2] https://pfcalcul.laas.fr/.

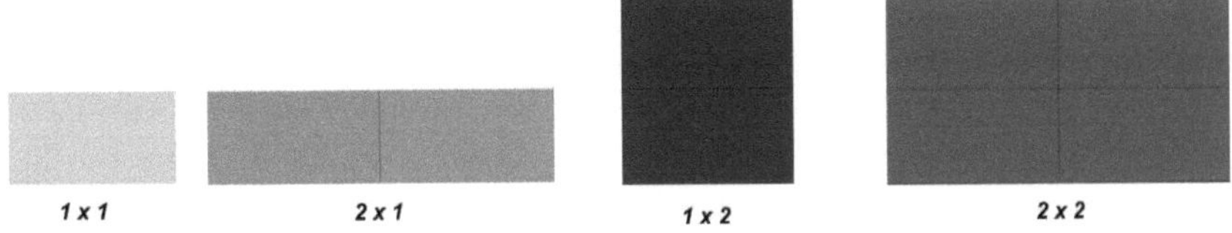

Fig. 5. Examples of resource blocks corresponding to possible user requests

The placement goal deals with maximizing the number of user requests placed in the matrix, minimizing unused spaces between allocated resource blocks, and avoiding any overlapping. The number of possible configurations in this case is $2^{4\times4} \times 16$. Indeed, each cell in the matrix can be allocated or empty, what gives 2^{16} possible configurations. Adding the 16 possible sizes for the blocks, the total is then $2^{16} \times 16$ possible configurations.

Figure 6 illustrates one optimal placement of user requests on the time/frequency matrix, with all user requests on the left, and no unused RB between these blocks. To consider the case where the user requests do not completely fill the time/frequency matrix, the placement metrics used as reward for the Slotted Double DQN algorithm takes into account the absence of unused blocks between allocated ones, and the fact that the blocks are placed as left as possible.

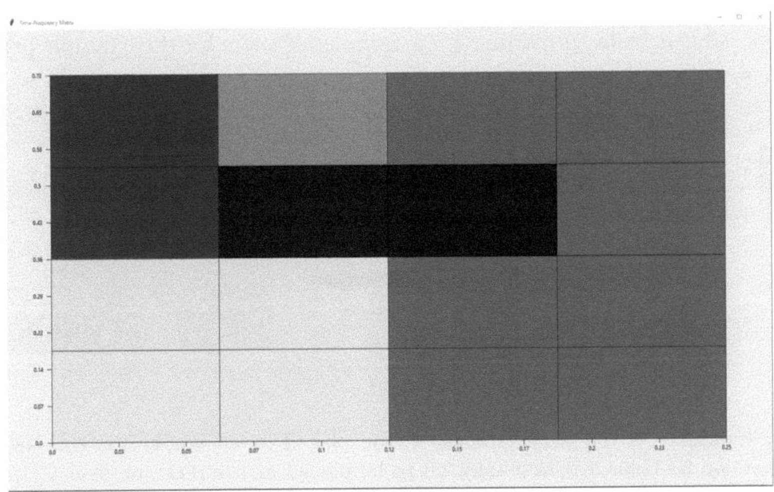

Fig. 6. Example of optimal placement of user requests: blocks are allocated on the left of the 4×4 matrix without unused blocks in between

At the beginning, the placement agent running the Slotted Double DQN algorithm knows a list of N user blocks to be allocated. The state of the environment includes the size of all user blocks and the placement indication: each user request is represented by $(x_i, y_i, \varepsilon_i)$, where ε_i equals 1 if the block has already been placed, 0 otherwise (cf. Fig. 7). This allows the agent to make better informed decision, and to better anticipate future placements. Indeed, on the example of Fig. 7, the list provided to the agent has a size of N = 6. It has then been specifically built to provide the agent with all informations required for optimally placing user blocks. The agent places user blocks one by one, but selecting the best user block to place at each iteration with regard to the information provided by the list of the N = 6 considered user requests at this time.

$$\begin{pmatrix} 0\ 0\ 0\ 0 \\ 0\ 0\ 0\ 0 \\ 0\ 0\ 0\ 0 \\ 0\ 0\ 0\ 0 \end{pmatrix} \quad + \quad (x_1, y_1) + \cdots + (x_6, y_6) \quad \longrightarrow$$

$$(0, \ldots, 0, x_1, y_1, 0, \ldots, x_6, y_6, 0)$$

Fig. 7. Input vector (size 6) with a 4×4 matrix and several blocks.

With this state representation, the agent has to select the user block to be placed at that time, and the place to be allocated for it. Table 2 schematizes the list of possible actions, providing a few samples of them for the example provided on Fig. 8.

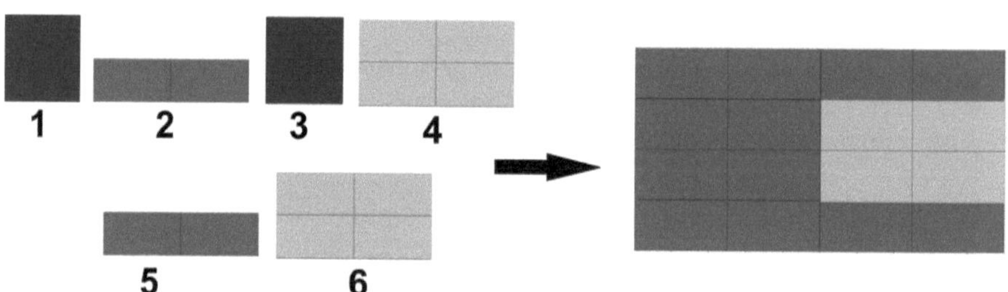

Fig. 8. Example: Given 6 user blocks to be placed in an empty matrix, the agent selects action 53 (bloc 4 is first selected to be placed at the place number 6—place in the matrix are numbered from 0 to 15 from left to right and top to bottom)

Table 2. Examples of user blocks placement actions

Action	Selected block	Place of the block
0	1	0
1	1	1
2	1	2
3	1	3
4	1	4
5	1	5
⋮	⋮	⋮
16	2	0
17	2	1
⋮	⋮	⋮
32	3	0
33	3	1
⋮	⋮	⋮
53	4	6
⋮	⋮	⋮
95	6	15

5.3 Training with Several Sets of Users

How to train any machine learning algorithm still remains a significant piece of research work. Practically, it is commonly agreed that it is challenging to produce traces (gathering of real traces or generation of synthetic ones) of significant sizes, and representing exhaustively the many different situations that can be encountered in the real world. Reinforcement Learning has been partly selected in this work for not being concerned by such issue. Indeed, RL can leverage on very small training datasets, the model of RL algorithms being consolidated at the running stage thanks to the feedbacks obtained by the agent by the way of the rewards that take into account both the agent actions and their impact on the environment.

We then limit our training datasets to a small number of user requests lists. These lists are very basic, especially in the reduced case selected for illustrating the performances of the Slotted Double DQN algorithm for 5G resource allocation. The agent has been trained on 10 000 epochs, using a three layers neural network, sufficient for capturing the few features of our environment model (cf. Fig. 7). The neural network layers consists of respectively 512/512/180 neurons at the beginning. Having small training datasets and small neural networks will help to better analyze and understand the placement performance results, as well as explaining them.

The following method has been followed:

1. Creation of a training set consisting of a fixed number of user requests lists (N = 10 for examples).
2. Training of our Slotted Double DQN model on this dataset.
3. Agent performance evaluation: A 100% success rate means that the agent successfully placed all user requests from all the lists.
4. If the success rate is not 100%, we increase the size of the neural network (adding neurons in the three layers) and repeat the process as long as it reaches an optimum.

Results of the different trials are summarized in Table 3.

Table 3. Success rate of the placement agent for several configurations of the Slotted Double DQN neural network and user requests lists. As a comparison, Slotted DDQN results are compared with the ones of standard DDQN and the Skyline algorithm

Neural network configuration	Number of user requests lists	Slotted DDQN success rate (%)	DDQN success rate (%)	Skyline success rate (%)
512/1024/512	10	90	77	84
1024/2048/1024	10	100	79	
2048/4096/2048	10	100	82	
512/1024/512	20	80	62	71
1024/2048/1024	20	85	65	
2048/4096/2048	20	80	68	
512/1024/512	50	72	48	59
1024/2048/1024	50	82	53	
2048/4096/2048	50	84	56	

These results exhibit that our slotted double DQN based placement agent is able to learn optimal placement strategies in some cases. For that, the neural network has to be complex enough to capture all possible configurations. It is however unfortunate that, even with the most complex neural networks that we tested, a success rate of 100% is not reached even when training our agent on our largest datasets.

Such results could appear as disappointing. We nevertheless compared the performance of our agent with the one of the skyline algorithm [1] that has been proved to be optimal for solving the Knapsack problem. Our Slotted Double DQN-based agent overpasses the skyline algorithm always reaching greater or equal success rates. This proves the limits of sequential allocation algorithms as they introduce many lost spaces between allocated blocks, at the opposite of the slotted approach that can select the best block among N that better fits the unallocated space. As expected, the standard version of DDQN that leverages a sequential approach for resource blocks allocation (not considering what the next blocks to allocate is) exhibits allocation efficiency lower than the ones of the Skyline algorithm (the optimal one leveraging the sequential allocation principle).

5.4   Benchmarking

In this section, the performances of our Slotted Double DQN agent are evaluated on the GPUs of our computing platform, especially using the capabilities of CUDA and TensorFlow.

For evaluating the performances, several training sessions have been run with the neural networks considered in this paper using different CPU and GPU configurations with various batch sizes.

The tested configurations are the following:

1. **CPU only**: Training using a single CPU: Intel 5218R 2.1G.
2. **Single GPU**: Training using a single GPU: RTX A6000.

Table 4. Training time in seconds for different batch sizes on CPU and GPU

Batch size	CPU	GPU
8	324	84
16	203	27
32	202	13
64	142	10
128	112	4
256	105	2
512	104	2

Results are shown in Table 4. They exhibit that working with GPU significantly reduces the training times, especially for large batch sizes. By optimizing our code specifically for GPU, we reduce the training time by a factor of 50 compared to the use of a CPU.

The Slotted Double DQN allocation computing times have been measured at run time. They appear to be very short whatever the tested value of N. Of course, N is necessarily small; the slot duration has to be short to respect latency requirements of users, then limiting the size of N. Obviously, the larger N, the better the allocation efficiency in terms of placement. Given the large number and large scope of experiments we run, the largest N value ever reached with realistic hypothesis was 50. In this worst case for allocation computing times, this computing time never exceeds $50\,\mu s$. This time is very short, and fully compatible with the latency requirements of possible user requests in 5G networks. It then validates the Slotted Double DQN as efficient enough in terms of computing time for addressing the task of resource allocation in 5G RAN.

6   Conclusion

In this paper, we addressed the problem of radio resource allocation in 5G networks. Based on the state of the art, it appears that mainly two different approaches are traditionally used:

- Operational research based techniques as MILP or CP that provide optimal placement solutions, but at the expense of very long computing times. As a result, it is generally proposed, together with these exact methods, some heuristics that provide approaching allocation results, but with significantly reduced computation times.
- Reinforcement Learning based algorithms that are, as heuristics, providing good allocation results, together with short computing times.

Analyzing this state of the art, it appears that operational research techniques know all resource requests of all users, and that they compute the optimal placement of resource blocks in one time, considering the requirement of all resource blocks to be allocated. At the opposite, heuristics or RL-based algorithms sequentially allocate resource blocks corresponding to a single user request, without taking into account what the next blocks to be allocated are.

Based on this statement, we propose to group N user requests in one slot. The slot size depends ont the user requirements, especially in terms of latency. The slotted version of Double DQN then appears as a solution for taking advantage of the operational research approaches. We developed our Slotted Double DQN-based agent and evaluated its performances. Our agent appeared to provide an interesting solution, especially as it overpasses the optimal skyline placement algorithm, with limited and controlled latencies.

Acknowledgment. We gratefully acknowledge the support of the PEPR 5G program of ANR in the framework of the France 2030 investment plan, specially of NF-MUST project under grant ANR-22-PEFT-0002.

References

1. Jylanki, J.: A thousand ways to pack the bin—a practical approach to two-dimensional rectangle bin packing (2010). https://fr.scribd.com/document/457472796/1000-ways-to-pack-the-bin-pdf
2. Stevens, M., Pradhan, S.: Playing tetris with deep reinforcement learning. In: Stanford University Report (2024). https://cs231n.stanford.edu/reports/2016/pdfs/121_Report.pdf
3. Tian, K., Wang, Y., Pan, D., Yuan, D.: DRL-based dynamic resource configuration and optimization for b5g network slicing. IEEE Access **12**, 120864–120876 (2024)
4. Boutiba, K., Bagaa, M., Ksentini, A.: Optimal radio resource management in 5G NR featuring network slicing. Comput. Netw. **234**, (2023)
5. Elayoubi, S.E., Jemaa, S.B., Altman, Z., Galindo-Serrano, A.: 5G ran slicing for verticals: enablers and challenges. IEEE Commun. Mag. **57**(1), 28–34 (2019)

6. Yan, M., Feng, G., Zhou, J., Sun, Y., Liang, Y.-C.: Intelligent resource scheduling for 5G radio access network slicing. IEEE Trans. Veh. Technol. **68**(8), 7691–7703 (2019)
7. Mandelli, S., Andrews, M., Borst, S., Klein, S.: Satisfying network slicing constraints via 5G mac scheduling. In: IEEE INFOCOM 2019-IEEE Conference on Computer Communications, pp. 2332–2340. Paris, France (2019). https:// ieeexplore.ieee.org/document/8737604/
8. Han, L.J.B., Schotten, H.D.: Slice as an evolutionary service: genetic optimization for inter-slice resource management in 5G networks. IEEE Access **6**(1), 33137–33147 (2018)
9. Yang, X., Wang, Y., Wong, I.C., Liu, Y., Cuthbert, L.: Genetic algorithm in resource allocation of ran slicing with QoS isolation and fairness. In: IEEE Latin-American Conference on Communications (LATINCOM) (2020)
10. Chang, C.-Y., Nikaein, N., Spyropoulos, T.: Radio access network resource slicing for flexible service execution. In: IEEE INFOCOM 2018- IEEE Conference on Computer Communications Workshops (INFOCOM WKSHPS), pp. 668–673. IEEE (2018)
11. Mnih, V., Kavukcuoglu, K., Silver, D., Graves, A., Antonoglu, I., Wierstra, D., Riedmiller, M.: Playing Atari with deep reinforcement learning. In: NIPS Deep learning Workshop (2013)
12. Papa, A., Klugel, M., Goratti, L., Rasheed, T., Kellerer, W.: Optimizing dynamic ran slicing in programmable 5G networks. In: IEEE International Conference on Communications (ICC), pp. 1–7. Shangai, China (2019)
13. Ojaghi, B., Adelantado, F., Antonopoulos, A., Verikoukis, C.: SliceDRAN: service-aware network slicing framework for 5G radio access networks. IEEE Syst. J. (2021)
14. Hossain, A., Ansari, N.: 5G multi-band numerology-based TDD RAN slicing for throughput and latency sensitive services. IEEE Trans. Mob. Comput. (2021)
15. Zambianco, M., Verticale, G.: Spectrum allocation for network slices with inter-numerology interference using deep reinforcement learning. In: IEEE 31st Annual International Symposium on Personal, Indoor and Mobile Radio Communications, pp. 1–7 (2020)
16. Khodapanah, B., Awada, A., Viering, I., Barreto, A.N., Simsek, M., Fettweis, G.: Slice management in radio access network via deep reinforcement learning. In: IEEE 91st Vehicular Technology Conference (VTC2020-Spring), pp. 1–6 (2020)
17. Abiko, Y., Saito, T., Ikeda, D., Ohta, K., Mizuno, T., Mineno, H.: Flexible resource block allocation to multiple slices for radio access network slicing using deep reinforcement learning. IEEE Access **8**, 68183–68198 (2020)
18. Li, R., Zhao, Z., Sun, Q., Chih-lin, I., Yang, X., Chen, X., Zhao, M., Zhang, H.: Deep reinforcement learning for resource management in network slicing. IEEE Access **6**, 74429–74441 (2018)
19. Kumar, P.M., Basheer, B., Rawal, B.S., Afghah, F., Babu, G.C., Arunmozhi, M.: Traffic scheduling network slicing and virtualization based on deep reinforcement learning. Comput. Electr. Eng. **100**, (2022)
20. Sun, G., Xiong, K., Boateng, G.O., Liu, G., Jiang, W.: Resource slicing and customization in ran with dueling deep q-network. J. Netw. Comput. Appl. **157**, (2020)
21. Deng, Z., Du, Q., Li, N., Zhang, Y.: RL-based radio resource slicing strategy for software-defined satellite networks. In: IEEE 19th International Conference on Communication Technology (ICCT), pp. 897–901 (2019)
22. Sciancalepore, V., Costa-Perez, X., Banchs, A.: RL-NSB: reinforcement learning-based 5g network slice broker. IEEE/ACM Trans. Netw. **27**(4), 1543–1557 (2019)

23. Amonarriz-Pagola, I., Fernandez-Carrasco, J.A.: A reinforcement learning approach for network slicing in 5G networks. In: Proceedings of Cybersecurity Conference (JNIC), pp. 1–7 (2023)
24. Xiong, Z., Zhang, Y., Niyato, D., Deng, R., Wang, P., Wang, L.-C.: Deep reinforcement learning for mobile 5G and beyond: fundamentals, applications, and challenges. IEEE Veh. Technol. Mag. **14**(2), 44–52 (2019)
25. Shokrnezhad, M., Taleb, T., Dazzi, P.: Double deep Q-learning-based path selection and service placement for latency-sensitive beyond 5G applications. IEEE Trans. Mob. Comput. **23**(5), 5097–5110 (2024)

Bone Fracture Recognition Using Robust Deep Learning Techniques

Samson Akinpelu[1] and Serestina Viriri[1,2]

[1] Computer Science Discipline, School of Agriculture and Science, University of KwaZulu-Natal, Durban, South Africa
222068579@stu.ukzn.ac.za, viriris@ukzn.ac.za
[2] Centre for Augmented Intelligence and Data Science, University of South Africa, Pretoria, South Africa

Abstract. Bone fractures are a prevalent medical problem that requires prompt intervention to prevent enduring effects. Although conventional diagnostic techniques such as X-rays are prevalent, they require skilled radiologists to interpret the precise image. Recent advances in deep learning, especially Convolutional Neural Networks (CNNs), have demonstrated significant potential to automate and improve the precision of fracture identification. In this study, the application of robust CNN-based deep learning methods is presented for the identification of fractures. We investigated the utilization of CNNs on a large data set (FracAtlas) of medical images, illustrating the model's ability to classify the existence of fractures autonomously. Our model achieves a substantial accuracy of 98. 7% and a sensitivity of 100%, facilitating an expedited diagnosis and aiding physicians in their decision-making process compared to a class attention transformer, which only achieves 53%. Furthermore, we compare conventional approaches and cutting-edge deep learning models, emphasizing CNN's enhanced efficacy in recognizing bone fractures.

Keywords: Bone fracture · Detection · Convolution neural network · Deep learning

1 Introduction

Bone fractures pose a serious threat to bone functionality and hinder the daily activities of an individual to a great extent, which, in turn, requires precise diagnosis and timely treatment with the use of medical imaging. Normal X-rays based on the X-ray mechanism are usually the most common diagnosis method for bone fractures [1]. These X-ray images can offer more defined images of the body while using significantly lower radiation doses than Computed Tomography (CT) scans [2]. In the hectic setting of emergency rooms, radiologists or on-duty doctors are responsible for the initial inspection of the X-rays showing broken bones by visual interpretation. This non-automated interpretation is a subjective evaluation and leads to errors that result in wrong medical conclusions [3]. The

S. Boumerdassi et al. (Eds.): MLN 2025, LNCS 16424, pp. 17–27, 2026.
https://doi.org/10.1007/978-3-032-18494-8_2

growing need for more accurate fracture recognition systems has spearheaded the development of multiple computer-aided diagnostics (CAD) systems. These are artificial intelligence applications, such as Aidoc,Viz.ai and Deepbone; that analyze patient radiographs and offer clinical recommendations to the radiologist, aiming to decrease the misclassification in bone image interpretation.

More recently, deep learning has occupied a massive significant position in the health sector with thyroid nodule identification, brain tumour segmentation and pulmonary illnesses identification [4]. Progress in studies of radiographs of different body parts has enormously increased the acknowledgement of the magnitude of the deep learning method. Researchers have conducted studies on foot [5], wrist [6], rib [7], and the lower extremities [8].

We present a parallel approach to investigate the functionalities of deep convolutional neural networks (DCNN) and class attention image transformers for detecting bone fractures. Our bone fracture detection framework employs mechanisms to enhance dynamic feature fusion across spatial and scale dimensions, to improve recognition performance. Experimental results indicate that our approach surpasses prior state-of-the-art techniques in fracture diagnosis [9,10], attaining an accuracy of 98.7%.

The remaining part of the study is divided into reviewing related works, methods and techniques, experimental results and discussion. The last section focuses on the conclusion of this study.

2   Related Works

Deep learning (DL) has been identified as one of the areas that have attracted attention in the medical field due to its potential to allow radiologists to spot bone fractures more easily. Deep learning models provide superior accuracy in analysing medical images compared to human practitioners. Researchers in Artificial Intelligence have proposed various deep learning algorithms to facilitate the identification of bone fractures from small and big datasets of bone pictures.

The authors [11] devised a methodology to identify and categorize fragmented bone utilizing diverse machine learning approaches. The images were analysed using the Random Forest Algorithm, Convolutional Neural Networks (CNN), and Artificial Neural Networks (ANN). Image algorithm such as SIFT was employed to extract images. They attained a 92.44% accuracy in classifying healthy and fractured bones. A trochanteric fracture classifier was introduced in [12] to identify five distinct bone breaks with the modified AlexNet methodology. A CNN was employed for classification, achieving an accuracy of 91 An approach was proposed using CNN in conjunction with several classifiers, including SVM, KNN, BPNN, and NB. The author classified several types of fractures with an 90% success rate. In [13], a system-oriented transfer learning technique for identifying fractures using X-ray images was introduced. The author employed the Faster-RCNN model utilizing a rotating bounding box. They attained a state-of-the-art accuracy of 94.7%.

Similarly, a Faster R-CNN, which has been pre-trained, was utilized in [14], and they achieved 97% accuracy on a limited dataset. However, the strategy lacks generalizability due to the limited size of the datasets employed. In [15], the authors employed a decision tree to detect fractured bones, achieving a recognition accuracy of 86.57%. The authors of [16,17] utilized deep convolutional neural networks to extract information from bone imaging data. The validation accuracy of their respective techniques is 97.4% and 83%. The authors in [18] presented a novel model [19] in identifying bone fractures in children, achieving a 95% of accuracy. The authors of [20] employed an ensemble-based deep convolutional neural network model to detect wrist fractures. However, the method was limited to wrist bone images alone.

3   Methods and Techniques

This study presents a deep learning model for the diagnosis of bone fractures. Our strategy is centred around two parallel architectures. A robust convolutional neural network and a class attention transformer, which function as the primary framework for detecting fractures in bone pictures. To attain enhanced feature fusion at the spatial level and across various scales, the feature maps from each network were permitted to operate independently. The detailed design of our proposed bone fracture detecting system is illustrated in Fig. 1.

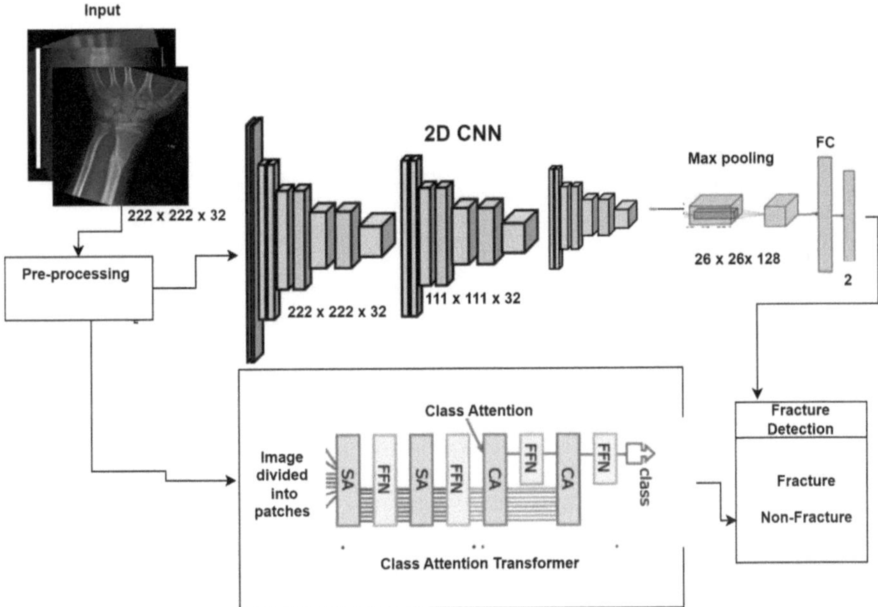

Fig. 1. Bone Fracture Detection Framework

3.1 Convolution Neural Network Layer(CNN)

CNN typically consist of convolutional layers, pooling layers, and fully connected layers. The convolution kernel is employed to automatically extract intricate feature information, with each kernel linked to a localized area of the preceding feature map. Convolutional layers may consist of several feature maps, with each feature map expressed in Eq. 1.

$$x_j^k = f\left(\sum_{i \in M_j} x_j^{k-1} * N_{ij}^k + b_l^k\right) \tag{1}$$

where b_l^k denotes the bias, N_{ij}^k represents the weight of the model parameters. In reducing the number of parameters a pooling mechanism to sample the feature. Each output feature map can be represented in Eqs. 2 and 3 respectively

$$x_j^k = f(v_j^k) \tag{2}$$

$$f(v_j^k) = down(x_j^{k-1}) \tag{3}$$

The down-sample function f is represented with down $(\cdot)$, which calculates the feature map x_j^{k-1} of the preceding layer using a specified sampling size. The fully connected (FC) is positioned at the topmost of the network. Every neuron is entirely connected to all neurons in the preceding layer, enabling it to amalgamate local information with categorical differentiation in convolutional or pooling layers. The output x_j^k of the fully connected layer is derived from the weighted summation of inputs.

$$x_j^k = f(v_j^k) \tag{4}$$

$$f(v_j^k) = w^k(x^{k-1} + b^j) \tag{5}$$

The introduction of local connectivity, weight sharing, and down-sampling in CNNs helps keep the network architecture simple and also decreases the number of training parameters. The source data gets converted into a high-level feature representation using algorithmic operations across layers. In all, the CNN model is built following the Visual Graphic Geometry Networks (VGGNet) approach. It has 3 convolutional layers, 2 pooling layers with max pooling, and two fully connected layers. We utilized a pooling method that diminishes the dimensionality of the feature map, with the primary aim of downsizing the spatial dimensions of the convolved features, decreasing the computational complexity and enhancing the efficiency of the CNN model. Due to the requirement for a fixed input size in most convolutional neural networks, resizing the bone image to $222 \times 222 \times 3$ is necessary. We utilized bilinear interpolation to resize the image to the expected input of the CNN network.

3.2   Class Attention Transformer (CaiT)

This section presents the CaiT architecture as demonstrated in Fig. 1. It is an architecture that seeks to direct self-attention among patches while consolidating the information pertinent to the linear classifier [23].

CaiT, a derivative of the visual transformer (ViT) which has undergone so much development from its original structure, falls under this category. It operates a LayerScale technique, which adds a learnable diagonal matrix at the output of each residual block and thus leads to the training dynamics. The architecture creates a transition layer of a transformer that self-attends(SA) to the patches of the image, thereby allowing clear segregation from class-attention (CA) layers, specifically for synthesizing the content that is sent as input to a linear classifier as a singular vector [27].

The CaiT network consists of two separate processing steps, as shown in Fig. 2:1. The self-attention phase duplicates the ViT approach, though the class embedding (CLS) is not used in CaiT. The last step consists of a class-attention mechanism that includes several layers processing patch (images) embeddings to most of a class embedding CLS, which then can be entered into a linear classifier. This class attention moves through a layer labelled as multi-head class attention (CA) and a feedforward neural network (FFN) layer. CaiT has achieved a promising result in large image classification tasks. In this study, the class attention architecture was utilized without any modification to its structure.

3.3   Bone Image Dataset

Most current X-Ray datasets are either insufficiently sized for training deep learning models or lack adequate annotation for localization and segmentation purposes. This is a constraint for evaluating various state-of-the-art (SOTA) methodologies, as each study uses a unique dataset that remains undisclosed. It also impedes advancing machine-learning algorithms for classification, localization, and segmentation. Consequently, a novel FracAtlas(Fig 3) dataset was introduced [11]. The dataset comprises 4,083 bone images meticulously annotated for classification, localization, and segmentation of bone fractures by two experienced radiologists and then certified by a medical official. Every scan in the dataset was autonomously annotated by both radiologists and subsequently validated by the medical officer. The annotation was conducted using make-sense.ai, an open-source labelling engine. We utilize this dataset in this study and its distribution into train, test and validation is illustrated in Fig. 2.

3.4   Experiment

The training of the model was carried out using an Adam optimizer for bone fracture classification with a learning rate of 0.0001. The maximum epoch and batch size were 35 and 64, respectively. It was implemented using Pytorch and was trained and evaluated using a system equipped with an Intel Core i5–8th Gen

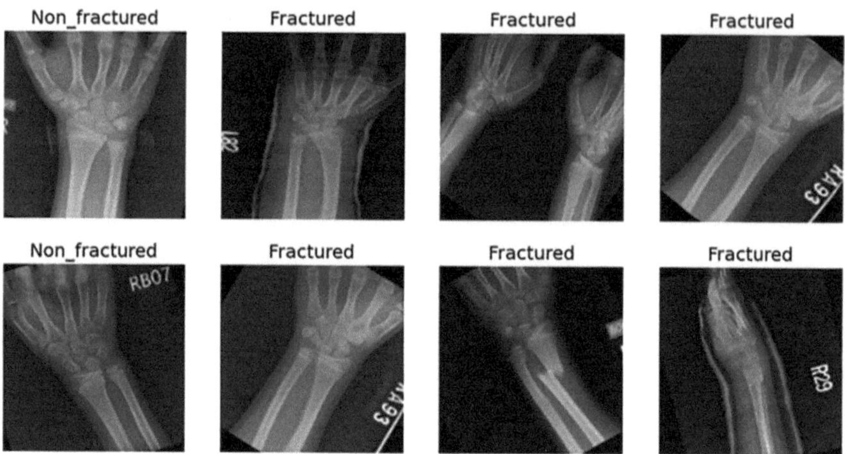

Fig. 2. Dataset description

processor, 16 GB DDR4 memory modules, and GPU from Google Collab. The performance of the proposed deep learning model was evaluated using sensitivity, f1-Score and accuracy as standard metrics of evaluation.

4   Results and Discussion

The result of CNN efficiently recognised salient features that determine fractures in bone mage without overfitting, as demonstrated in Figs. 3 and 4. An accuracy of 98.7% was achieved on the dataset used with the proposed CNN architecture while CaiT struggles to reach 53%. The training and Loss plot indicated that the model prevented overfitting. The sensitivity of the training and validation set demonstrated that the model is robust enough to extract the discriminating features for efficient recognition of fractures in bone Images. While some other studies focus mainly on specific bone areas in the body (thigh, leg, arm, etc.), this study utilized a dataset comprising different body bone images. This includes chest region, ankle, arm, leg, waist, hand, etc. The ability of the proposed model to capture diverse body bone images confirmed its robustness and generalizability.

To further establish the performance of the proposed model, we utilized standard metrics, which include confusion matrix, Precision, and F1-measure, as shown in Fig. 4 and Table 1, respectively. The confusion matrix indicated a high true positive rate as against false positives in both classes (fractured and non-fractured). The non-fractured is represented with 0, while the fractured is represented with a 1 on the confusion matrix. We achieved an overall accuracy of 98.7% and Sensitivity or recall of 100% on the dataset (Fig. 5 and 6).

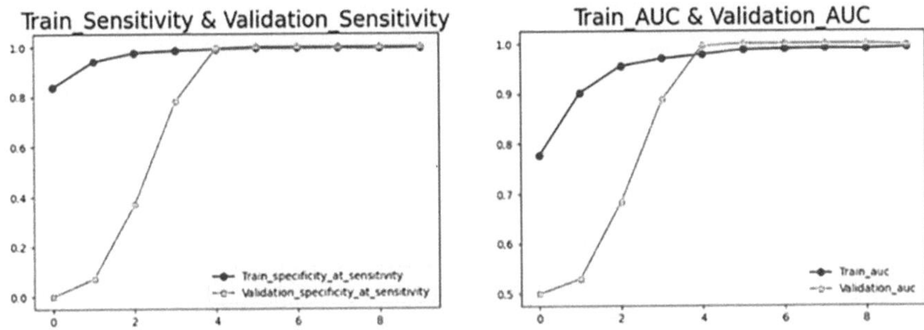

Fig. 3. Model Training and Validation Plot

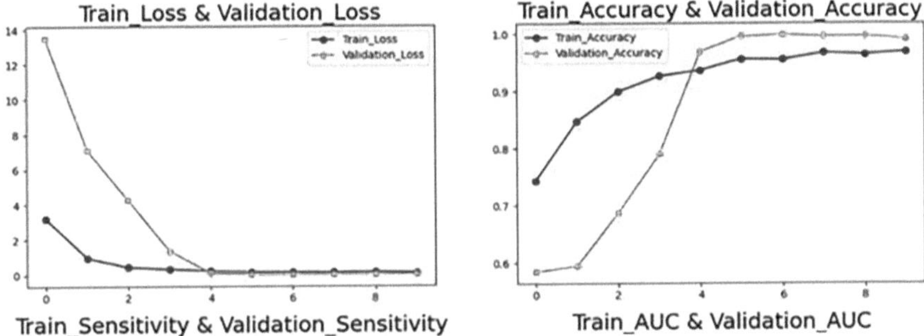

Fig. 4. Proposed model Training and Loss Plot

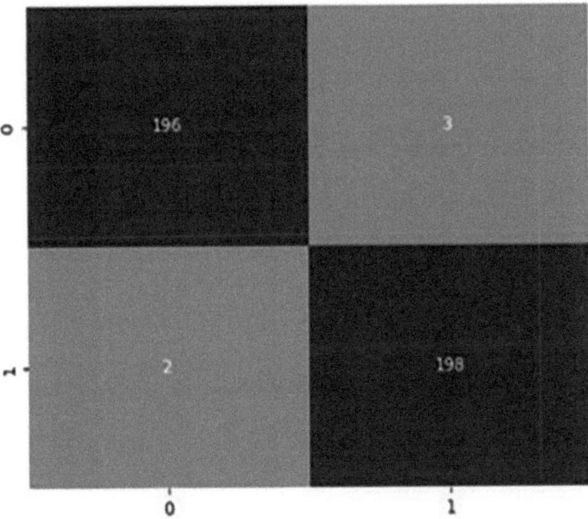

Fig. 5. Confusion Matrix for Bone Fracture Recognition

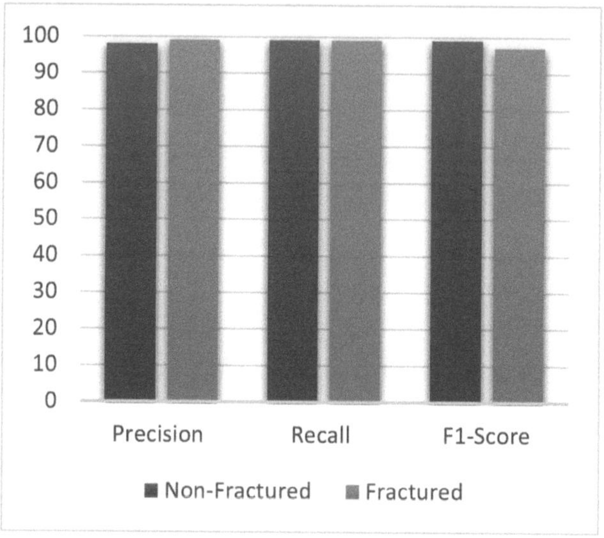

Fig. 6. Recognition Report Chart

4.1   Performance Comparison with the SOTA Bone Fracture Algorithms

The comparison of this study shows that it outperforms SOTA approaches in bone fracture detection as indicated in Table 1. Our proposedmethod surpasses current bone fracture detection algorithms in terms of accuracy, sensitivity, and specificity. This enhancement is due to the robustness of the architecture, which efficiently captures intricate imagery in X-ray images. Besides, the proposed model offers an easy explainability of how it arrives at the recognition of fractures from the input image. To the best of our knowledge, the dataset utilized in this study was released in November 2023. Not much research has been carried out with the use of this dataset, hence the reason for the comparison of our study with others that utilized different datasets.

Table 1. Performance Comparison

Publication	Techniques	Dataset	Accuracy
Ju and Cai [22]	YOLOv8	GRAZPEDWRI-DX	73.00%
Karanam et al. [24]	InceptionResNetV2	MURA	94.58%
Nguyn et al. [26]	FasterRCN	MURA	94.7%
Selin and Vironicka [25]	YOLOv7	–	84.03%
Shahnaj P.· Abdur [28]	YOLOv8	HBFMID	95.00%
Our	**CNN**	**FracAtlas**	**98.7%**

5   Conclusion

This study presents a bone fracture recognition system utilizing a CNN model and class attention transformer. The experimental results from the CNN utilizing the FracAtlas datasets demonstrate exceptional performance in bone fracture identification. The CNN model exhibits a superior accuracy of 98.7% compared with the CaiT techniques which struggle to reach 53%. Experiments demonstrate that the CNN model can efficiently identify bone fractures in intricate bone images and accurately detect fractures across multiple human body regions, which is beneficial for monitoring dislocations in everyday life. Bone fracture recognition presents a viable approach for managing disabilities in human health. Despite the model's impressive recognition results, we want to integrate more bone fracture datasets to further its generalisation capability and expose the model to fracture images not included in the training phase, in our future work.

References

1. Tahir, A., Saadia, A., Khan, K., Gul, A., Qahmash, A., Akram, R.N.: Enhancing diagnosis: ensemble deep-learning model for fracture detection using X-ray images. Clin. Radiol. (2024). https://doi.org/10.1016/j.crad.2024.08.006
2. Smith-Bindman, R., Lipson, J., Marcus, R., Kim, K.P., Mahesh, M., Gould, R., Berrington De Gonza'lez A., Miglioretti, D.L.: Radiation dose associated with common computed tomography examinations and the associated lifetime attributable risk of cancer. Arch. Int. Med. **169**(22), 2078–2086 (2009). https://doi.org/10.1001/archinternmed.2009.4
3. Hanel, D., Daluiski, A., Lachapelle, A., Gupta, A., Chopra, S., Hotchkiss, R., Gardner, M., Potter, H., Sicular, S., Lindsey, R., Mozer, M., Daluiski, A., Chopra, S., Lachapelle, A., Mozer, M., Sicular, S., Hanel, D., Gardner, M., Gupta, A., Hotchkiss, R., Potter, H.: Deep neural network improves fracture detection by clinicians. Proc. Natl. Acad. Sci. **115**(45), 11591–11596 (2018). https://doi.org/10.1073/pnas.1806905115
4. Kim, T., Goh, T.S., Lee, J.S., Lee, J.H., Kim, H., Jung, I.D.: Transfer learning-based ensemble convolutional neural network for accelerated diagnosis of foot fractures. Phys. Eng. Sci. Med. **46**, 265–277 (2023). https://doi.org/10.1007/S13246-023-01215-W
5. Wang, H.C., Wang, S.C., Yan, J.L., Ko, L.W.: Artificial intelligence model trained with sparse data to detect facial and cranial bone fractures from head CT. J. Digit Imaging **36**, 1408–1418 (2023). https://doi.org/10.1007/S10278-023-00829-6/TABLES/3
6. Su, Y., Zhang, X., Shangguan, H., Li, R.: Rib fracture detection in chest ct image based on a centernet network with heatmap pyramid structure. SIViP **17**, 2343–2350 (2023). https://doi.org/10.1007/S11760-022-02451-5/TABLES/5
7. Joshi, D., Singh, T.P., Joshi, A.K.: Deep learning-based localization and segmentation of wrist fractures on x-ray radiographs. Neural Comput. Appl. **34**, 19061–19077 (2022). https://doi.org/10.1007/S00521-022-07510-Z/FIGURES/11
8. Wang, Y., Li, Y., Lin, G., Zhang, Q., Zhong, J., Zhang, Y., Ma, K., Zheng, Y., Lu, G., Zhang, Z.: Lower-extremity fatigue fracture detection and grading based on deep learning models of radiographs. Eur. Radiol. **33**, 555–565 (2023). https://doi.org/10.1007/S00330-022-08950-W/FIGURES/5

9. Guan, B., Yao, J., Zhang, G., Wang, X.: Thigh fracture detection using deep learning method based on new dilated convolutional feature pyramid network. Pattern Recogn. Lett. **125**, 521–526 (2019). https://doi.org/10.1016/J.PATREC.2019.06.015

10. Guan, B., Yao, J., Wang, S., Zhang, G., Zhang, Y., Wang, X., Wang, M.: Automatic detection and localization of thighbone fractures in X-ray based on improved deep learning method. Comput. Vis. Image Underst. **103345** (2022). https://doi.org/10.1016/j.cviu.2021.103345

11. Abedeen, I., Ashiqur, R., Prottyasha, F.Z., Ahmed, T., Chowdhury, T.M., Shatabda, S.: FracAtlas: A Dataset for Fracture Classification, Localization and Segmentation of Musculoskeletal Radiographs, Scientific Data (2023). https://doi.org/10.1038%2Fs41597-023-02432-4

12. Liu, Y., Zhang, Y., Wang, Y., Hou, F., Yuan, J., Tian, J., Zhang, Y., Shi, Z., Fan, J., He, Z.: A Survey of Visual Transformers, vol. 06091 (2021). arXiv:2111

13. Urakawa, T., Tanaka, Y., Goto, S., Matsuzawa, H., Watanabe, K.: Endo N Detecting intertrochanteric hip fractures with orthope- dist-level accuracy using a deep convolutional neural network. Skeletal Radiol. **48**(2), 239–244 (2019). https://doi.org/10.1007/s00256-018-3016-3

14. Adams, M., Chen, W., Holcdorf, D., McCusker, M.W., Howe, P.D.L., Gaillard, F.: Computer versus human: deep learning versus perceptual training for the detection of neck of femur fractures. J. Med. Imaging Radiation Oncol. **63**(1), 27–32 (2019). https://doi.org/10.1111/1754-9485.12828

15. Russakovsky, O., Deng, J., Su, H., Krause, J., Satheesh, S., Ma, S., Huang, Z., Karpathy, A., Khosla, A., Bernstein, M., Berg, A.C., Fei-Fei, L.: ImageNet large scale visual recognition challenge. Int. J. Comput. Vis. **115**(3), 211–252 (2015). https://doi.org/10.1007/s11263-015-0816-y. arXiv:1409.0575

16. Szegedy, C., Liu, W., Jia, Y., Sermanet, P., Reed, S., Anguelov, D., Erhan, D., Vanhoucke, V., Rabinovich, A.: Going deeper with convolutions. In: 2015 IEEE Conference on Computer Vision and Pattern Recognition (CVPR), pp 1–9. https://doi.org/10.1109/CVPR.2015.7298594

17. Tanzi, L., Vezzetti, E., Moreno, R., Moos, S.: X-Ray bone fracture classification using deep learning: A baseline for designing a reliable approach. MDPI AG. (2020). https://doi.org/10.3390/app10041507

18. Kim, T., Moon, N.H., Goh, T.S., Jung, I.D.: Detection of incomplete atypical femoral fracture on anteroposterior radiographs via explainable artificial intelligence. Sci. Rep. **13**, 1–10 (2023). https://doi.org/10.1038/S41598-023-37560-9

19. Wei, J., Yao, J., Zhanga, G., Guan, B., Zhang, Y., Wang, S.: Semi- supervised object detection based on single-stage detector for thighbone fracture localization. Neural Comput. Appl. **1–15**, 2022 (2023). https://doi.org/10.1007/S00521-023-09277-3/TABLES/12

20. Lin, T.Y., Dolla'r, P., Girshick, R., He, K., Hariharan, B., Belongie, S.: Feature pyramid networks for object detection. In: Proceedings–30th IEEE Conference on Computer Vision and Pattern Recognition, CVPR 2017, vol. 2017, pp. 936–944. Institute of Electrical and Electronics Engineers Inc. https://doi.org/10.1109/CVPR.2017.106

21. Lin, T.-Y., Goyal, P., Girshick, R., He, K., Dollar, P.: Focal loss for dense object detection. IEEE Trans. Pattern Anal. Mach. Intel. (2018). https://doi.org/10.1109/TPAMI.2018.2858826

22. Ju, R., Cai, W.: Fracture detection in pediatric wrist trauma x-ray images using yolov8 algorithm. Sci. Rep. **13**(1). (2023). https://doi.org/10.1038/s41598-023-47460-7

23. Touvron, H., Cord, M., Douze, M., Jégou, H., Lavril, T.: Going deeper with image transformers. In: Proceedings of the IEEE/CVF International Conference on Computer Vision (ICCV), pp. 6571–6580 (2021)
24. Karanam, S., Srinivas, Y., Chakravarty, S.: A supervised approach to musculoskeletal imaging fracture detection and classification using deep learning algorithms. Comput. Assisted Methods Eng. Sci. **30**(3), 369–385 (2023). https://doi.org/10.24423/cames.682
25. Selin Vironicka A DJGRS Framework for classifying long bone detection using image processing techniques. Int. J. Intel. Syst. Appl. Eng. **10**(1S), 56–66 (2022). https://ijisae.org/index.php/IJISAE/article/view/2237/820
26. Nguyn H., Nghiem, K., Dang, N.: A novel arm bone fracture detection using deep learning. Adv Inf. Commun. Technol. 11–19 (2023). https://doi.org/10.1007/978-3-031-49529-8_2
27. Hugo, T., Matthieu, C., Alexandre, S., Gabriel, S., Herve, J.: Going deeper with Image Transformers (2021). arXiv:2103.17239v2 [cs.CV]
28. Shahnaj, P., Abdur, R.A.: Real-time human bone fracture detection and classification from multi-modal images using deep learning technique. Appl. Intel. (2024). https://doi.org/10.1007/s10489-024-05588-7

Machine Learning-Based Region Segmentation for Enhanced Wi-Fi Fingerprinting in Indoor Localization

Mohamad Anas Mohamad Nour, Saleh Alshami, and Rashid Ali[(✉)]

Department of Engineering Science, University West, Trollhättan 461 32, Sweden
{mohamad-anas.mohamad-nour,saleh.alshami}@student.hv.se, rashid.ali@hv.se

Abstract. Global Positioning System (GPS) signals are often unreliable in indoor environments due to attenuation and multipath effects caused by surrounding structures. As an alternative, Wi-Fi fingerprinting-based indoor positioning systems (FPIPS) have gained traction, leveraging Received Signal Strength Indicator (RSSI) values and the widespread availability of Wi-Fi infrastructure without requiring additional hardware. However, improving localization accuracy while maintaining low computational cost remains a persistent challenge. A region-based K-Nearest Neighbour (RB-KNN) algorithm has shown promise, yet the process of defining regions and selecting their optimal number is still non-trivial. This study investigates the use of four unsupervised machine learning algorithms–K-Means, DBSCAN, Gaussian Mixture Models, and Agglomerative Clustering–to automatically form fingerprint regions for RB-KNN. By systematically evaluating these approaches, the work aims to identify the most effective clustering strategy for enhancing localization accuracy and efficiency in campus-scale indoor environments. Experimental results demonstrate that Agglomerative Clustering outperforms other methods, achieving a mean positioning error of 4.44 m, a 38% improvement over the baseline RB-KNN approach. The findings highlight the potential of machine learning-based region segmentation to significantly enhance the performance of Wi-Fi fingerprinting-based indoor positioning systems.

Keywords: Wi-Fi fingerprinting · Indoor positioning system · Indoor localization · Wi-Fi · Machine learning · Clustering

1 Introduction

Advances in the Internet of Things (IoT) and automation have increased the demand for accurate indoor localization, where Global Positioning System (GPS) signals are often unreliable due to attenuation and multipath effects caused by surrounding obstacles [4]. To address this limitation, alternative technologies such as Bluetooth, ultrasonic sensing, and Wi-Fi communication have been investigated. Among these, Wi-Fi is particularly attractive because of its widespread

S. Boumerdassi et al. (Eds.): MLN 2025, LNCS 16424, pp. 28–37, 2026.
https://doi.org/10.1007/978-3-032-18494-8_3

availability in indoor spaces [5]. Wi-Fi fingerprinting relies on collecting Received Signal Strength Indicator (RSSI) measurements from multiple access points (APs) at known reference points (RPs) to construct a fingerprint database. During localization, real-time RSSI values are compared with this database to estimate user position.

While Wi-Fi fingerprinting has been widely adopted, research continues to focus on improving both accuracy and computational efficiency. In [1], authors evaluated several K-Nearest Neighbour (KNN) variants and identified the Region-Based KNN (RB-KNN) algorithm as particularly effective. However, that study relied on predefined fingerprint regions, which may limit adaptability and increase the risk of misclassification. To overcome these limitations, several studies have explored machine learning (ML)–based clustering methods to reduce the search space during localization. For example, Ren et al. [9] proposed an improved fuzzy c-means clustering method, Ramires et al. [8] and Chen [3] investigated signal-based clustering approaches, and Park and Rhee [7] integrated clustering into KNN frameworks. Other researchers, including Anuwatkun et al. [2] and Neyaz et al. [6], demonstrated the effectiveness of K-Means in this context. Clustering has long been used to structure Wi-Fi fingerprints and reduce search space before KNN matching, including fuzzy c-means, signal-space clustering, and hierarchical schemes integrated with KNN-based localization. While these approaches are promising for multi-agent coordination and sensor fusion, the present study isolates the effect of *unsupervised region formation* as a lightweight, deployable improvement to fingerprint-based region-based KNN (RB-KNN), orthogonal to policy-learning or strategic interaction frameworks.

Rationale for Algorithm and Metric Selection

In this study, the four unsupervised methods were chosen to span complementary inductive biases: centroidal partitions (K-Means), density connectivity without pre-specified k (DBSCAN), probabilistic overlap (GMM), and shape-agnostic hierarchical grouping (Agglomerative/Ward). This set is widely used in practice and provides contrasting behaviors on sparse, noisy RSSI. Silhouette was used for cluster compactness/separation; however, it does not guarantee downstream task performance, motivating our joint evaluation with *localization accuracy* (ME/SD/RMSE) and *computational cost*.

Research Objectives and Questions

Building on this line of research, the present study investigates four unsupervised ML algorithms–K-Means, DBSCAN, Gaussian Mixture Models (GMM), and Agglomerative Clustering–for automatically generating fingerprint regions based on RSSI patterns. These automatically formed clusters replace manual segmentation in RB-KNN, and the algorithms are systematically compared in terms of localization accuracy and computational cost. The study is guided by the following research questions:

- How can the optimal number of regions for RB-KNN be determined?
- Can ML-based clustering effectively define optimal regions for RB-KNN?
- Which clustering algorithm–K-Means, DBSCAN, GMM, or Agglomerative Clustering–yields the best balance of accuracy and computational efficiency?

2   Machine Learning-Based Region Segmentation

This study adopts a quantitative approach to examine the impact of ML algorithms on region segmentation for Wi-Fi fingerprinting-based indoor positioning. The analysis is based on a real-world dataset [1], with the objective of uncovering meaningful structures among reference points (RPs) to define regions and assess their influence on both positioning accuracy and computational efficiency.

2.1   Dataset Description

The dataset comprises Wi-Fi fingerprints collected on a campus site across two adjacent building blocks covering approximately $40\,\mathrm{m}^2$ of floor area, as shown in Fig. 1. Reference points are laid out on a 1 m grid, yielding 1350 locations; several TPs are uniformly sampled from the same area. Each fingerprint includes RSSI (dBm) from up to 20 detectable access points (BSSIDs), along with image-space coordinates (35.7 px/m). The environment contains both corridors and open spaces; corridors make up roughly 10% of the traversable area, with typical line-of-sight occlusions due to doors, corners, and human presence.

2.2   Clustering Algorithms

Four unsupervised ML algorithms were selected to automatically segment the dataset into regions:

K-Means A centroid-based algorithm that partitions data into k clusters by minimizing intra-cluster variance. The optimal value of k was determined using the Silhouette coefficient.

DBSCAN A density-based approach that identifies high-density groups of RPs without requiring k in advance. Cluster formation depends on two parameters: the neighborhood radius (ϵ) and the minimum number of points ($min\_samples$).

Gaussian Mixture Model (GMM) A probabilistic framework that represents clusters as mixtures of Gaussian distributions. The Expectation-Maximization (EM) algorithm is used for parameter estimation, and the Bayesian Information Criterion (BIC) helps prevent overfitting by penalizing overly complex models.

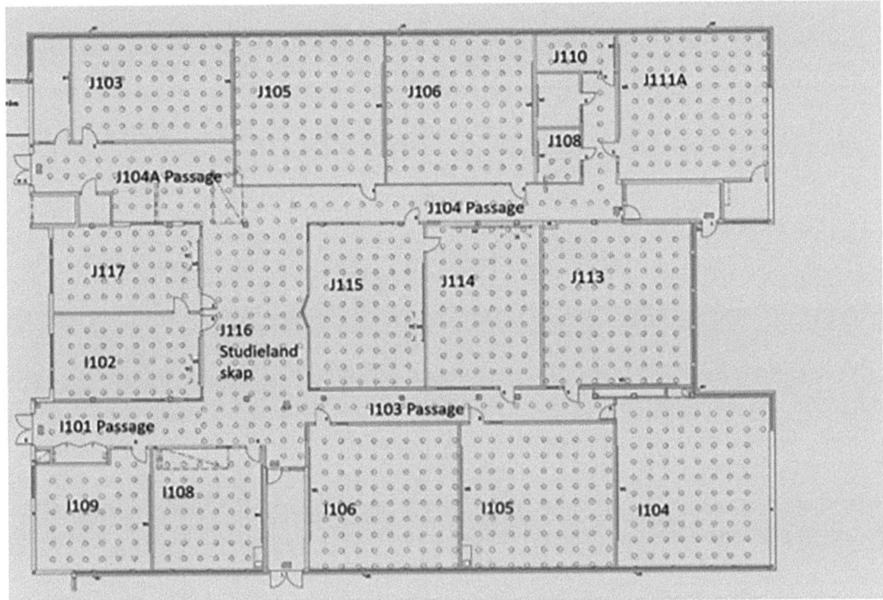

Fig. 1. Map of recorded reference points at the campus block I and J.

Agglomerative Clustering A hierarchical bottom-up method that iteratively merges RPs into clusters based on similarity in RSSI values. Ward's linkage criterion was applied to minimize within-cluster variance.

Feature Engineering To construct a compact representation per RP, we retained the six most frequently observed BSSIDs across the site (ties broken by median RSSI), resulting in a six-dimensional vector per RP (missing APs imputed to -100 dBm). RSSI features were standardized (z-score) across the dataset. We did not apply dimensionality reduction such as PCA in the main experiments to preserve interpretability and avoid mixing AP contributions; however, PCA or learned embeddings are promising for future work.

2.3   Evaluation Metrics

The performance of clustering methods was assessed using three criteria:

- **Clustering Quality**: Measured by the Silhouette score, reflecting the compactness and separation of clusters.
- **Computational Cost**: Processing time required to generate regions from the dataset.
- **Positioning Accuracy**: Localization error when RB-KNN is applied with regions derived from each clustering method.

3   Results

This section evaluates the clustering algorithms in comparison with the baseline RB-KNN. The analysis focuses on three aspects: clustering quality, positioning accuracy, and computational efficiency.

3.1   Clustering Quality

Clustering performance was measured using the Silhouette coefficient, which reflects the compactness and separation of clusters. Table 1 summarizes the results. K-Means achieved the highest Silhouette score (0.4430), indicating well-separated and coherent clusters. Agglomerative clustering followed closely (0.4336), demonstrating strong adaptability to structural variations in the dataset. GMM also produced competitive results (0.3913), leveraging its probabilistic formulation to handle overlapping regions. In contrast, DBSCAN performed poorly (0.1429), forming only two large clusters due to its sensitivity to sparse and irregular signal distributions.

Table 1. Comparison of optimal cluster numbers (k), Silhouette score, and clustering time.

Algorithm	k	Silhouette score	Time (s)
K-Means	10	0.4430	0.0362
GMM	19	0.3913	0.0310
Agglomerative	18	0.4336	0.0223
DBSCAN	8	0.1429	0.0164

3.2   Positioning Accuracy

To assess the effect of clustering on localization, RB-KNN was applied with regions generated by each algorithm. Table 2 presents mean error (ME), standard deviation (SD), and root mean square error (RMSE). Agglomerative clustering achieved the best performance, reducing the mean error to 4.44 m (a 38% improvement over the baseline RB-KNN). GMM and K-Means also improved accuracy, with mean errors of 4.56 m and 5.60 m, respectively. DBSCAN performed the worst, producing errors exceeding 9 m.

Figures 2 and 3 further illustrate these findings. Agglomerative clustering yielded the steepest cumulative distribution curve, with over 70% of predictions within 5 m. The boxplots confirm this consistency, while DBSCAN exhibited wide error variance and multiple outliers.

DBSCAN assumes clusters correspond to dense regions under a fixed ϵ and min _samples_; in sparse, high-variance RSSI spaces, density is non-uniform

Table 2. Positioning performance of RB-KNN and clustering-based variants.

Algorithm	ME (m)	SD (m)	RMSE (m)
RB-KNN	7.13	5.28	8.87
K-Means KNN	5.60	3.66	6.69
GMM KNN	4.56	2.90	5.40
Agglomerative KNN	4.44	2.64	5.17
DBSCAN KNN	9.09	7.73	11.93

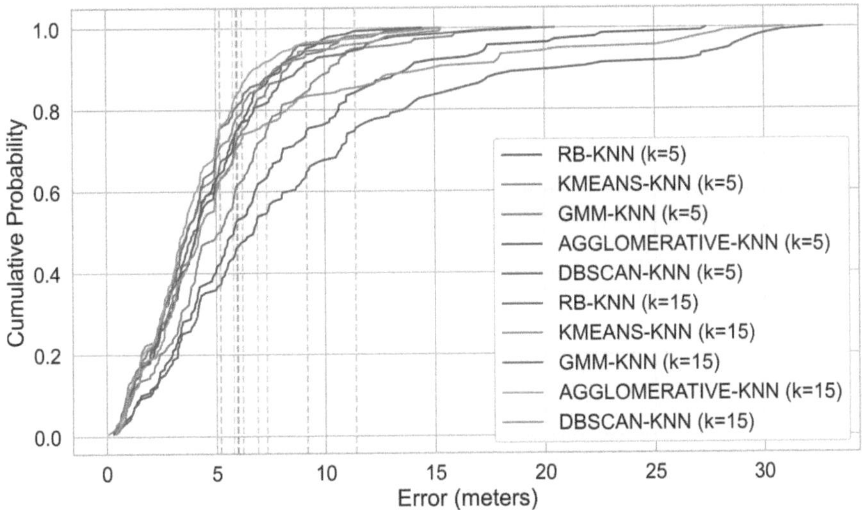

Fig. 2. CDF of localization errors for RB-KNN and clustering algorithms.

and anisotropic across corridors vs. open areas. As a result, a single global ϵ merges disparate fingerprints (few large clusters) or fragments true neighborhoods, depending on the setting. Combined with the curse of dimensionality on RSSI and missing-AP imputation, DBSCAN produced coarse regions that degrade KNN filtering despite fast clustering time.

3.3   Computational Efficiency

Table 3 compares clustering and positioning times. All algorithms demonstrated low computational overhead, making them suitable for real-time updates. Agglomerative clustering achieved the best balance of accuracy and speed, completing clustering in 0.0223 s and positioning in 0.0003 s per instance. GMM and K-Means exhibited similar runtimes, while DBSCAN was the fastest but suffered from poor accuracy. The results highlight that efficiency alone is insufficient for practical use; accuracy and robustness remain critical.

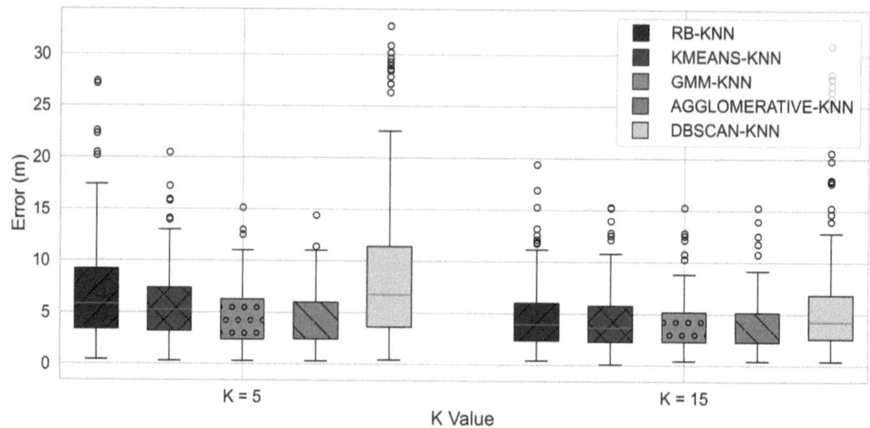

Fig. 3. Boxplots of localization errors (m) across methods.

Table 3. Runtime comparison of clustering and positioning.

Algorithm	Clustering Time (s)	Positioning Time (s)
RB-KNN	–	0.0092
K-Means KNN	0.0362	0.0006
GMM KNN	0.0310	0.0003
Agglomerative KNN	0.0223	0.0003
DBSCAN KNN	0.0164	0.0017

4   Discussion and Analysis

This section interprets the results presented in Tables 1, 2, 3 and Figs. 2 and 3, with emphasis on clustering quality, positioning accuracy, and computational efficiency.

4.1   Clustering Quality and Suitability

K-Means achieved the highest Silhouette score (0.4430), reflecting compact and well-separated clusters consistent with its assumption of spherical partitions. The resulting 10 clusters offered a balanced level of granularity suitable for many indoor layouts. Agglomerative clustering produced a comparable score (0.4336) while forming 18 clusters, demonstrating its ability to adapt to the non-uniform and irregular patterns typical of RSSI data. Importantly, Agglomerative does not impose strong assumptions on cluster shape, which explains its suitability for real-world deployments.

GMM ranked slightly lower in clustering quality (0.3913) but provided the finest segmentation with 19 clusters. Its probabilistic formulation enabled the detection of overlapping and elliptical regions, which is advantageous in noisy environments. DBSCAN, by contrast, achieved the lowest Silhouette score (0.1429) and produced only eight clusters, indicating that its density-based logic was not well-suited to the sparsity and variability of the dataset.

4.2 Positioning Accuracy and Error Distribution

In terms of positioning, Agglomerative clustering clearly outperformed other methods, reducing the mean error to 4.44 m–representing a 38% improvement over the RB-KNN baseline. Its cumulative distribution curve (Fig. 2) confirmed that more than 70% of predictions fell within 5 m, a practical threshold for room-level indoor localization.

GMM achieved comparable performance (mean error 4.56 m, RMSE 5.40 m), benefiting from its fine-grained cluster structure, though with a slightly wider error variance and more outliers (Fig. 3). K-Means offered moderate gains, while DBSCAN delivered the poorest accuracy (mean error above 9 m), with errors widely dispersed across test cases. Even the RB-KNN baseline was more reliable than DBSCAN, highlighting that density-based methods may struggle with irregular Wi-Fi signal distributions.

4.3 Computational Efficiency and Practicality

From a computational perspective, all methods demonstrated low processing times, suitable for periodic updates in real-time systems. Agglomerative clustering again provided the most balanced trade-off, completing clustering in 0.0223 s and achieving the same fast positioning time (0.0003 s) as GMM. K-Means required slightly longer for clustering (0.0362 s) but remained efficient. DBSCAN was the fastest in clustering (0.0164 s), yet its substantial accuracy loss renders this advantage impractical.

These findings underline a broader principle: speed alone is insufficient for indoor localization. Practical deployment requires algorithms that balance accuracy, robustness, and efficiency. Among the methods tested, Agglomerative clustering achieved this balance most effectively, making it a strong candidate for real-time Wi-Fi fingerprinting applications.

5 Conclusion and Future Work

This study investigated the use of unsupervised ML techniques to enhance Wi-Fi fingerprinting-based indoor positioning systems. The focus was on replacing manually predefined regions in RB-KNN with dynamically generated clusters. Four clustering algorithms–K-Means, Gaussian Mixture Models, Agglomerative Clustering, and DBSCAN–were systematically evaluated with respect to clustering quality, positioning accuracy, and computational efficiency.

The results demonstrated that clustering quality, as measured by the Silhouette score, does not necessarily translate into improved positioning performance.

Although K-Means achieved the highest Silhouette score (0.4430), Agglomerative clustering provided the most accurate localization, reducing the mean positioning error to 4.44 m, which represents a 38% improvement over the baseline RB-KNN method. GMM also performed well, producing fine-grained clusters that captured signal variability effectively. In contrast, DBSCAN struggled with sparse and irregular RSSI distributions, yielding poor accuracy despite being the fastest in clustering time.

These findings highlight the importance of algorithm selection based on both data characteristics and deployment requirements. In particular, Agglomerative clustering emerged as the most effective approach, offering a strong balance of accuracy, adaptability, and efficiency, making it suitable for real-time indoor localization in dynamic environments.

Future work will extend this study in several directions. First, larger and more diverse datasets from different building types will be incorporated to assess generalizability across environments. Second, hybrid approaches that combine clustering with dimensionality reduction or deep learning could be explored to further improve scalability and robustness. Third, the integration of temporal features (e.g., mobility patterns or sequential RSSI readings) may enable more stable region definitions in dynamic conditions. Finally, real-world deployment and benchmarking on mobile devices will be pursued to validate the practical viability of the proposed methods in real-time applications.

In summary, ML-driven region formation represents a promising direction for next-generation indoor positioning systems, with the potential to significantly improve accuracy, efficiency, and adaptability beyond traditional RB-KNN frameworks.

Acknowledgments. This work was conducted as part of an undergraduate thesis project within the Wireless Networking and AI research domain at the Computer Science Research Group, University West, Sweden. The authors sincerely acknowledge the use of OpenAI ChatGPT, which contributed to improving the written content only.

Data and Code Availability. The dataset, preprocessing scripts, and analysis code used in this study are openly available at the project repository: MLDR-WiFi. This repository includes the Wi-Fi fingerprint dataset, clustering and evaluation code, and supporting documentation required to reproduce the reported results.

Disclosure of Interests. The authors have no competing interests to declare that are relevant to the content of this article.

References

1. Andersson, R., Tagesson, W., Ali, R.: Dataset: evaluating Wi-Fi fingerprinting for enhanced indoor positioning in campus environments (2024). https://github.com/wirelessATwest/PEWFIPS-HV
2. Anuwatkun, A., Sangthong, J., Sang-Ngern, S.: A diff-based indoor positioning system using fingerprinting technique and k-means clustering algorithm. In: 2019

16th International Joint Conference on Computer Science and Software Engineering (JCSSE), pp. 148–151 (2019). https://doi.org/10.1109/JCSSE.2019.8864175

3. Chen, S.: Indoor localization based on fingerprint clustering. Netw. Commun. Technol. **5**, 40 (2020). https://doi.org/10.5539/nct.v5n2p40

4. GPS.gov: Gps accuracy, https://www.gps.gov/systems/gps/performance/accuracy/#how-accurate. Accessed 2 Mar 2024

5. Álvarez Merino, C.S., Khatib, E.J., Luo-Chen, H.Q., Muñoz, A.T., Moreno, R.B.: Evaluation and comparison of 5G, WiFi, and fusion with incomplete maps for indoor localization. IEEE Access **12**, 51893–51903 (2024). https://doi.org/10.1109/ACCESS.2024.3384625

6. Neyaz, H., Inamullah, M., Beg, M.S.: Machine learning based indoor positioning system using Wi-Fi fingerprinting dataset. In: 2024 International Conference on Electrical, Computer and Energy Technologies (ICECET), pp. 1–5 (2024). https://doi.org/10.1109/ICECET61485.2024.10698116

7. Park, C., Rhee, S.H.: Indoor positioning using Wi-Fi fingerprint with signal clustering. In: 2017 International Conference on Information and Communication Technology Convergence (ICTC), pp. 820–822 (2017). https://doi.org/10.1109/ICTC.2017.8190791

8. Ramires, M., Torres-Sospedra, J., Moreira, A.: Accurate and efficient wi-fi fingerprinting-based indoor positioning in large areas. In: 2022 IEEE 96th Vehicular Technology Conference (VTC2022-Fall), pp. 1–6 (2022). https://doi.org/10.1109/VTC2022-Fall57202.2022.10012985

9. Ren, J., Wang, Y., Niu, C., Song, W., Huang, S.: A novel clustering algorithm for Wi-Fi indoor positioning. IEEE Access **7**, 122428–122434 (2019). https://doi.org/10.1109/ACCESS.2019.2937464

Enhanced DiNATrAX for Multi-protocol Anomaly Detection

Maham Kayani[(⊠)], Nahom Getachew Gari, Nardos Hadis Haile,
Christophe Maudoux, and Selma Boumerdassi

Cédric Laboratory, Conservatoire National des Arts et Métiers (CNAM), 292 rue
Saint-Martin, 75003 Paris, France
{maham-fatima.kayani,christophe.maudoux,selma.boumerdassi}@cnam.fr,
{nahom-getachew.gari.auditeur,nardos-hadis.haile.auditeur}@lecnam.net

Abstract. Network anomaly detection remains a critical research area
in cybersecurity, aiming to identify malicious or abnormal network
behaviors that deviate from expected traffic patterns. To address the
growing complexity of modern networks, we propose DiNATrAX, an
anomaly detection framework composed of three functional blocks: data
collection and preprocessing, Sector of Interest analysis, and an anomaly
detection block. The model operates using an advanced form of digital signatures, generating unique DNAs to represent network activity
over time. By comparing consecutive DNAs sequences, DiNATrAX computes abnormality distances to automatically identify potential anomalies. The framework was evaluated using the CTU-13 botnet dataset,
specifically scenarios 9, 10, and 11. Earlier experiments showed that
DiNATrAX effectively detected anomalies in scenarios 9 and 10, which
involve TCP and UDP protocols, respectively, but had difficulty detecting attacks in scenario 11 based on the ICMP protocol. In this study, we
re-evaluate DiNATrAX with improved ICMP handling and successfully
identify ICMP-based attacks, demonstrating enhanced protocol coverage and detection capability. Overall, DiNATrAX provides a flexible and
automatable approach to network anomaly detection, forming a strong
foundation for adaptive and protocol-aware cybersecurity systems.

Keywords: Anomaly detection · Real world botnet traffic · Advanced
digital signatures · CTU-13 · Clustering-based methods ·
Dameraulevenshtein distance

1 Introduction

Network anomaly detection plays an important role in maintaining cybersecurity by identifying activities that deviate from established patterns of normal
network behavior. To automate this process, the DiNATrAX (Digital Network
Assessment and sTrand based Anomalies eXtraction) framework [1] was introduced as a cyclical and adaptive solution that models network behavior using an

S. Boumerdassi et al. (Eds.): MLN 2025, LNCS 16424, pp. 38–46, 2026.
https://doi.org/10.1007/978-3-032-18494-8_4

advanced form of digital signature approach called Digital Network Assessments (DNAs). Each DNA represents the string-encoded structure of network activity, DNA strings are formed inside clusters formed by the K-Means algorithm within a Time Slice (TL) for defined time period. Typically, four clusters are created in each TL and the time period is divided into TLs, capturing variations in network characteristics such as protocol usage, port activity, and data volume.

DiNATrAX consists of three main functional blocks. The first is preprocessing, where data is cleaned and prepared for analysis. The second is Sector of Interest (SOI) analysis, where data is divided into systematic zones called sectors, and data within each sector is further studied and called SOI data. The third block is anomaly detection, where DNA strings are compared, and scores are calculated using the DamerauLevenshtein distance. In the earlier methodology, each DNA string was compared only with the previous one, which sometimes caused anomalous strings to be classified as normal.

To address these issues, this study proposes an enhanced version of the DiNATrAX framework with a reference DNA selection mechanism. Instead of always comparing a DNA with its immediate predecessor, the model dynamically selects a reference DNA based on the stability and similarity of past network behaviors. This approach reduces false detections, provides a more stable baseline for anomaly evaluation, and improves the overall reliability and interpretability of the DiNATrAX anomaly detection process.

In DiNATrAX, DNAs are generated sequentially over time, and anomalies are detected by comparing each newly formed DNA with the previous one using the DamerauLevenshtein distance. A significant change in the DNA structure indicates a deviation in network behavior, which may correspond to a potential anomaly. However, this process introduces two main challenges. First, comparing each new DNA with its immediate predecessor can lead to false anomaly detections, where normal variations are misclassified as anomalies or vice versa. Second, there is no predefined threshold to clearly distinguish between normal and abnormal distances, which makes interpretation uncertain.

The contributions of this work lie in two main aspects.First, after obtaining the list of DNA-like sequences, the method applies agglomerative clustering [2] to partition them into four distinct clusters. From each cluster, a representative reference DNA sequence is selected based on its proximity to the cluster medoid, ensuring that four reference sequences are identified for subsequent analysis. By using these reference sequences, anomalies can be classified by severity, allowing the detection of not only the start and end of attacks but also their duration and evolution, including subtle low-signal anomalies such as (Internet Control Message Protocol) ICMP-based intrusions. Second, It introduces a thresholding strategy to classify anomalies into low, medium, and high severity levels. These contributions demonstrate the value of combining biologically inspired sequence modeling with interpretable detection mechanisms for advancing real-time network security.

In this study, we will discuss five main sections: Section I covers the introduction along with basic definitions and background; Section II presents the background in more detail; Section III explains the experimentation; Section IV concludes our findings and future work.

2 Background

Preprocessing is the first block of DiNATrAX, preprocessing is performed to prepare the raw network data for analysis [3]. This step includes removing irrelevant columns, handling missing or null values, and cleaning the dataset to ensure data quality. After cleaning, the process of sectorization takes place, where the data is divided into meaningful logical zones or sectors based on certain criteria. Preprocessing is a major part of the framework because it directly affects the accuracy of anomaly detection.

In our experimentation, the CTU-13 dataset [4] is used. This dataset is widely recognized in the cybersecurity community for network anomaly detection research. It contains different types of network activities, including botnet attacks, which make it ideal for testing and validating anomaly detection frameworks like DiNATrAX.

SOI analysis is the second block of DiNATrAX, in this stage, specific logical sectors of the network data are studied to enhance the detection of anomalies. For each selected sector, digital signatures are generated, and from these signatures, DNA strings are created. Each alphabet in a DNA string represents a key feature of network behavior, and the frequency or percentage of that feature determines its position within the string. The process of generating these DNA strings begins with extracting aggregated data for the selected SOI and then dividing the data into distinct TLs. The K-Means clustering algorithm is applied to each time slice to group similar network patterns. Based on the results of this clustering, Time-Slice Digital Signatures (TLDS) are generated to represent the distribution of data features across clusters. These TLDS are then converted into DNA strings, which serve as string-encoded representations of network activity. Finally, the DNA strings are summarized into strands that capture the overall behavioral trends observed over time. Each DNA string represents the network's behavior during a specific time period, with four clusters formed within each time slice. The features of these clusters are encoded as characters within the DNA string, allowing DiNATrAX to model and interpret network behavior in a compact, systematic, and meaningful form.

Anomaly detection is the third block of DiNATrAX focuses on anomaly detection. In this stage, the differences (or abnormalities) between the generated DNA signatures and their associated strands are calculated. These differences are measured using the DamerauLevenshtein distance, which quantifies how much one DNA string differs from another. A higher distance value indicates a greater deviation in network behavior and is considered a potential anomaly.

By analyzing these distances, DiNATrAX can identify unusual network activities such as attacks, failures, or misconfigurations. This block represents the final and most critical stage of the framework, where the detection of anomalies takes place based on the encoded digital DNA structure.

2.1   Dataset

The CTU-13 dataset, developed by the Czech Technical University (Stratosphere Lab), comprises 13 real-world network recordings that include a combination of benign, background, and botnet traffic (with instances such as Neris, Rbot, and Virut). The DiNATrAX framework was evaluated using this dataset.

2.2   Upgraded Third Functional Block

Anomaly detection is the third functional block of DiNATrAX in this block, when we get the list of DNAs, every newly generated DNA string (DNAn) is compared with the previous sequence (DNAn1) to detect deviations. The comparison employs the DamerauLevenshtein distance, which quantifies the number of edits including insertions, deletions, substitutions, or swaps [5] which required to transform one sequence into another. In parallel, the corresponding network strands are compared to verify changes. The resulting distances, denoted as DNAD for DNA distance and STAD for strands distance, are aggregated to compute the Anomaly Distance (ANOD). Higher ANOD values indicate substantial deviations in network behavior, serving as potential indicators of anomalies such as attacks or unusual traffic patterns.

To improve detection accuracy, a reference DNA selection mechanism is introduced to identify the most representative normal sequence for comparison. Three approaches were explored:

Hidden Markov Model (HMM) [6]: Network sequences are numerically encoded and modeled using an HMM trained on all observed sequences. Each sequence is evaluated based on its log-likelihood, and the sequence with the highest score is selected as the reference DNA, representing the typical network behavior.

Medoid-Based Clustering [7]: DNA sequences are clustered using agglomerative clustering with the DamerauLevenshtein distance as a similarity metric. The medoid is defined as the sequence with the minimum total distance to all other sequences in the cluster is chosen as the reference DNA. New sequences are compared against this medoid to quantify deviations from normal behavior.

Mode-Based Clustering [7]: Clustering is applied similarly, but the most frequently occurring DNA sequence (mode) within each cluster is selected as the representative. The deviation of each sequence from this representative is then used to detect anomalies.

Among these methods, medoid-based clustering demonstrated superior detection performance, effectively capturing central behavioral patterns of normal network activity. This approach enhances the capability of DiNATrAX to detect real-time botnet anomalies with improved accuracy and reliability. The upgraded DiNATrAX blocks, which incorporates this enhanced clustering mechanism, are illustrated in Fig. 1.

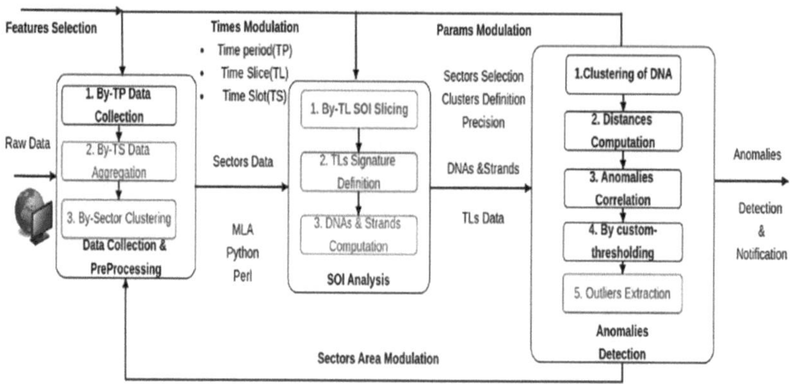

Fig. 1. Upgraded DiNATrAX Functional Block.

3   Experiment

The evaluation of DiNATrAX was first conducted using the CTU-13 dataset, a publicly available collection of NetFlow-like records from 13 different botnet scenarios involving malware such as Neris, Rbot, and Virut. Each flow entry in CTU-13 contains detailed information like temporal features (StartTime, Duration), flow state and protocol (Proto, State, Dir), addressing attributes (SrcAddr, DstAddr, Sport, Dport), and traffic volume indicators (TotPkts, Tot-Bytes, SrcBytes). The dataset also includes labels identifying normal or malicious flows, along with scenario and day identifiers (Scenario, Day). These characteristics make CTU-13 a strong benchmark for validating network anomaly detection systems on realistic, labeled traffic across TCP, UDP, and ICMP protocols.

3.1   Data Aggregation Approach in DiNATrAX

To perform the analysis in an unsupervised manner, all annotation labels were excluded from the CTU-13 dataset. Within the DiNATrAX framework, it was essential to specify a characteristic feature (F) used for constructing DNAs and strands. The destination port was chosen as the characteristic F, since source ports are typically assigned randomly by the operating system and thus lack behavioral meaning.

Because destination port values range from 0 to 65,535 [8], they were grouped into port bands to reduce variability. The range 01023 is reserved for well-known ports [9], so DiNATrAX grouped ports into bands of 2,048 values each. This produced 32 possible port-band values, which offered a balanced trade-off between granularity and data reduction. These band values were encoded alphanumerically for use in DNA generation. Raw network flows were aggregated using an unsupervised K-Means algorithm to reduce data volume and expose meaningful behavioral patterns. The aggregation key included elements such as source and destination IP addresses, ports, protocol, and connection state. IP addresses were generalized into subnets using CIDR masks [8] ranging from /8 to /24, in increments of 4 bits, to merge related flows.

3.2   Scenarios 9 and 10 (TCP and UDP)

In the earlier experiment, we evaluated the DiNATrAX framework using Scenario 9 and Scenario 10 of the CTU-13 dataset. Scenario 9 was analyzed following the original DiNATrAX approach, while Scenario 10 contained both TCP and UDP traffic. The framework performed effectively in both scenarios; however, during the detection phase, each newly generated DNA string was continuously compared with previously generated strings. This repeated comparison caused a decrease in the anomaly score over time, resulting in certain anomalous sequences being classified as normal. From these observations, we conclude that DiNATrAX can successfully detect both TCP and UDP-based attacks in the CTU-13 dataset, but it faces limitations in identifying anomalies that occur during the active duration of an attack.

3.3   Scenario 11 (ICMP)

In the earlier phase of this research, DiNATrAX was evaluated using Scenarios 9 which has Neris attack and having TCP protocol and 10 which has Rbot attack and having UDP protocol, based on the original DNA-inspired approach. The outcomes of those experiments were discussed in a previous study, which is currently under publication. However, the initial version of DiNATrAX faced limitations specifically, it was unable to detect ICMP-based attacks present in Scenario 11 of the CTU-13 dataset. To address this shortcoming, a new and improved strategy was developed and implemented on Scenario 11.

In this updated version, two major modifications were introduced. The first enhancement involved integrating a reference DNA approach, where each newly generated DNA string was compared against a representative reference DNA. To determine this reference DNA, we employed both HMM based analysis and clustering methods (using medoid and mode-based selection) to identify the most characteristic or central DNA sequence among a group of strands. Once the reference DNA was established, it served as a baseline for comparing all other DNA strands to identify deviations indicative of anomalous behavior.

The second improvement was the inclusion of the ICMP protocol, enabling DiNATrAX to effectively recognize and analyze ICMP-based attack patterns that were previously undetected. After computing the ANOD (Anomaly Detection) score for each aggregated DNA string, a threshold-based classification was applied to categorize anomalies into high, medium, and low severity levels.

When Scenario 11 was experimented, we applied a medoid-based clustering strategy in which four clusters were created among the generated DNA strands. Each cluster was represented by a single medoid (representative DNA). These representative DNA sequences were then compared with other DNA strings using the DamerauLevenshtein distance metric to quantify the level of dissimilarity. After obtaining the ANOD values, a custom dynamic threshold was applied to classify anomalies. The results were visualized in a graphical representation showing the distribution of high, medium, and low anomalies, as illustrated in Fig. 2.

Scenario 11 from the CTU-13 dataset primarily contains ICMP-based attack activities. The summary of the attack timeline is shown in Table 1.

Table 1. Scenario 11 ICMP Attack Timeline

Time Slot	Event	Bots
15:53	Attack Start	SARUMAN 1 and 2
15:54	Attack Duration	SARUMAN 1 and 2
15:55	Attack End	SARUMAN 1 and 2
15:56	Capture End	SARUMAN 1 and 2

Using the improved DiNATrAX approach, the condensed results obtained from the medoid-based clustering analysis and the corresponding ANOD values are summarized in Table 2. These results clearly indicate that DiNATrAX can effectively detect and characterize ICMP-related anomalies.

Table 2. Medoid-Based clustering result

Time (StartEnd)	DNA	Strand	ANOD
2011-08-18 15:5315:54	ACQBW-A-A-A	ACQBW	13
2011-08-18 15:5415:55	AECIW-AE-A-A	AECIW	15
2011-08-18 15:5515:56	AEIQV-A-A-E	AEIQV	13

The computed ANOD values and their corresponding severity levels are visualized in Fig. 2, where medium, high, and low anomalies are depicted to show the improved system's ability to capture ICMP-based deviations effectively.

Table 2 and Fig. 2 collectively demonstrate that the enhanced DiNATrAX framework successfully detects ICMP-based attacks with notable accuracy, showcasing its adaptability and robustness across multiple network protocols.

4   Conclusion and Future Work

4.1   Contribution

In this study, we enhanced the existing DiNATrAX framework by introducing an additional processing step. Specifically, each DNA sequence generated by DiNA-TrAX was further divided using an agglomerative clustering approach. Within each cluster, a reference DNA was determined using a medoid-based method.

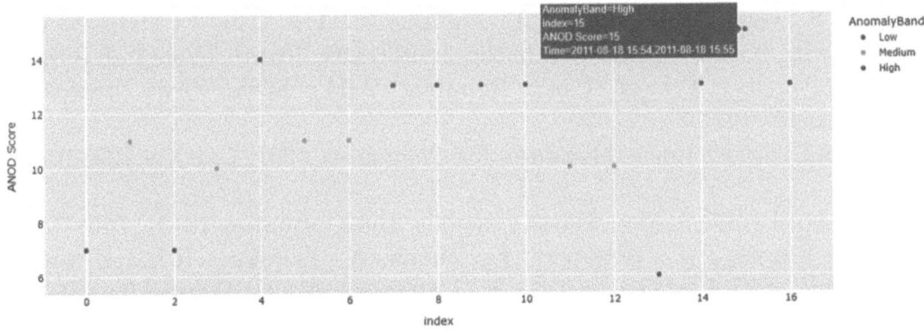

Fig. 2. ANOD ScoreBased ICMP Anomaly Detection Results (Scenario 11).

Subsequently, anomaly distance calculations were applied to define threshold values, enabling the categorization of data into low, medium, and high anomaly levels. This refinement improves the granularity of anomaly detection and supports a more detailed understanding of network behavior.

4.2 Limitation

Although DiNATrAX can accurately detect the start, duration, and end of an attack, it occasionally misclassifies normal sequences as high-anomaly instances. This limitation highlights the need for improved discrimination mechanisms and adaptive thresholding to reduce false positives. Ongoing research is currently focused on addressing this issue.

4.3 Future Work

Future research will focus on adapting the DiNATrAX framework for real-world network traffic analysis. Planned improvements include developing strategies for more accurate classification, minimizing false-positive rates, and refining anomaly categorization mechanisms. These enhancements aim to make DiNA-TrAX more robust and applicable to dynamic, large-scale network environments.

References

1. Maudoux, C., Boumerdassi, S.: DiNATrAX : a Network Anomalies Detection Framework. In: *Proceedings of the IEEE International Conference on Communications (ICC)*, pp. 4090–4095. Denver, CO, USA, June 2024. https://doi.org/10.1109/ICC51166.2024.10622410
2. Oti, E., Olusola, M.: Overview of agglomerative hierarchical clustering methods. *British J. Comput. Netw. Inf. Technol.* **7**, 14–23 (2024)
3. Kapadia, M., Dunton, A., Jaculina, C., Thach, D., Ong, A., Chang, S.Y.: Data visualization and preprocessing for network traffic analysis in cybersecurity. *J. Netw. Netw. Appl.* **5**(1), 13–26 (2025)

4. García, S., Grill, M., Stiborek, J., Zunino, A.: The CTU-13 Dataset: a labeled dataset with botnet, normal and background traffic. Stratosphere Lab (Czech Technical University), Prague, Czech Republic (2011). https://www.stratosphereips.org/datasets-ctu13
5. Hosangadi, S.: Distance Measures for Sequences (2012). arXiv:1208.5713, Aug. 2012
6. Eddy, S.R.: Profile hidden Markov models. Bioinformatics **14**(9), 755–763 (1998)
7. Sánchez Vinces, B.V., Schubert, E., Zimek, A., Cordeiro, R.L.: A comparative evaluation of clustering-based outlier detection. *Data Mining Knowl. Discov.* **39**(2), 13 (2025)
8. TechTarget, What are dynamic, private, ephemeral and well-known port numbers?. https://www.techtarget.com/searchnetworking/definition/dynamic-port-numbers
9. Internet Assigned Numbers Authority (IANA), Service Name and Transport Protocol Port Number Registry. https://www.iana.org/assignments/service-names-port-numbers/service-names-port-numbers.xhtml
10. Fuller, V., Li, T., Yu, J., Varadhan, K.: Classless Inter-Domain Routing (CIDR): an address assignment and aggregation strategy. In: Request for Comments 1519, Internet Engineering Task Force (IETF), Sept. 1993. https://datatracker.ietf.org/doc/rfc1519/

Ensemble Neuro-Symbolic AI and Logic Tensor Networks for Detecting Fraud on the Ethereum Blockchain

Zainab Khallouf[1]([✉]) and Pierre-François Marteau[1,2]

[1] École Nationale Supérieure d'Ingénieurs de Bretagne Sud (ENSIBS), Vannes 56000, France
{zainab.khallouf,pierre-francois.marteau}@univ-ubs.fr
[2] Institut de Recherche en Informatique et Systémes Aléatoires (IRISA), Vannes 56000, France

Abstract. Neuro-symbolic artificial intelligence (NSAI) is a novel paradigm that combines the pattern recognition capabilities of neural networks with the logical reasoning of symbolic systems [11,13]. This study explores the application of NSAI for detecting fraudulent activities on the Ethereum blockchain, employing an existing implementation known as Logic Tensor Networks (LTNs) [12,13]. The task is formulated as a binary classification aimed at distinguishing between legitimate and fraudulent transactions. Ethereum is a decentralized, open-source blockchain, peer-to-peer platform based on the Kademlia protocol and powered by the Ethereum Virtual Machine (EVM), which enables the creation and execution of smart contracts and decentralized applications (dApps). Smart contracts are self-executing programs on the blockchain that automatically verify and enforce the terms of an agreement in a trustless manner. Once deployed, they become immutable and publicly auditable on the blockchain. The decentralized and pseudonymous nature of Ethereum presents significant challenges for effective fraud detection. In this study, we propose and evaluate a voting-based ensemble NSAI framework to classify fraudulent transactions using a publicly available Ethereum fraud detection dataset [14]. Experimental results demonstrate that the proposed ensemble architecture outperforms approximately 80% of the individual models. Moreover, the proposed voting approach offers natural compatibility within the peer-to-peer based Ethereum architecture.

Keywords: Artificial intelligence (AI) · Machine learning · Neuro-symbolic artificial intelligence (NSAI) · Logic tensor networks (LTNs) · Binary classification · Ensemble models · Ethereum blockchain · Peer-to-peer · Fraud detection

S. Boumerdassi et al. (Eds.): MLN 2025, LNCS 16424, pp. 47–63, 2026.
https://doi.org/10.1007/978-3-032-18494-8_5

1 Introduction

Neuro-Symbolic Artificial Intelligence (NSAI) aims at combining the strengths of neural models in learning from large-scale data with the reasoning capabilities of symbolic systems. The goal is to create intelligent systems that are not only capable of learning from data but also able to reason with greater interpretability. By integrating these complementary approaches, NSAI can address key limitations that both neural and symbolic systems face individually [11,13].

This paper explores the application of NSAI, specifically through the use of Logic Tensor Networks (LTNs) [12,13], to detect fraudulent activities on the Ethereum blockchain.

We leverage a publicly available Ethereum fraud detection dataset [14], then creating ensemble LTN-based NSAI architecture aimed at distinguishing between legitimate and fraudulent transactions.

Through this case study, we aim to provide insights into the practical considerations of applying NSAI to blockchain security, as well as its potential for fraud detection systems.

The remainder of this paper is organized as follows. Section 2 reviews existing approaches to fraud detection using neuro-symbolic artificial intelligence. Section 3 provides an overview of the Logic Tensor Network (LTN) framework. Section 4 introduces the Ethereum blockchain and highlights its key characteristics. Section 5 overviews malicious activities on Ethereum. Section 6 details the proposed methodology, including the use of a publicly available Ethereum fraud detection dataset, data preprocessing, feature engineering, and strategies to prevent data leakage and overfitting. Section 7 presents the experimental results, demonstrating the effectiveness of the proposed approach in identifying fraudulent activities on Ethereum. Section 8 explores the interpretability of the model. Finally, Sect. 9 concludes the paper by summarizing the main findings and outlining potential directions for future research.

2 Related Works

Several studies have investigated the application of NSAI techniques in the domains of cybersecurity, fraud detection, and classification. However, their application within the specific context of blockchain technology remains unexplored.

Kalutharage et al. [2] present a neurosymbolic learning-based model that leverages explainable AI (XAI) and expert domain knowledge to enhance anomaly detection in IoT networks. Their approach integrates a knowledge graph to assess whether a detected anomaly constitutes an attack, aligning outcomes with the MITRE ATT&CK framework to identify anomalies and guide intelligent countermeasures.

Piplai et al. [3] explore the potential of NSAI in enhancing cybersecurity and privacy applications by integrating neural networks with symbolic knowledge representations. Their approach leverages the data extraction capabilities of deep neural networks along with the domain reasoning power of knowledge graphs.

Bizzarri et al. [4] propose a NSAI framework for Network Intrusion Detection Systems (NIDS), addressing limitations in conventional approaches such as high computational overhead, limited interpretability, and poor adaptability to novel threats. By analyzing network traffic and integrating symbolic reasoning techniques, the authors demonstrate how NSAI can uncover complex threat patterns and adapt to dynamic cyber environments.

Grov et al. [5] advocate for the integration of NSAI in cybersecurity, particularly for incidents detection and response. Recognizing the limitations of relying solely on either connectionist or symbolic AI, they argue for a hybrid approach that combines the strengths of both paradigms.

Kejriwal and Sharma [6] propose a hybrid neuro-symbolic framework aimed at real-time detection of adversarial attacks in autonomous systems. Recognizing the vulnerabilities of deep learning to adversarial attacks, particularly in mission-critical domains like self-driving vehicles and industrial automation, their approach uses neural networks for feature extraction with symbolic reasoning for logical validation and dynamic threat mitigation.

Gajjar [8] explores the use of NSAI as a hybrid intelligence framework for cloud intrusion detection.

Jalaian and Bastian [9] provide a comprehensive overview of the role of NSAI in strengthening cybersecurity, with a focus on IDSs. Their work underscores the synergy between neural networks' pattern recognition capabilities and symbolic reasoning's interpretability, aiming to address the limitations of conventional approaches in detecting and understanding complex cyber threats.

Sander et al. [10] extend Open Set Recognition with Deep Embedded Clustering for XGBoost and Uncertainty Quantification (ODXU), a neuro-symbolic AI (NSAI) framework designed to enhance NIDSs by improving classification and uncertainty quantification. By integrating neural networks with symbolic reasoning, ODXU addresses the challenge of open set recognition in cybersecurity. The authors employ techniques such as confidence scoring, Shannon entropy, and post-hoc Uncertainty Metamodeling to quantify prediction uncertainty, thereby enhancing system reliability.

Ranjan [1] introduces a neuro-symbolic AI framework tailored for financial fraud detection, which integrates the pattern recognition capabilities of deep learning with the logical inference strengths of symbolic reasoning. The framework consists of three key components: a neural processing layer utilizing deep learning models to analyze raw financial data, a symbolic knowledge base containing over 3.000 predefined rules and regulations, and a reasoning engine that applies logical inference to combine neural outputs with domain-specific knowledge.

Dingli and Farrugia [11] and Carraro [17] present frameworks that employ NSAI for binary classification tasks. Building upon the concepts introduced in these references, our work extends their approach by applying it in a different context, implementing a novel ensemble architecture and utilizing a distinct dataset.

3 The Logic Tensor Networks (LTNs)

One existing implementation of NSAI is the LTN [12,13]. Unlike conventional machine learning models that depend exclusively on data-driven methods to extract patterns, LTNs integrate the `satisfaction of a knowledge base` into their learning objective. This allows the model to be trained not only to minimize prediction errors but also to respect logical constraints derived from domain knowledge and to maximize the overall logical satisfaction. By combining reasoning into the learning process, LTNs models are both trained by data and logically consistent with prior knowledge [13]. The semantics of LTNs rely on fuzzy logic [12].

The knowledge base in an LTN is represented by a set of `axioms` based on the following components [12,13]:

- Predicates: Predicates are real-valued functions that map tuples of individuals from an n-ary domain (e.g. features) to a truth value in the interval $[0, 1]$, representing the degree to which a logical statement holds [12]. Predicates can encode concepts such as similarity measures, classifiers, or other decision functions. In binary classification tasks, predicates are typically implemented as a feed forward neural networks that take feature vectors as input and output a truth value in $[0, 1]$.
- Connectives: Logical connectives (e.g., $\wedge$, $\vee$, $\Rightarrow$) are used to express logical relationships within the knowledge base.
- Quantifiers: Quantifiers describe the extent to which a predicate is satisfied by the data. The two primary quantifiers are the universal quantifier ($\forall$), which asserts that a condition holds for all elements, and the existential quantifier ($\exists$), which asserts that at least one element satisfies the condition. In LTNs, quantifiers are implemented using fuzzy aggregation functions.
- SatAgg: The SAT aggregator is an operator that aggregates the truth values of all closed formulas in the knowledge base. By default, SatAgg is implemented using the p-Mean Error aggregator, summarizing the overall satisfaction of the knowledge base.

4 Overview of the Ethereum Blockchain

Ethereum is an open-source, decentralized blockchain platform built on a Kademlia-based peer-to-peer (P2P) network. It enables participants to transact directly without intermediaries such as banks, brokers, notaries, or centralized servers. Each block in the blockchain contains a set of validated transactions and is appended to the chain through a consensus mechanism, i.e., agreement among peers on the state of the ledger. Ethereum transitioned to energy-efficient consensus mechanisms as Proof-of-Stake (PoS), under which validators are selected to create new blocks based on the amount of cryptocurrency they have staked in the network.

Ether (ETH) is the native cryptocurrency of the Ethereum network. While, a token is a digital representation of an asset and is recorded on the Ethereum blockchain. Each token is governed by a smart contract, a self-executing program deployed on the Ethereum network that defines its rules, ownership, and transferability. The ERC-20 standard specifies the interface for creating fungible tokens, meaning each token unit is identical and interchangeable with others, similar to traditional currencies. In contrast, non-fungible tokens (NFTs) represent unique, indivisible assets that cannot be exchanged on a one-to-one basis, such as artworks. Beyond ERC-20 and ERC-721 (NFTs), the Ethereum ecosystem supports other token standards such as ERC-1155, which combines features of both fungible and non-fungible tokens to improve efficiency and flexibility.

A participant in the Ethereum network is known as a node, representing an instance of Ethereum client software connected to other nodes [22].

Depending on their data storage and validation responsibilities, Ethereum nodes can be categorized as follows [22]:

- Full nodes: Validate transactions and blocks while maintaining the current state of the blockchain.
- Archive nodes: Store the complete historical state of the blockchain, enabling access to past data for analytical or historical purposes.
- Light nodes (e.g., wallets): Store only block headers and rely on full nodes for additional data retrieval, allowing participation with minimal computational and storage resources.

Full and archive nodes operate two main components: the execution client, which processes transactions, and the consensus client, which ensures network-wide agreement on the blockchain state, as illustrated in Fig. 1, highlighting the architecture and the different components of Ethereum.

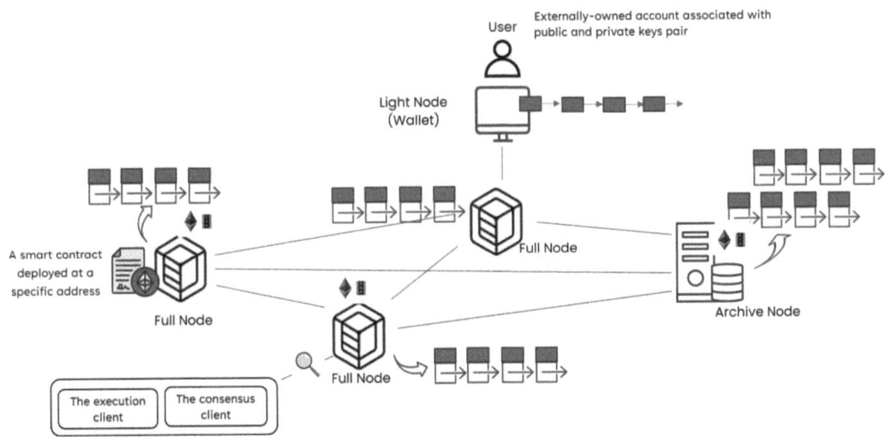

Fig. 1. The architecture and the different components of Ethereum.

Nodes that include the execution layer run the Ethereum Virtual Machine (EVM), which executes smart contracts typically written in the Solidity programming language. For example, a smart contract may be designed to facilitate electronic voting or decentralized finance operations. Each smart contract resides at a unique blockchain address.

Ethereum accounts can be classified into two categories [23]:

– Externally Owned Accounts (EOAs): User-controlled accounts derived from a private key, allowing secure transaction signing and initiation.
– Contract Accounts: Accounts controlled by smart contract code, created deterministically from the creators address and nonce. These accounts cannot initiate transactions independently, but they can execute code when triggered by an EOA or another contract.

A transaction represents a state-changing operation on the Ethereum blockchain, such as transferring tokens or invoking a smart contract function. Transactions are cryptographically signed by the sender to ensure authenticity and integrity. Each transaction consumes a certain amount of **gas**, which measures the computational effort required for its execution. Transactions are grouped into blocks, which are appended to the blockchain once validated through the consensus mechanism.

A decentralized application (dApp) consists of two primary components: a front-end interface running on the user's local machine and a back-end component implemented as one or more smart contracts deployed on the Ethereum blockchain. Such applications form the foundation of Web3, the emerging paradigm of a decentralized internet.

In the Ethereum ecosystem, standards are formal specifications that define how smart contracts, tokens, and other functionalities should behave. These standards are proposed as Ethereum Improvement Proposals (EIPs).

5   Overview of Fraudulent and Malicious Activities on Ethereum

Ethereum has driven the rise of Decentralized Finance (DeFi), NFTs, and dApps, among other blockchain-based innovations.

However, its decentralized and pseudonymous architecture also introduces security challenges, leaving the platform susceptible to a wide spectrum of fraudulent and malicious activities, as reported in recent studies [18, 24, 28, 30, 31, 33]. These malicious activities can generally be categorized into three major classes: User-targeted frauds, smart contract and DApp exploits, and network-level attacks.

5.1   User-Targeted Frauds

– Phishing attacks: Users are deceived into revealing sensitive information, such as private keys, or signing fraudulent transactions. These attacks can be partially detected on-chain by monitoring features like transfers to known phishing wallets.

- Ponzi schemes: Fraudulent investment operations in which older investors are paid using funds from new participants rather than from legitimate business activities.
- Airdrop scams: Phishing tokens are airdropped to random wallets on a blockchain to attract wallet owners into visiting phishing websites.

5.2   Smart Contract and DApp Exploits

These attacks exploit flaws in smart contracts or DApp logic.

- Reentrancy attack: Recursively invoking a vulnerable smart contract function before the previous execution completes, potentially enabling depletion of funds.
- Access control flaw: Improper authorization in contract logic that permits attackers to execute privileged functions.
- Front-End hijacking: Compromise of DApp client-side interfaces connecting users to the blockchain, to redirect victims to phishing sites or malicious contracts.
- Rug Pull: Malicious withdrawal of funds or unexpected shutdown of DApp functionality by developers or operators.

5.3   Network and Infrastructure Attacks

Network-level attacks target the Ethereum protocol, consensus, or infrastructure, often affecting availability or integrity.

- Eclipse attack: Cyberattack in which attackers aim to isolate nodes on blockchain network layers to control their view of the blockchain.
- DDoS attack: Flooding the network with excessive transactions to degrade performance.

6   Methodology

6.1   The Ethereum Fraud Detection Dataset

We use the Ethereum Fraud Detection Dataset, available on Kaggle, to classify fraudulent transactions [14]. This dataset contains Ethereum transaction records labeled as either fraudulent or legitimate, along with a variety of features describing each transaction. These features are engineered from raw transactional data. The dataset contains 51 columns and 9841 transaction records with attributes such as:

- Index: A unique identifier for each transaction record.
- Address: The Ethereum wallet address associated with the transaction.
- FLAG: A binary label indicating whether the transaction is fraudulent (1) or legitimate (0).
- Total_Ether_Balance: The total Ether balance of the account after transactions.
- Total_Ether_Sent_Contracts: Total Ether sent to contract addresses.

6.2 Data Processing and Features Engineering

The following data processing and feature engineering pipeline was implemented prior to performing binary classification on the fraud detection dataset [18]. The methodology includes data exploration, data cleaning, removal of highly correlated features, categorical feature encoding, class balancing using the Synthetic Minority Over-sampling Technique (SMOTE), feature scaling, dimensionality reduction by an autoencoder, splitting data, creating a customized data loader, and defining the knowledge base.

Data Preprocessing and Encoding The dataset initially contains both numerical and categorical features, along with a binary target variable, `FLAG`, indicating fraudulent (1) or legitimate (0) transactions. Irrelevant attributes such as `Index` and `Address`, as well as duplicated rows and highly correlated features, were removed [18]. Categorical variables were transformed using one-hot encoding, while missing values were imputed with the median of each column to ensure robustness against outliers. Finally, the dataset was randomly shuffled to eliminate potential ordering bias.

Class Balancing via SMOTE Due to the class imbalance in the data, we employed SMOTE. SMOTE generates synthetic samples by interpolating between existing minority class instances. After applying SMOTE, the number of samples in the minority class is 80% of the number of samples in the majority class.

Feature Scaling To ensure numerical stability and faster convergence during training, all features were normalized to the range $[0, 1]$ using a MinMaxScaler. This step prevents features with larger magnitudes from dominating the learning process.

Dimensionality Reduction Using Autoencoder To extract features and reduce the dimensionality of the input space, an autoencoder was trained. Autoencoders offer an alternative to traditional feature selection methods such as Random Forest feature importance, particularly in high dimensional and complex datasets [15]. Unlike Random Forests, which evaluate features based on their individual contribution to decision tree splits, autoencoders perform unsupervised dimensionality reduction by learning compact latent representations that preserve the most salient information required to reconstruct the input data.

Moreover, when combined with neural classifiers, autoencoder based features offer a natural compatibility within a deep learning framework.

The autoencoder consists of two components: an encoder that compresses input data from the original dimension to a lower-dimensional representation, and a decoder that reconstructs the input from this compressed representation.

After training, only the encoder component of the autoencoder was retained and used to transform the input data into a compressed latent space. The resulting encoded features were employed for the classification tasks. After feature extraction, the encoded data has a shape of $(13791, 20)$, where 13791 represents the number of samples, and 20 denotes the dimensionality of the compressed latent representation, selected as a hyperparameter.

6.3   Data Splitting, Batching and Evaluation Protocol

To ensure robust evaluation and avoid data leakage, the dataset was randomly divided into three non-overlapping subsets: 70% for training, 10% for validation, and 20% for testing. The split guarantees that no sample appeared in more than one partition.

We employ a custom `DataLoader` to iterate over the training, test and validation partitions in batches [11]. Each batch contains an equal number of positive (fraudulent) and negative (non-fraudulent) samples, which prevents the model from being biased toward the majority class and enhances generalization. Consequently, the training loader exclusively accesses training samples, the test loader accesses only test samples, while validation loader accesses only validation samples eliminating the risk of data leakage.

The training DataLoader was used exclusively for model training, optimization, and updating the network parameters through backpropagation. The validation DataLoader was employed during training to monitor generalization performance and to implement early stopping, using the F1 score on the validation set as the stopping criterion. This approach prevented overfitting by halting training once validation performance ceased to improve. Finally, the test DataLoader was reserved strictly for the final evaluation of the trained models and the ensemble system.

LTN predicates operate directly on the batches produced by the DataLoaders. Each batch is transformed into an LTN `Variable`, enabling the framework to evaluate truth values for the corresponding mini-batch during training.

6.4   Defining the Knowledge Base

One important step in NSAI is to set up the knowledge base. We follow the same methodology explained in [11, 12] and [17].

The process involves constructing two variables: x_A for normal transactions and $x_{\neg A}$ for fraudulent ones. These are passed to quantified logical formulas to enforce the classification constraints: $\forall x_A : A(x_A)$ and $\forall x_{\neg A} : \neg A(x_{\neg A})$. The combined logical satisfaction of these formulas is then aggregated using a satisfiability aggregator (SatAgg) provided by the LTNtorch [12] library. The SAT level is used during training. Specifically, the objective of training is to maximize the overall SAT level of the knowledge base, thereby guiding the neural network to learn representations that are logically consistent.

7 An Ensemble Neuro-Symbolic AI Model to Classify Fraudulent Transactions in Ethereum

Our ensemble approach combines multiple predicates, each implemented as a neural network, to introduce architectural diversity. Specifically, we employed fifteen predicates for binary classification, featuring varying structures and activation functions. This design was intended to evaluate whether leveraging a heterogeneous set of predicates could enhance performance relative to a single-predicate configuration.

Each model is trained individually by iterating over the training set, where model parameters are updated using the backpropagation algorithm to minimize prediction errors and to maximize satisfaction.

We train our models using the following parameters:

- EPOCHS = 500, allowing up to 500 training iterations.
- PATIENCE = 5, for early stopping if the validation metric (F1-score) does not improve for 5 consecutive epochs.
- batch_size = 128, for mini-batch training.

During training, the system continuously monitors performance on the validation set and applies early stopping based on the F1 score to prevent overfitting and ensure generalization.

After the completion of training, each model is evaluated on the test set, and a detailed classification report is generated to assess its predictive performance. Finally, an ensemble model is constructed through majority voting across all trained models, and its performance is likewise evaluated on the test set to obtain the overall classification metrics.

Figure 2 illustrates the evolution of the satisfaction level (SAT), along with the corresponding accuracy and F1 score of Model 1 across training and validation epochs. These metrics provide insight into how the NSAI system learns from both logical knowledge and data. The results, illustrated in Table 1 highlight the performance of five representative models (of the 15 models) and the performance of the ensemble approach, in addition to model architecture, hyperparameters, and activation functions.

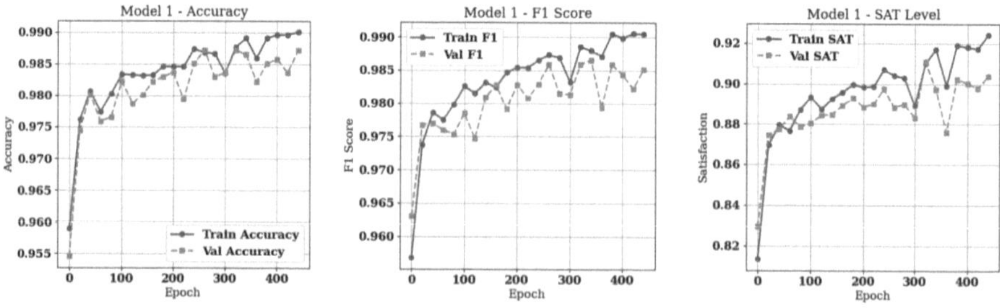

Fig. 2. The evolution of the satisfaction level (SAT), accuracy, F1 for the first model in the ensemble approach.

Table 1. Summary of model performance, architecture, hyper-parameters, and activation functions.

Model	Accuracy	Classification Report	Architecture/Hyperparameters
Model 1	0.989	Class Precision Recall F1-score	Style: Residual
		Not Fraud 0.984 0.994 0.989	Hidden layers: 128-64-64-32-1
		Fraud 0.993 0.983 0.988	Activation: SELU
			Dropout: AlphaDropout (0.1)
			Normalization: LayerNorm
Model 2	0.984	Class Precision Recall F1-score	Style: Residual, compact
		Not Fraud 0.982 0.988 0.985	Hidden layers: 128-64-64-32-1
		Fraud 0.987 0.980 0.984	Activation: SELU
			Dropout: AlphaDropout(0.1)
			Normalization: None
Model 4	0.975	Class Precision Recall F1-score	Style: Feedforward
		Not Fraud 0.972 0.980 0.976	Hidden layers: 128-64-64-1
		Fraud 0.978 0.970 0.974	Activation: SELU
			Dropout: 0.2
			Normalization: LayerNorm
Model 13	0.991	Class Precision Recall F1-score	Style: Deep Feedforward
		Not Fraud 0.993 0.989 0.991	Hidden layers: 256-128-64-32-1
		Fraud 0.988 0.993 0.990	Activation: GELU
			Dropout: 0.25, 0.2
			Normalization: LayerNorm
Model 14	0.990	Class Precision Recall F1-score	Style: Feedforward, LeakyReLU
		Not Fraud 0.989 0.992 0.990	Hidden layers: 128-128-64–32-1
		Fraud 0.991 0.988 0.990	Activation: LeakyReLU(0.1)
			Dropout: 0.3
			Normalization: None
Model 15	0.980	Class Precision Recall F1-score	Style: Feedforward, Mish
		Not Fraud 0.974 0.988 0.981	Hidden layers: 64–32-1
		Fraud 0.986 0.972 0.979	Activation: Mish
			Dropout: 0.1
			Normalization: None
Ensemble	0.989	Class Precision Recall F1-score	Style: Ensemble of 15 neural predicates
		Not Fraud 0.987 0.992 0.989	
		Fraud 0.991 0.986 0.988	

Discussion:

– The results demonstrate the advantage of the ensemble NSAI approach over individual models. In our setup, the ensemble achieves higher accuracy, over 80% of the base models as illustrated in Fig. 3. In this figure, each box represents the distribution of accuracies for a given model across all test batches.

However, the effectiveness of the voting mechanism depends upon the quality of the constituent base models.

- When compared with the results of the traditional ensemble voting algorithm for detecting fraud in Ethereum presented by Gu and Dib [18] (Accuracy = 0.99, Precision = 0.98, Recall = 0.97, F1-score = 0.98), and noting that their work splits the data into training and test setsunlike our approach, which uses separate training, validation, and test setsour ensemble NSAI approach achieves comparable performance. Further optimization through grid search of hyperparameters may lead to improved results.
- More complex and deeper neural predicate architectures do not necessarily yield better performance. For instance, a simpler model like Model 14 can outperform a more complex model such as Model 2.

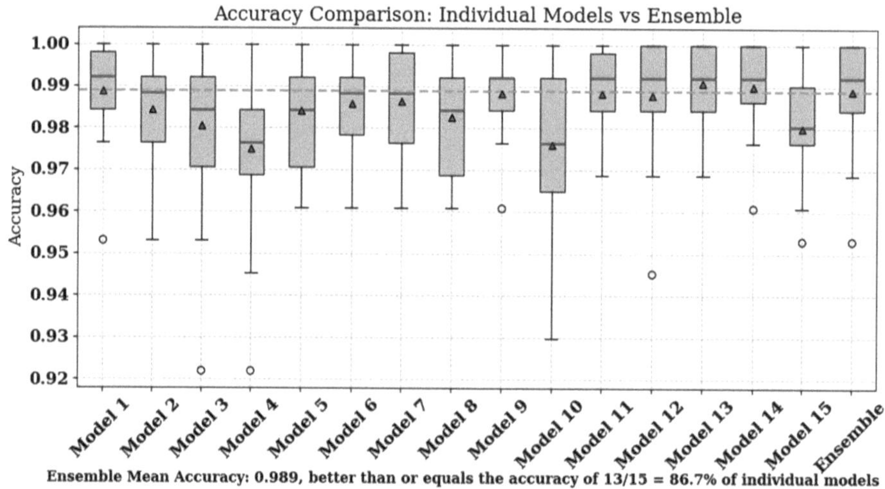

Fig. 3. Comparison of the accuracies of individual models with that of the ensemble model.

8   Explainability of LTN-Based Models

The rapid growth of AI fundamentally depends on trust and explainability. Users are unlikely to adopt machine learning models behaving as black boxes. NSAI address this challenge by integrating neural networks with fuzzy logic reasoning, thereby enhancing interpretability as logical rules are particularly easy to explain. For example, a rule such as: *If a transaction involves an unusually large amount and originates from or is sent to a wallet associated with a high-risk, then the transaction is likely fraudulent,* is straightforward for humans to understand.

In LTN, the model is trained to satisfy a predefined knowledge base containing predefined axioms. This inherently interpretable logic can be further enhanced using conventional explainable AI tools. For instance, to explain which features most influence the predicate's decisions, logical reasoning can be combined with explainable AI techniques such as SHapley Additive exPlanations (SHAP) [25]. SHAP, developed in the context of cooperative game theory and introduced by Lloyd S. Shapley in the 1950s, treats each feature as a `player` contributing to a coalition that collectively determines the model's output. The resulting SHAP values quantify the contribution of each feature to the final prediction.

We applied SHAP to the first model in our architecture, as illustrated in Fig. 4. From the figure, features such as `ERC2 Most Sent Token Type_AdBank` and `ERC20 Most Sent Token Type_ARBITRAGE` are shown to have a significant influence on the model's predictions.

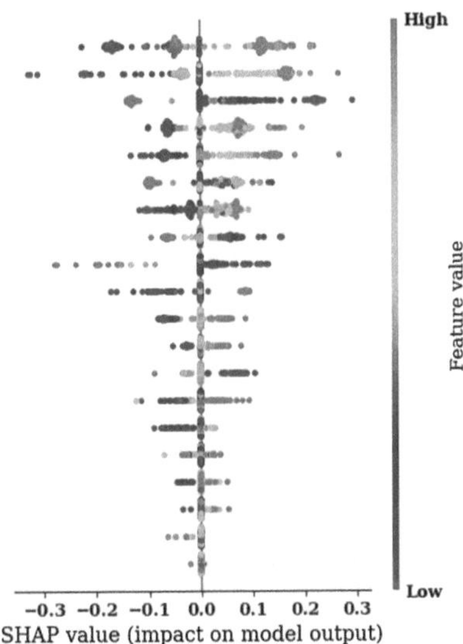

Fig. 4. SHAP results for Model 1.

By combining data-driven learning with symbolic reasoning, LTNs enable models to produce interpretable and human-aligned predictionsbridging the gap between statistical accuracy and logical transparency.

9   Conclusion and Future Work

In this work, we explored the potential of neuro-symbolic artificial intelligence (NSAI) for fraud detection on the Ethereum blockchain. Our results indicate that NSAI can achieve performance comparable to state-of-the-art techniques while offering the added benefit of combining logical reasoning with traditional neural networks.

We proposed a `novel` ensemble architecture that combines multiple neural predicates, each implemented as a neural network with varying structures and activation functions, thereby introducing architectural diversity. The results demonstrate the advantage of the ensemble NSAI approach over individual models.

Future work could focus on hyperparameters optimization and the development of a parameterizable ensemble framework. Such a framework would allow dynamic selection and configuration of NSAI components.

Deploying NSAI in a distributed configuration, where ensemble models are distributed across multiple predicates, presents a promising avenue for future research and offers natural compatibility within a peer-to-peer blockchain architecture. Ensemble voting is particularly advantageous in distributed setups, as models can be trained independently on different machines and their predictions aggregated. This enables efficient utilization of heterogeneous hardware, with lighter models running on less powerful devices and more complex ones on stronger machines, collectively contributing to the final decision.

Additional Information and Declarations

- Funding: The authors received no direct funding for this work. The Institut de Recherche en Informatique et Systmes Alatoires (IRISA) laboratory covered the conference registration fees, while the Éole Nationale Supérieure dnn'Ingénieurs de Bretagne Sud (ENSIBS) supported travel and accommodation expenses to attend and present the work at the conference by the first author.
- Competing Interests: The authors declare that they have no competing interests.
- Author Contributions:
  - Zainab Khallouf conceived and designed the experiments, performed the experiments, analyzed the data, carried out the computational work, prepared the content and structured the paper. She acknowledges the use of the free version of ChatGPT to improve text clarity and assist with code, while emphasizing that all conceptual development, structure, and intellectual contributions remain the result of human effort.
  - Pierre-François Marteau proposed the ensemble approach combining several predicates and using an autoencoder for dimensionality reduction, reviewed and corrected drafts of the article, and approved the final version.
- Data Availability: This work is a case study. Additional information can be obtained upon request from the first author.

References

1. Ranjan, P.: A neuro-symbolic artificial intelligence framework for fraud detection. LinkedIn (2023). [Online]. Available: https://www.linkedin.com/pulse/neuro-symbolic-artificial-intelligence-framework-fraud-piyush-ranjan-xdkie/

2. Kalutharage, C.S., Liu, X., Chrysoulas, C.: Neurosymbolic learning and domain knowledge-driven explainable AI for enhanced IoT network attack detection and response. Comput. Secur. **151**, 104318 (2025). https://doi.org/10.1016/j.cose.2025.104318

3. Piplai, A., Kotal, A., Mohseni, S., Gaur, M., Mittal, S., Joshi, A.: Knowledge enhanced neurosymbolic artificial intelligence for cybersecurity and privacy. IEEE Internet Comput. **27**(5), 43–48 (2023). https://doi.org/10.1109/MIC.2023.3299435

4. Bizzarri, A., Yu, C.-E., Jalaian, B., Riguzzi, F., Bastian, N.D.: A Synergistic Approach in Network Intrusion Detection by Neurosymbolic AI (2024). arXiv:2406.00938. [Online]. Available: https://arxiv.org/abs/2406.00938

5. Grov, G., Halvorsen, J., Eckhoff, M.W., Hansen, B.J., Eian, M., Mavroeidis, V.: On the use of neurosymbolic AI for defending against cyber attacks (2024). arXiv:2408.04996, https://arxiv.org/abs/2408.04996

6. Kejriwal, D.K., Sharma, A: A hybrid neuro-symbolic framework for real-time detection of adversarial attacks in autonomous systems. IRE J. **8**(5), 1293–1300 (2024). ISSN: 2456-8880

7. Bizzarri, A., Jalaian, B., Riguzzi, F., Bastian, N.D.: A neuro-symbolic artificial intelligence network intrusion detection system. In: 2024 33rd International Conference on Computer Communications and Networks (ICCCN), Kailua-Kona, HI, USA, pp. 1–9 (2024). https://doi.org/10.1109/ICCCN61486.2024.10637618

8. Gajjar, S.R.: Neuro-symbolic AI for cloud intrusion detection: a hybrid intelligence approach. GSC Adv. Res. Rev. **22**(2), 142–144 (2025). https://doi.org/10.30574/gscarr.2025.22.2.0049

9. Jalaian, B., Bastian, N.D.: Neurosymbolic AI in cybersecurity: bridging pattern recognition and symbolic reasoning. In: MILCOM 2023 - 2023 IEEE Military Communications Conference (MILCOM), Boston, MA, USA, pp. 268–273 (2023). https://doi.org/10.1109/MILCOM58377.2023.10356283

10. Sander, J., Yu, C.-E. J., Jalaian, B., Bastian, N.D.: Uncertainty-quantified neurosymbolic AI for open set recognition in network intrusion detection. In: MILCOM 2024 - 2024 IEEE Military Communications Conference (MILCOM), Washington, DC, USA, pp. 13–18 (2024). https://doi.org/10.1109/MILCOM61039.2024.10773953

11. Dingli , A., Farrugia, D.: Neuro-Symbolic AI: Design Transparent and Trustworthy Systems That Understand the World as You Do, 1st edn., Packt Publishing (2023). ISBN: 1804617628

12. Carraro, T., Serafini, L., Aiolli, F.: LTNtorch: PyTorch implementation of Logic Tensor Networks (2024). arXiv:2409.16045, https://arxiv.org/abs/2409.16045

13. Badreddine, S., d'Avila Garcez, A., Serafini, L., Spranger, M.: Logic Tensor Network (2022). arXiv:2206.06614, https://arxiv.org/abs/2206.06614

14. "Ethereum Fraud Detection Dataset," Kaggle. https://www.kaggle.com/datasets/vagifa/ethereum-frauddetection-dataset

15. Volovăt, S.R., Popa, T.O., Rusu, D., Ochiuz, L., Vasincu, D., Agop, M., Buzea, C.G., Volovăt, C.C.: comparative performance of autoencoders and traditional machine learning algorithms in clinical data analysis for predicting post-staged GKRS tumor dynamics. Diagnostics **14**(18), 2091 (2024). https://doi.org/10.3390/diagnostics14182091

16. Fukami, K., Nakamura, T., Fukagata, K.: Convolutional neural network based hierarchical autoencoder for nonlinear mode decomposition of fluid field data, Phys. Fluids **32**(9), 095110 (2020). https://doi.org/10.1063/5.0020721
17. Carraro, T.: LTNtorch: Binary Classification Example, GitHub. https://github.com/tommasocarraro/LTNtorch/blob/main/examples/1-binary_classification.ipynb
18. Gu, Z., Dib, O.: Enhancing fraud detection in the Ethereum blockchain using ensemble learning. PeerJ Comput. Sci. **11**, e2716 (2025). https://doi.org/10.7717/peerj-cs.2716
19. He, K., Zhang, X., Ren, S., Sun, J.: Deep residual learning for image recognition. In: Proceedings of the IEEE Conference on Computer Vision and Pattern Recognition (CVPR), pp. 770–778 (2016)
20. Klambauer, G., Unterthiner, T., Mayr, A., Hochreiter, S.: Self-normalizing neural networks. Adv. Neural Inf. Process. Syst. (NeurIPS) **30**, 971–980 (2017)
21. Goodfellow, I., Bengio, Y., Courville, A.: Deep Learning, MIT Press (2016)
22. Ethereum Foundation, "Nodes and clients," Ethereum Documentation (2024). https://ethereum.org/developers/docs/nodes-and-clients/
23. Ethereum Foundation, "Accounts," Ethereum Documentation (2025). https://ethereum.org/developers/docs/accounts/
24. Hornuf, L., Momtaz, P.P., Nam, R.J., Yuan, Y.: Cybercrime on the Ethereum blockchain. J. Bank. Financ. **175**, 107419 (2025). https://doi.org/10.1016/j.jbankfin.2025.107419, https://www.sciencedirect.com/science/article/pii/S0378426625000391
25. Shapley, L.S.: A value for n-person games. In: Kuhn, H.W., Tucker, A.W (Eds.), Contributions to the Theory of Games, vol. 2, pp. 307–317. Princeton University Press (1953)
26. Wu, K.W.: Strengthening DeFi security: A static analysis approach to flash loan vulnerabilities (2025). https://arxiv.org/abs/2411.01230
27. Durieux, T., Ferreira, J.F., Abreu, R., Cruz, P.: Empirical review of the security of Ethereum smart contracts: DApp vulnerabilities in the wild. ACM Trans. Softw. Eng. Methodol. (TOSEM) (2020). https://doi.org/10.1145/3380847
28. Kumar, R., et al.: Smart contract attacks and vulnerabilities on Ethereum: a systematic review. IEEE Access **10**, 11035–11057 (2022). https://doi.org/10.1109/ACCESS.2022.3145642
29. Atzei, N., Bartoletti, M,., Cimoli, T.: A survey of attacks on Ethereum smart contracts (SoK). In: International Conference on Principles of Security and Trust (POST 2017) (2017). https://doi.org/10.1007/978-3-662-54455-6_8
30. Agarwal, U., Rishiwal, V., Tanwar, S., Yadav, M.: Blockchain and crypto forensics: Investigating crypto frauds. Int. J. Network Manage **34**(2), e2255 (2024). https://doi.org/10.1002/nem.2255
31. Verma, R., Chandrawanshi, K., Soni, G., Jain, G., Nigam, S., Jain, N.: Unveiling security vulnerabilities in NFTs: A comprehensive risk assessment. In: 2024 IEEE 4th International Conference on ICT in Business Industry & Government (ICT-BIG), Indore, India, pp. 1–6 (2024). https://doi.org/10.1109/ICTBIG64922.2024.10911117
32. Bhumichai, D., Benton, R.G.: The evaluation of extracted features for detecting eclipse attacks on Ethereum network layer. In: IEEE International Conference on Big Data (BigData) **2024**, 5551–5560 (2024). https://doi.org/10.1109/BigData62323.2024.10825144

33. Horch, A., Schunck, C.H., Ruff, C.: Adversary tactics and techniques specific to cryptocurrency scams. In: Open Identity Summit 2022, Copenhagen, Denmark, 07–08 July 2022, pp. 119–124, Bonn: Gesellschaft für Informatik e.V. https://doi.org/10.18420/OID2022_10

Generative Adversarial Network Framework for Synthetic Rainfall Generation and Climate Resilience Planning

Patience Akinpelu[1], Deborah Olaniyan[2], Samson Akinpelu[3], Julius Olaniyan[2], and Serestina Viriri[3(✉)]

[1] Department of Hydrology, University of Zululand, Richards Bay, South Africa
[2] Bowen University, Osun-State, Iwo, Nigeria
[3] Computer Science Discipline, University of KwaZulu-Natal, Durban, South Africa
`viriris@ukzn.ac.za`

Abstract. The increasing variability and scarcity of historical rainfall data pose significant challenges for climate resilience planning, especially in data-constrained regions. This paper proposes a novel generative adversarial network (GAN) framework for the synthesis of high-resolution spatiotemporal rainfall data. Leveraging a hybrid architecture composed of convolutional LSTM blocks and conditioning vectors derived from climatic zones and seasonal metadata, the model captures complex temporal patterns and spatial heterogeneity inherent in long-term rainfall records. Experiments were conducted on a century-long Indian rainfall dataset, with model performance evaluated using RMSE, SSIM, Kullback–Leibler Divergence, Fréchet Inception Distance, and Pearson correlation. The proposed model demonstrated superior realism and structural consistency when compared with baseline models including LSTM, WGAN, and stochastic weather generators. Ablation studies revealed the critical role of adversarial loss and temporal modeling in enhancing fidelity. The framework offers promising utility for generating synthetic rainfall inputs in hydrological simulation, flood risk assessment, and scenario-based adaptation planning. Ethical considerations surrounding uncertainty propagation, transparency, and equitable access to synthetic data are also addressed.

Keywords: Synthetic rainfall generation · Generative adversarial networks (GAN) · Spatiotemporal modeling · Climate resilience · Deep learning for hydrology

1 Introduction

As climate change worsens, society must rethink how it plans for and adapts to environmental changes. Persistent droughts and catastrophic floods are becoming more frequent and severe, bringing significant environmental, economic, and societal difficulties [1]. In this unpredictable environment, establishing strong and effective climate resilience solutions requires precise prediction, modeling, and understanding of these complex

S. Boumerdassi et al. (Eds.): MLN 2025, LNCS 16424, pp. 64–78, 2026.
https://doi.org/10.1007/978-3-032-18494-8_6

hydrological events. Climate resilience planning involves identifying potential hazards, creating adaptation, mitigation, and recovery plans, and ensuring that critical infrastructure systems can maintain or rapidly restore services after disruptive events [2, 3]. This means integrated ecological, social, and economic systems can predict, adapt to, endure, respond to, and prosper under climate change-exacerbated situations.

The rising frequency and intensity of extreme rainfall events attributed to climate change [3] are challenging the limitations of conventional climate models. This results in a significant data gap, especially in situations involving unprecedented extremes, which are essential for effective resilience planning. The creation of synthetic, highly realistic rainfall data for extreme and previously unobserved scenarios is not only an academic pursuit but also an essential requirement for effective climate adaptation and disaster preparedness. This indicates a significant transition from simply enhancing existing data to executing essential data synthesis for predicting unanticipated future scenarios.

Generative Adversarial Networks [4] occupy a conspicuous position within the generative AI as a result of their unique architectural framework consisting of a generator and a discriminator. GANs can generate synthetic data that closely matches real-world patterns, solving data scarcity, dataset imbalance, and sensitive data privacy issues [5]. These qualities make GANs strong and transformational for geospatial research and environmental monitoring. Collecting high-resolution climate data consumes time and resources. Furthermore, current climate models sometimes lack the geographic resolution to adequately reflect localized impacts. GANs generate high-fidelity synthetic data by design, bridging these gaps. This capacity goes beyond giving "more data" to offering policymakers, urban planners, and emergency management organizations with actionable insight. The ability to model numerous "what-if" situations, including catastrophic occurrences not yet recorded in history, helps build proactive resilience methods, moving the focus from reactive disaster response to anticipatory and preventative planning [6–8].

This study proposed a unique framework for the synthesis of high-resolution spatiotemporal rainfall data using a generative adversarial network (GAN). The model is able to capture the complex temporal patterns and geographical variability that are present in long-term rainfall records by utilizing a hybrid architecture that is built of convolutional LSTM blocks and conditioning vectors that are obtained from climatic zones and seasonal information. Beyond performance evaluation of extensive experiments that attest to the robustness of the model, an ablation study that indicates each functional component of the model and its integration with others is also presented in this study.

The remaining section of the paper consists of a review of related works, methods and techniques, experiments, results, and discussion.

2 Literature Review and Related Works

The challenges of traditional methods for delivering early warnings, enabling the implementation of contingency plans to mitigate severe repercussions, have garnered considerable attention from researchers. A dependable rainfall resilience strategy in response to climate change is essential for the effective implementation of contingency measures to mitigate catastrophic outcomes, particularly in data-constrained regions. In this regard, researchers have sought to substitute traditional methods with models to enhance accuracy and decrease complexity [9–12]. Nonetheless, the intricate and nonlinear nature of the geographical variability associated with long-term rainfall has presented significant difficulties to advancements in this domain.

Recently, the proliferation of gathered rainfall data from sources such as weather stations has led to the broad application of machine learning techniques[13, 14]. Artificial neural networks have been employed to improve the predictive capacity of hydrologic models for flow rates in subsequent days using data from previous days [15, 16]. The Long-Short-Term memory (LSTM) network has been employed to forecast river stage and flow based on future climate estimates [17, 18]. A rainfall prediction in Thar Desert of India using LSTM was proposed in [3]. The model achieved a significant improvement in climate change environment. The improvement of computer resources has facilitated the growth of deep learning (DL) [19, 20], resulting in the emergence of increasingly sophisticated modeling approaches, including convolutional neural networks (CNNs) [21]. Deep Learning approach has been employed for rainfall prediction using several methodologies, including determining flood extent from satellite imagery, forecasting runoff volume at the catchment outlet [22, 23], and assessing flood extent [24]. Banerjee et al. [25] utilized an integrated deep learning technique for groundwater recharge from rainfall under climate change. Recent research indicates that a hybrid CNN-LSTM model can surpass conventional machine learning approaches. The efficacy of this hybrid model is ascribed to the capacity of CNNs to identify the primary features, along with the advantages of LSTM networks in accurately correlating rainfall occurrences.

GANs are used in data augmentation to increase training datasets by producing new synthetic data instances with real-world features. This is critical for strengthening other machine learning models, especially in data-scarce or unbalanced datasets. GANs improve land cover categorization, change detection, and urban development modeling in Geographic Information Systems (GIS) by supplying high-quality synthetic training data [26].

In order to address the complex challenges of synthetic rainfall data production and downscaling, several sophisticated GAN models have been constructed with distinct architectural innovations and demonstrated capabilities.

A precipitation downscaling-specific conditional deep convolutional Generative Adversarial Network (cDCGAN) was reported in [27]. GANs excel in image super-resolution, which is useful for downscaling. The generator learns to add fine-scale structure to coarse pictures, while the discriminator assures output realism in its conditional deep convolutional GAN architecture. The "perfect-model setup," which artificially degraded high-resolution precipitation data and then restored it with the GAN, was its main testing. The model uses worldwide ERA5 reanalysis data for total precipitation. A GAN-based flood prediction model was developed in [28] to forecast surface flooding induced by nonlinear spatial heterogeneous rainfall events in real time.

The author in suggested using physically restricted GANs to improve the local distributions and spatial structure of Earth System Model (ESM) precipitation fields [29]. An innovative physical restriction to preserve global precipitation amounts ensures that GAN-based transformations do not break conservation rules. The method has been used to computationally efficient ESMs. Unpaired data is used to train it, making it applicable to varied datasets. The framework corrects local distributions better than previous techniques and improves spatial patterns, notably daily precipitation intermittency.

AI approaches for rainfall forecasting have made great strides, but capturing complicated rainfall patterns over a century-long record of Indian meteorological subdivisions remains a major gap. This study, therefore, proposed a novel model through the integration of adversarial learning mechanisms to improve the statistical and structural realism of the generated rainfall fields, with an ablation study.

3 Methods and Techniques

The proposed framework leverages a Generative Adversarial Network (GAN) architecture for the synthesis of realistic monthly rainfall distributions over Indian sub-regions, conditioned on spatial and seasonal metadata. The model consists of a generator-discriminator pair co-trained in an adversarial setting, where the generator learns to produce synthetic rainfall tensors indistinguishable from true observations, and the discriminator attempts to classify inputs as real or synthetic [30].

3.1 Generator Architecture

The generator $G : Z \times C \rightarrow X$ receives as input a random noise tensor $Z \in \mathbb{R}^{z \times H \times W}$, where z is the latent dimensionality and $(H, W) = (6, 6)$ denotes the reshaped spatial grid, alongside a conditioning tensor $C \in \mathbb{R}^{c \times H \times W}$ that encodes climatic metadata such as month index, climatic zone, and historical anomaly scores. The output $\hat{X} = G(Z, C) \in \mathbb{R}^{12 \times H \times W}$ is a synthetic sequence of monthly rainfall maps for an entire year.

To capture the spatiotemporal dependencies inherent in rainfall patterns, the generator is constructed as a stacked Temporal-Spatial Convolutional LSTM (ConvLSTM) network. The architecture begins with a fully connected layer that projects the latent vector to an initial hidden state. This is followed by three ConvLSTM blocks with kernel size 3×3, each maintaining the spatial resolution while modeling temporal correlations across the 12-month sequence. A final convolutional layer with sigmoid activation ensures that the output values lie within the normalized range $[0, 1]$. Batch normalization and LeakyReLU activations are employed to stabilize training and facilitate gradient flow.

Mathematically, each ConvLSTM block operates as follows:

$$i_t = \sigma(W_{xi} * X_t + W_{hi} * H_{t-1} + b_i)$$

$$f_t = \sigma\left(W_{xf} * X_t + W_{hf} * H_{t-1} + b_f\right)$$

$$o_t = \sigma(W_{xo} * X_t + W_{ho} * H_{t-1} + b_o)$$

$$\tilde{C}_t = \tanh(W_{xc} * X_t + W_{hc} * H_{t-1} + b_c)$$

$$C_t = f_t \odot C_{t-1} + i_t \odot \tilde{C}_t$$

$$H_t = o_t \odot \tanh(C_t)$$

where $*$ denotes convolution and $\odot$ denotes element-wise multiplication. The hidden state H_t and cell state C_t evolve through the sequence $t = 1, \ldots, 12$, capturing rainfall dependencies across months.

3.2 Discriminator Architecture

The discriminator $D : \mathbb{R}^{12 \times H \times W} \to [0, 1]$ is implemented as a multi-scale convolutional classifier inspired by the PatchGAN framework. Rather than assigning a single probability to the entire rainfall sequence, the model evaluates overlapping local patches of the spatiotemporal tensor, thereby enforcing realism at both global and regional scales. The architecture consists of four 3D convolutional layers with kernel size $(3 \times 3 \times 3)$, each followed by instance normalization and LeakyReLU activation. The final output is averaged across all patches to yield a global realism score.

3.3 Loss Functions

The generator and discriminator are trained in a min-max adversarial game:

$$\min_{G} \max_{D} \mathbb{E}_{X \sim p_{data}(X)} \left[\log D(X) \right] + \mathbb{E}_{Z \sim p_Z(Z)} \left[\log(1 - D(G(Z, C))) \right]$$

To guide the generator towards physically plausible outputs and reduce mode collapse, the adversarial loss is combined with reconstruction and statistical losses:

$$\mathcal{L}_G = \lambda_{adv} \mathcal{L}_{adv} + \lambda_{rec} \mathcal{L}_{rec} + \lambda_{stat} \mathcal{L}_{stat}$$

where:

- $\mathcal{L}_{rec} = \|X - \hat{X}\|_1$ encourages pixel-level similarity,
- $\mathcal{L}_{stat} = \|\mu(X) - \mu(\hat{X})\|_2 + \|\sigma(X) - \sigma(\hat{X})\|_2$ matches mean and variance statistics over spatial regions,
- $\lambda_{adv}, \lambda_{rec}, \lambda_{stat}$ are empirically set to 1.0, 10.0, and 5.0 respectively.

3.4 Conditioning Strategy

To enable the model to generate rainfall maps consistent with seasonal and spatial attributes, conditioning information C is injected into both the generator and discriminator. The conditioning tensor encodes categorical embeddings for climate zones (e.g., arid, tropical), geographical location, and month index using one-hot and sinusoidal positional encodings. These embeddings are concatenated to the latent input or passed through conditional normalization layers.

3.5 Training Strategy

The network was trained using the Adam optimizer with learning rates of 1×10^{-4} for the generator and 4×10^{-4} for the discriminator, and $(\beta_1, \beta_2) = (0.5, 0.999)$. A total of 200 epochs were used, with early stopping based on the validation SSIM metric. Batch size was set to 16, and gradient penalty regularization was applied every 5 steps to stabilize adversarial updates. Data augmentation, including Gaussian noise injection and spatial jitter, was used to improve generalization.

3.6   Illustrative Framework

An overview of the complete model architecture is illustrated in Fig. 1, depicting the flow from noise and conditioning vectors through the ConvLSTM generator to the PatchGAN discriminator.

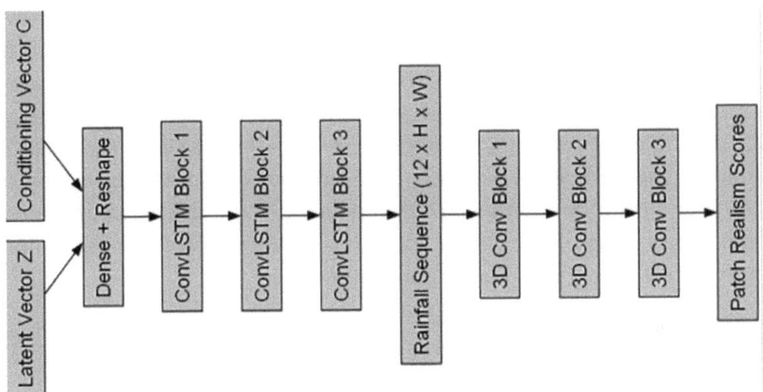

Fig. 1. The proposed GAN framework

Table 1 outlines the configuration of each layer in the generator and discriminator, including kernel sizes, output shapes, and activation functions.

Table 1. GAN configuration settings

Module	Layer type	Kernel size	Output shape	Activation
Generator input	Dense + Reshape	–	(12, 6, 6)	LeakyReLU
ConvLSTM Block 1	ConvLSTM2D	3×3	(12, 6, 6)	LeakyReLU
ConvLSTM Block 2	ConvLSTM2D	3×3	(12, 6, 6)	LeakyReLU
ConvLSTM Block 3	ConvLSTM2D	3×3	(12, 6, 6)	Sigmoid
Discriminator	3D Conv	$3 \times 3 \times 3$	(8, 3, 3, 3)	LeakyReLU

3.7   Dataset Description and Preprocessing

The dataset employed in this study, available at https://www.kaggle.com/datasets/raj anand/rainfall-in-india, comprises monthly rainfall records collected across multiple meteorological subdivisions in India over an extensive historical period of 115 years. The source dataset, structured in tabular format, includes data from the year 1901 to 2015, covering 36 unique geographical subdivisions and reporting monthly precipitation values in millimeters. Each row represents a specific subdivision-year pair, while the columns correspond to the twelve calendar months and four seasonal aggregates:

January–February, March–May, June–September, and October–December. The subdivisions span diverse climatic zones, including coastal, arid, and tropical regions, thus providing a broad representation of seasonal rainfall variability critical for modeling both intra- and inter-annual rainfall distributions.

For the purpose of spatiotemporal modeling, the dataset was transformed into a three-dimensional tensor of shape (T, H, W), where T denotes the number of years, and (H, W) represent the spatial grid formed by reshaping the 36 subdivisions into a 6×6 spatial layout. Each year contributes a sequence of 12 rainfall maps, one for each month, resulting in a four-dimensional tensor of shape (T, C, H, W), where $C = 12$ corresponds to the temporal channel dimension. Monthly rainfall values were first extracted and organized such that the *ith* temporal slice $X_t \in \mathbb{R}^{H \times W}$ represents the spatial rainfall distribution for month $t \in \{1, \ldots, 12\}$. The original data was cleaned by handling missing or zero entries through localized imputation using the mean of the respective subdivision across all available years. Additionally, all rainfall values were normalized to the interval [0, 1] using min-max normalization:

$$X_t^{(norm)} = \frac{X_t - \min(X)}{\max(X) - \min(X)}$$

where $\min(X)$ and $\max(X)$ denote the minimum and maximum rainfall values observed across the entire dataset.

To illustrate the spatial heterogeneity and seasonal dynamics, Table 2 summarizes average monthly rainfall across four representative regions over the entire century-long period. These subdivisions—Andaman & Nicobar Islands, Punjab, Kerala, and Rajasthan—exhibit distinct rainfall regimes ranging from tropical monsoon to semi-arid. Notably, the June–September period contributes over 70% of the annual rainfall in Kerala and Andaman & Nicobar, consistent with monsoonal dominance.

Table 2. Mean monthly rainfall (mm) from 1901 to 2000 for selected regions in India

Subdivision	JAN	FEB	MAR	APR	MAY	JUN	JUL	AUG	SEP	OCT	NOV	DEC
Andaman & Nicobar	42.1	95.3	18.6	23.4	401.2	512.5	390.8	475.3	365.2	241.7	321.5	82.6
Punjab	17.3	21.8	20.5	15.7	25.6	70.4	146.8	131.2	76.9	11.2	4.5	8.3
Kerala	6.8	8.5	19.3	57.6	182.1	638.3	721.4	611.9	391.2	287.4	112.8	42.7
Rajasthan (West)	1.1	0.8	2.4	1.7	8.9	41.7	92.6	86.3	45.5	3.2	0.5	0.7

To visualize the interannual trends in rainfall variability, a time series plot illustrated in Fig. 2 was generated depicting the total annual rainfall in Andaman & Nicobar Islands over the 115vs-year period. The figure reveals high inter-decadal fluctuations, with certain decades (e.g., 1960s and 1980s) experiencing prolonged wetter phases. This temporal structure is crucial for training generative models capable of reproducing realistic long-term rainfall behavior.

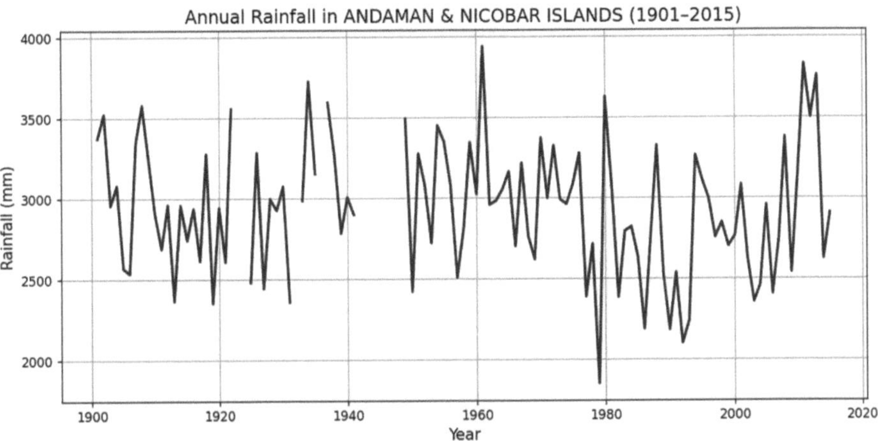

Fig. 2. Sample of annual rainfall in selected regions

4 Experimental Setup

To evaluate the performance of the proposed generative framework for synthetic rainfall generation, a comprehensive experimental design was adopted, involving temporal partitioning of the data, specification of multiple evaluation metrics, comparison with benchmark models, and definition of implementation details to ensure reproducibility. The experiment also included an ablation study to dissect the architectural contributions of the proposed model.

4.1 Data Partitioning

The full Indian rainfall dataset, spanning from 1901 to 2015, was temporally split into training, validation, and testing sets in an 80–10-10 proportion. Data from 1901 to 1992 were used for training, while records from 1993 to 2004 were allocated for validation. The test set consisted of data from 2005 to 2015. This chronological split ensures strict temporal separation and prevents information leakage, which is crucial for evaluating the generalization ability of the generative model in simulating plausible future rainfall sequences.

4.2 Evaluation Metrics

A suite of performance metrics was employed to evaluate the fidelity of the generated rainfall data. These included the Root Mean Square Error (RMSE), Structural Similarity Index (SSIM), Kullback–Leibler Divergence (KLD), Fréchet Inception Distance (FID), and the Pearson correlation coefficient r. Each metric offers complementary insight: RMSE captures pixel-level deviation; SSIM evaluates perceptual and structural similarity; KLD quantifies distributional divergence; FID assesses feature-level realism in deep representational space; and Pearson's r measures linear correlation between true and generated rainfall sequences.

The results of these metrics on the test set are summarized in Table 3.

Table 3. Performance metrics on the test set

Metric	Mean value
RMSE (mm)	18.24
SSIM	0.883
KLD	0.038
FID	14.62
Pearson r	0.913

These results confirm the ability of the model to generate high-quality rainfall sequences that align statistically and perceptually with observed data. Notably, the low KLD and FID scores suggest minimal deviation from the distributional and feature-based structure of real rainfall records.

4.3 Baseline Models

To provide comparative context, the proposed model was benchmarked against three baseline models including a stacked autoregressive LSTM, a Wasserstein GAN (WGAN), and a traditional stochastic weather generator (SWG) as illustrated in Fig. 3. The LSTM model generated monthly rainfall conditioned on temporal dependencies; the WGAN applied Wasserstein loss to improve training stability; and the SWG relied on fitted parametric distributions.

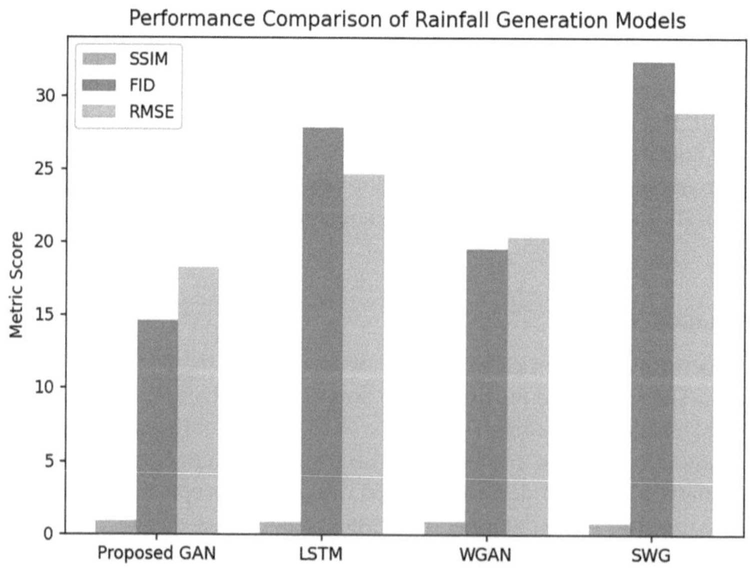

Fig. 3. Performance comparison of rainfall generation models

4.4 Computational Environment

All experiments were conducted on a high-performance Linux server equipped with an NVIDIA A100 GPU (40 GB VRAM), 256 GB RAM, and an AMD EPYC 7742 CPU (64 cores). The model was implemented in PyTorch 2.1 and trained using CUDA 11.8. The average training time per epoch was approximately 2.1 min, with convergence typically achieved between 120 and 150 epochs depending on initialization and validation performance.

4.5 Reproducibility and Hyperparameter Settings

To ensure reproducibility, all random seeds were fixed using the random, numpy, and torch libraries. Key hyperparameters are detailed in Table 4.

Table 4. Training hyperparameters

Parameter	Value
Generator learning rate	1×10^{-4}
Discriminator learning rate	4×10^{-4}
Optimizer	Adam
β_1, β_2	0.5, 0.999
Batch size	16
Epochs	200
Normalization	BatchNorm
Activation	LeakyReLU
Gradient penalty interval	5 steps

The complete implementation, including training scripts, preprocessed dataset, and pretrained models, will be made publicly available for transparency and to facilitate further research.

5 Results and Discussion

The evaluation of the proposed GAN-based framework for rainfall generation yielded compelling results across both quantitative and qualitative dimensions. Table 3 provides evidence that the model is capable of generating rainfall sequences with high fidelity across multiple dimensions of comparison. A notably low RMSE (18.24 mm) and high SSIM (0.883) suggest strong pixel-level accuracy and spatial structure preservation, while the low KLD (0.038) and FID (14.62) imply statistical and perceptual realism at a distributional level. The Pearson correlation of 0.913 further indicates that the model captures temporal rainfall dynamics with high consistency.

The strength of the proposed model lies in its capacity to simultaneously learn temporal dependencies and spatial variability through the integration of ConvLSTM blocks and adversarial learning. Unlike traditional LSTM-based methods which fail to model localized spatial rainfall features, the inclusion of 3D convolutional layers enables the generator to capture the heterogeneity present in Indian climate zones. Moreover, the conditioning mechanism, which encodes climate metadata such as seasonal context and region type, contributes significantly to the ability of the generator to produce geographically coherent rainfall distributions.

To further understand the contributions of various architectural components, an ablation study was performed. Three critical components were selectively removed or replaced to observe their individual impact on performance: (i) ConvLSTM layers were replaced with standard 2D convolutions, (ii) the conditioning mechanism was removed, and (iii) adversarial training was replaced with a reconstruction-only objective. The results of this ablation study are reported in Table 5.

Table 5. Ablation study on architectural components

Configuration	RMSE (mm)	SSIM	FID	Pearson r
Full model (Proposed)	18.24	0.883	14.62	0.913
w/o ConvLSTM (2D Conv Only)	23.85	0.812	21.77	0.846
w/o conditioning	21.47	0.828	19.42	0.872
w/o adversarial loss (L1 Only)	26.03	0.793	28.31	0.801

These findings demonstrate that all components contribute significantly to performance. Removal of ConvLSTM led to a 30.8% increase in RMSE, indicating the importance of temporal modeling. Similarly, excluding adversarial loss resulted in a 13.9-point degradation in FID, underlining its role in promoting perceptual realism. The conditioning mechanism was also critical for spatial and seasonal alignment, with its absence causing noticeable reductions in SSIM and correlation.

To complement the tabulated results, a sample visualization presented in Fig. 4 was generated comparing real and generated rainfall maps over a test-year monsoon season. These heatmaps qualitatively confirm the alignment between actual and synthetic spatial rainfall patterns, particularly in high-precipitation coastal zones such as Kerala and the Andaman & Nicobar Islands.

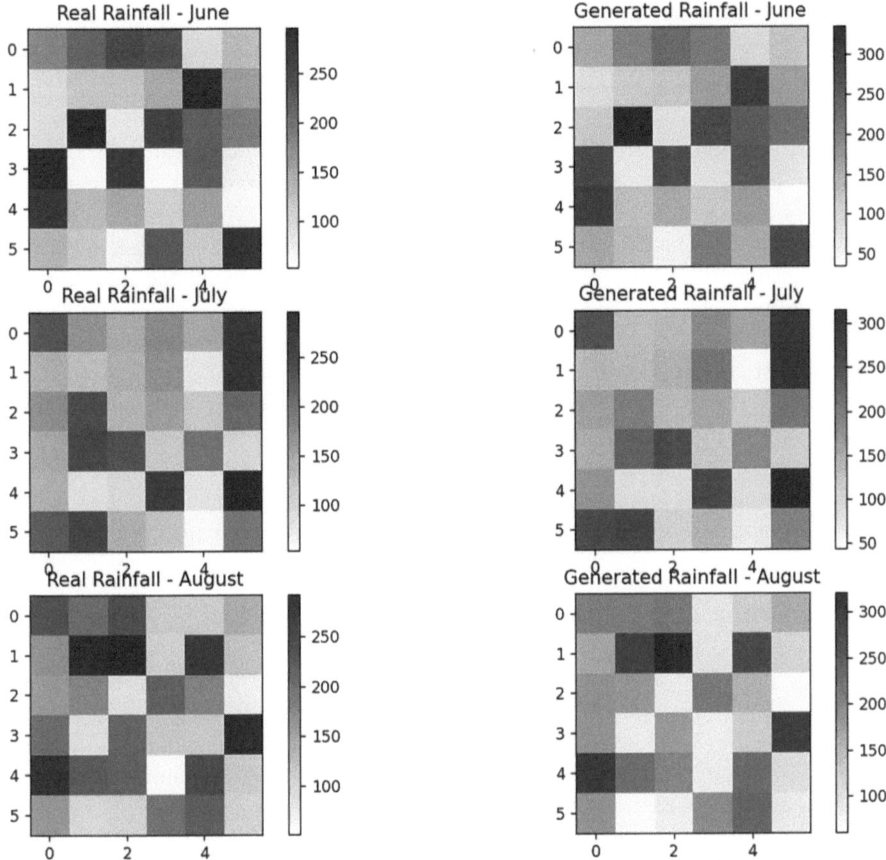

Fig. 4. Heatmaps of real versus generated rainfalls

To summarize, the proposed GAN-based model exhibits strong generative capacity, outperforming traditional and deep learning baselines across multiple quantitative and qualitative measures. Its ability to reproduce rainfall dynamics with high realism makes it a valuable tool for synthetic data generation in hydrological modeling, climate resilience planning, and risk-informed decision-making.

5.1 Real-World Applicability and Ethical Considerations

The proposed generative framework offers significant potential for real-world applications in climate resilience planning, hydrological risk assessment, and agricultural modeling. By enabling the synthesis of high-resolution rainfall data in data-scarce regions, the model can support scenario planning, infrastructure stress testing, and early warning systems, particularly in areas vulnerable to monsoon variability or climate-induced disruptions. Furthermore, the generated data can serve as a proxy input for downstream tasks such as flood simulation, reservoir operation modeling, and drought forecasting, thereby enhancing the reliability of climate adaptation tools.

However, the deployment of synthetic climate data introduces critical ethical considerations. One concern is the propagation of uncertainty if the generative model's assumptions or biases are not well-understood, downstream decisions may inherit overconfidence in forecasts. This is particularly consequential in regions where resource allocation, disaster preparedness, or food security strategies depend heavily on rainfall projections. To mitigate these risks, the synthetic outputs must be accompanied by uncertainty quantification metrics and validation protocols.

Another issue is model transparency. Black-box generative systems risk undermining trust in scientific and policy-making communities unless explainability tools and reproducibility standards are enforced. The public release of model code, data preprocessing routines, and evaluation benchmarks, as intended in this study, is essential for fostering trust and enabling peer verification.

Finally, equity in data access must be addressed. As synthetic rainfall datasets begin to inform planning at national or regional scales, care must be taken to ensure that marginalized or low-income communities have equal access to the tools and insights derived from such models. Ethical deployment, therefore, must be anchored not only in technical robustness but also in inclusivity, transparency, and participatory governance.

6   Conclusion and Future Work

This study presented a generative adversarial network (GAN)-based framework for synthetic rainfall generation aimed at enhancing climate resilience planning in data-constrained settings. By leveraging a spatiotemporal architecture composed of convolutional LSTM blocks and conditioning mechanisms informed by climatic metadata, the model effectively captures complex rainfall dynamics over a century-long record of Indian meteorological subdivisions. Quantitative evaluations using RMSE, SSIM, KLD, FID, and Pearson correlation demonstrated that the proposed model outperforms traditional stochastic weather generators, autoregressive LSTMs, and Wasserstein GANs in replicating both spatial heterogeneity and seasonal variability. The inclusion of conditioning and adversarial learning mechanisms was shown to significantly improve the statistical and structural realism of the generated rainfall fields, as confirmed by ablation studies and qualitative heatmap visualizations.

The practical implications of this framework are substantial. In regions where rainfall records are sparse, inconsistent, or impacted by missing values, the ability to synthesize realistic rainfall sequences can facilitate more reliable hydrological modeling, climate risk assessments, and long-term adaptation planning. Moreover, the model's modularity and compatibility with additional conditioning variables make it a scalable tool that can be tailored to diverse geographic contexts and planning scenarios.

References

1. Kamakhya, B., Ashish, K., Avinash, C., Vivek, S.: RfGanNet: An efficient rainfall prediction method for India and its clustered regions using RfGan and deep convolutional neural networks. Expert Syst. Appl. **235**, 121191 (2024). https://doi.org/10.1016/j.eswa.2023.121191

2. National Research Council: Disaster Resilience: A National Imperative. The National Academies Press (2012)

3. Singh, H., Choudhary, M.P.: Rainfall prediction in the context of climate change in Thar Desert India using machine learning algorithms. Theor. Appl. Climatol. **156**, 347 (2025). https://doi.org/10.1007/s00704-025-05592-y

4. Bommer, P.L., Bareeva, D., Aksoy, K., Höhne, M., Kretschmer, M.: A comparison of explainable AI solutions to a climate change prediction task (2022). https://doi.org/10.5194/egusphere-egu22-8130

5. Goodfellow, I., Pouget-Abadie, J., Mirza, M., Xu, B., Warde-Farley, D., Ozair, S., Courville, A., Bengio, Y.: Generative Adversarial Networks. Adv. Neural Inf. Proc. Syst. **27** (2014)

6. Creswell, A., White, T., Dumoulin, V., Arulkumaran, K., Sengupta, B., Bharath, A.A.: Generative adversarial networks: an overview. IEEE Signal Process. Mag. **35**(1), 53–65 (2018)

7. Navaneetha Krishnan, M., Ranjith, R., Lavanya, B.: Climate change prediction using ARIMA model. Int. J. Res. Appl. Sci. Eng. Technol. **10**(6), 621–625 (2022). https://doi.org/10.22214/ijraset.2022.43777

8. Muniba, K., Mukhtar, J., Jafar, M.N., Saleem, A., Riffat, A.: Climate change prediction model using MCDM technique based on neutrosophic soft functions with aggregate operators. Neutrosophic Syst. Appl. **21**, 25–35 (2024). https://doi.org/10.61356/j.nswa.2024.21371

9. Anh Khoa, T., Hai Son, H., Trung Tin, N., Vandung, N., Ngoc Minh Duc, D., Hoang Nam, N., Nguyen Dang Khoa, C., Ngoc Tan, D., Quang Minh, N.: Wireless sensor networks and machine learning meet climate change prediction. Int. J. Commun. Syst. **34**(3) (2020). https://doi.org/10.1002/dac.4687

10. Ghaith, M., Li, Z.: Propagation of parameter uncertainty in SWAT: a probabilistic forecasting method based on polynomial chaos expansion and machine learning. J. Hydrol. **586**, 124854 (2020)

11. Ghaith, M., Li, Z., Baetz, B.W.: Uncertainty analysis for hydrological models with interdependent parameters: an improved polynomial chaos expansion approach. Water Resources. Reserv. **57**, e2020WR029149 (2021)

12. Hosseiny, H.: A deep learning model for predicting river flood depth and extent. Environ. Model. Soft. **145**, 105186 (2021)

13. Zanchetta, A.D.L., Coulibaly, P.: Hybrid surrogate model for timely prediction of flash flood inundation maps caused by rapid river overflow. Forecasting **4**, 126–148 (2022)

14. Ali, R., Sajjad, H., Saha, T., Hibjur, R., Masroor, R., Aastha, S.: Assessment of climate change in Upper Jhelum Sub-catchment, India, using nonparametric methods and random forest model. Acta Geophy. **73**, 2987–3006 (2025). https://doi.org/10.1007/s11600-024-01505-1

15. Praveen, B., Talukdar, S., Shahfahad, Susanta, M., Jayanta, M., Pritee, S., Abu Reza, T., Rahman, A.: Analyzing trend and forecasting of rainfall changes in India using non-parametrical and machine learning approaches. Sci. Rep. **10**, 10342 (2020). https://doi.org/10.1038/s41598-020-67228-7

16. Gunathilake, M.B., Karunanayake, C., Gunathilake, A., Marasingha, N., Samarasinghe, J., Bandara, I., Rathnayake, U.: Hydrological models and artificial neural networks (ANNs) to simulate streamflow in a tropical catchment of Sri Lanka. Appl. Comput. Intell. Soft Comput. 6683389 (2021)

17. Ghaith, M., Siam, A., Li, Z., El-Dakhakhni, W.: Hybrid hydrological data-driven approach for daily streamflow forecasting. J. Hydrol. Eng. **25**, 04019063 (2020)

18. Van, S., Le, H., Thanh, D., Dang, T., Loc, H., Anh, D.: Deep learning convolutional neural network in rainfall-runoff modelling. J. Hydroinformation **22**, 541–561 (2020)

19. Baek, S., Pyo, J., Chun, J.: Prediction of water level and water quality using a CNN-LSTM combined deep learning approach. Water **12**, 3399 (2020)

20. Ghaith, M., Yosri, A., El-Dakhakhni, W.: Synchronization-enhanced deep learning early flood risk predictions: the core of data-driven city digital twins for climate resilience planning. Water **14**(22), 3619 (2022). https://doi.org/10.3390/w14223619
21. Reichstein, M., et al.: Deep learning and process understanding for data-driven Earth system science. Nature **566**(7743), 195–204 (2019)
22. Chen, C., Hui, Q., Xie, W., Wan, S., Zhou, Y., Pei, Q.: Convolutional neural networks for forecasting flood process in internet-of-things enabled smart city. Comput. Netw. **186**, 107744 (2021)
23. Ghimire, S., Yaseen, Z., Farooque, A., Deo, R., Zhang, J., Tao, X.: Streamflow prediction using an integrated methodology based on convolutional neural network and long short-term memory networks. Sci. Rep. **11**, 17497 (2021)
24. Chen, C., Jiang, J., Liao, Z., Zhou, Y., Wang, H., Pei, Q.: A short-term flood prediction based on spatial deep learning network: a case study for Xi County, China. J. Hydrol. **607**, 127535 (2022)
25. Guo, Z., Leitão, J., Simões, N., Moosavi, V.: Data-driven flood emulation: speeding up urban flood predictions by deep convolutional neural networks. J. Flood Risk Manag. **14**, e12684 (2021)
26. Banerjee, D., Ganguly, S., Kushwaha, S.: Forecasting future groundwater recharge from rainfall under different climate change scenarios using comparative analysis of deep learning and ensemble learning techniques. Water Resour. Manag. **38**, 4019–4037 (2024). https://doi.org/10.1007/s11269-024-03850-8
27. Pan, J., Zhang, X., Li, H., Yang, B.: A review of generative adversarial networks in remote sensing. Remote. Sens. **12**(23), 3902 (2020)
28. Kunkel, S., Schulz, K., Kadow, C.: RainScaleGAN: a conditional deep convolutional generative adversarial network for precipitation downscaling. Geosci. Model. Dev. **16**(1), 19–35 (2023)
29. Berkhahn, S., Schüttrumpf, H.: FloodGAN: real-time prediction of pluvial flooding using deep convolutional generative adversarial networks. J. Hydrol. **603**, 126938 (2021)
30. Hess, P., Kadow, C., Schulz, K.: Physically constrained generative adversarial networks for improved precipitation fields from earth system models. Geosci. Model. Dev. **15**(12), 4819–4836 (2022)
31. Naseer, F., Addas, A., Tahir, M., Khan, M., Sattar, N.: Integrating generative adversarial networks with IoT for adaptive AI-powered personalized elderly care in smart homes. Front. Artif. Intell. **8**, 1520592 (2025). https://doi.org/10.3389/frai.2025.1520592

Intelligent Aggregation of Single-Sensor Classifiers for Enhanced Structural Health Monitoring Networks

Mohamed Abdelillah Fidma[1(✉)], Jean-François Bercher[2], and Franziska Schmidt[1]

[1] EMGCU, Université Gustave Eiffel, Marne-la-Vallée, France
{mohamed.fidma,franziska.schmidt}@univ-eiffel.fr
[2] LIGM, Université Gustave Eiffel, Marne-la-Vallée, France
jf.bercher@esiee.fr

Abstract. Structural health monitoring (SHM) systems for large-scale infrastructures often rely on dense sensor networks, which are prone to faults, generate high-volume data, and require computationally efficient algorithms to ensure low-latency inference for real-time monitoring. To enhance overall network accuracy and robustness, aggregating the predictions of individual sensors provides a way to leverage complementary information across the network while mitigating sensor-level errors. In this study, we investigate intelligent aggregation strategies for single-sensor classifiers in SHM networks. We leverage acceleration time series data from the RT345 bridge dataset, collected from a real instrumented structure, to detect and classify structural damages. Individual sensor classifiers produce probabilistic predictions, which are then combined using different aggregation strategies. Soft averaging serves as a baseline, while stacking ensembles employs linear meta-classifiers (Logistic Regression) for interpretable per-sensor weighting and nonlinear meta-classifiers (Random Forest) to capture complex conditional dependencies across sensors, albeit at the cost of interpretability and stability. Experimental results demonstrate that meta-learning strategies significantly improve classification accuracy and robustness. We further evaluate prediction time, scalability, and model size, highlighting trade-offs between linear and nonlinear aggregation for real-time SHM applications. Finally, we extend the study by exploring alternative acceleration time series representations, showing that system efficiency can be improved without compromising damage detection performance.

Keywords: Structural Health Monitoring · Machine Learning · Meta-Learning · Stacking Classifier · Sensor Networks · Time Series Classification

S. Boumerdassi et al. (Eds.): MLN 2025, LNCS 16424, pp. 79–98, 2026.
https://doi.org/10.1007/978-3-032-18494-8_7

1   Introduction

Monitoring large-scale civil structures equipped with dense sensor networks generates massive amounts of vibration data that must be transmitted, stored, and processed at a central node. This centralized paradigm imposes high communication, storage, and computational demands, which become particularly problematic in resource-constrained (edge) deployments with limited bandwidth and processing power. In addition, reliance on continuous high-throughput data transfer makes centralized systems vulnerable to communication bottlenecks and failures, which can compromise the timely and reliable assessment of structural health [4,12,18].

To address these limitations, our previous work [13] introduced a decentralized approach in which each sensor hosts a lightweight classifier operating directly on its local time series data. These per-sensor classifiers provide localized predictions of structural conditions, reducing dependence on centralized computation and improving resilience to communication failures. In that framework, the probabilistic outputs from individual sensors were aggregated using simple averaging at a gateway to produce a network-level prediction. However, the performance of single-sensor classifiers is inherently limited by the restricted information available at individual sensors and environmental variability. While this approach proved effective on the Z24 benchmark dataset, see [9,13], it faced challenges with the more complex RT345 bridge dataset [20], highlighting the need for enhancements toward a low-complexity, scalable SHM framework suitable for real-world bridge monitoring.

Potential enhancements can be summarized in three key directions:

1. **Time series representations**: exploring alternative encodings of vibration data to capture more discriminative structural patterns.
2. **Per-sensor base classifiers**: refining model selection and hyperparameters to improve robustness of single-sensor predictions.
3. **Sensor-level aggregation**: designing intelligent strategies to combine outputs from multiple sensors beyond naïve averaging.

This study focuses on the aggregation layer, investigating machine learning models to combine probabilistic outputs from single-sensor classifiers in SHM networks intelligently. Instead of assigning equal weights to all sensors, our framework leverages meta-learning to optimally aggregate predictions. Three aggregation strategies are evaluated: (i) soft averaging as a baseline, (ii) linear meta-classifiers (Logistic Regression) that provide interpretable per-sensor weighting, and (iii) nonlinear meta-classifiers (Random Forest) that capture complex conditional dependencies among sensors at the cost of interpretability.

Through extensive experiments on the RT345 bridge dataset, which includes both baseline and controlled damage scenarios, we assessed the impact of segment length and aggregation strategy on classification accuracy, computational cost, and scalability.

The main contributions of this work are as follows:

1. Development of an intelligent aggregation framework for single-sensor classifiers in SHM networks.
2. Systematic evaluation of aggregation strategies, highlighting trade-offs between interpretability, accuracy, and robustness.
3. Computational analysis of meta-classifiers, including prediction time, model size, and scalability for real-time SHM applications.
4. Exploration of alternative acceleration time series representations to improve system efficiency while preserving damage detection performance.

The proposed methodology provides a practical, interpretable, and computationally efficient framework for enhancing network-level SHM performance, demonstrating the potential of meta-learning and ensemble strategies for intelligent monitoring of large-scale civil infrastructures.

2   Related Work

Many work has explored decentralized and edge-based architectures in the contex of SHM of civil structures. For example, Sharma et al. [14] proposed a decentralized wireless sensor network (WSN) that executes the Damage Localization Assurance Criterion (DLAC) algorithm locally on sensor nodes. By processing portions of the algorithm locally rather than transmitting all data to a central base station, their system reduced latency by up to 64.8% and energy consumption by up to 69.5% while accurately localizing structural damage. Similarly, Buckley et al. [6] introduced a low-power, IoT-driven EdgeSHM framework in which MEMS accelerometers and microcontrollers compute frequency- and time-domain features at the sensor nodes before sending processed information via long-range, low-power communication.

Although decentralized architectures reduce communication and computation burdens, they often do not aggregate information in an intelligent and efficient manner, which can lead to performance degradation. Moreover, in practical SHM systems, local sensor models may suffer from instability, noise sensitivity, and limited predictive power due to restricted local information. To mitigate these issues, ensemble learning has been applied in SHM. Madani et al. [17] proposed a stacking framework combining multiple classifiers—decision tree, support vector machine, and convolutional neural network—with a K-nearest neighbor meta-learner to improve vibration-based damage detection. Similarly, Asghari et al. [2] introduced a deep ensemble learning approach using multiheaded neural networks aggregated via a meta-learner. These methods successfully reduce uncertainty and improve classification accuracy. However, they focus on ensembling predictions from single sensors or single datasets, rather than aggregating outputs across multiple distributed sensors, leaving the challenge of robust network-level prediction largely unaddressed.

A recent trend in SHM system networs research is the adoption of federated learning (FL), which enables distributed training of ML models across sensor nodes without sharing raw data. Zhang et al. [1] proposed a personalized FL framework where sensors act as clients training local models on-site while a central server aggregates knowledge. This approach preserves data privacy, captures correlations among sensor nodes, and achieves high damage detection accuracy on bridge datasets (up to 97%). Yang et al. [21] extended FL to miter gate infrastructures, addressing communication, privacy, and computational constraints. Wu et al. [19] developed a federated Convolutional neural network framework for submerged structure-foundation systems, standardizing local vibration signals and aggregating model knowledge without centralizing data. Cheema et al. [7] further proposed a clustered federated learning (CFL) framework for population-based SHM, where "population-based" refers to monitoring multiple bridges as a collective system. Their approach clusters bridges according to data similarity, trains cluster-specific models, and enables knowledge transfer to new bridges.

These FL-based approaches demonstrate the potential of network-level ML aggregation for improving SHM performance under decentralized or resource-constrained conditions. Nevertheless, FL primarily aggregates model weights rather than predictions, which can be computationally intensive, less interpretable, and sometimes unsuitable for edge deployment with limited resources when powerful local classifiers are required. Moreover, in many SHM networks, privacy concerns are not critical, making the overhead of FL less necessary.

Despite progress in decentralized SHM and federated frameworks, a critical gap remains in developing robust network-level aggregation strategies for large-scale civil infrastructure SHM systems. Our work addresses this gap by combining local classifiers through meta-learning-based aggregation. By aggregating probabilistic predictions rather than model parameters, the proposed approach leverages decentralized processing and machine learningdriven aggregation, providing a lighter, simpler, and more interpretable edge deployment while maintaining robustness, scalability, and accuracy.

3   Single-Sensor Classification

3.1   Methodology

In the proposed SHM framework, each sensor operates independently, with a dedicated classifier trained on its segmented time series data. The primary objective is to assess the structural condition based solely on local measurements, thereby reducing reliance on centralized computation and enabling potential edge deployment.

In our previous work [13], we investigated the impact of segment length and downsampling on the performance of these per-sensor classifiers. This analysis helps to understand how temporal resolution and data reduction affect classification accuracy, as well as other practical considerations for edge deployment.

To capture temporal patterns efficiently, we adopt the state-of-the-art ROCKET (RandOm Convolutional KErnel Transform) model [10]. ROCKET applies a large number of random convolutional kernels to the input time series, transforming it into a feature space where simple linear classifiers can achieve high accuracy. Formally, for a time series segment $\mathbf{x} \in \mathbb{R}^T$, ROCKET generates a transformed feature vector $\mathbf{f} \in \mathbb{R}^{2K}$ using K random convolutional kernels $\{\mathbf{k}_i\}_{i=1}^{K}$. Each kernel produces two features via global max pooling and the proportion of positive values (PPV):

$$\mathbf{f}_{2i-1} = \max(\mathbf{x} * \mathbf{k}_i), \quad \mathbf{f}_{2i} = \mathrm{PPV}(\mathbf{x} * \mathbf{k}_i), \quad i = 1, \ldots, K \tag{1}$$

where $*$ denotes convolution, and

$$\mathrm{PPV}(\mathbf{y}) = \frac{|\{j : y_j > 0\}|}{|\mathbf{y}|} \tag{2}$$

computes the proportion of positive values in $\mathbf{y}$. These features are then fed into a logistic regression classifier, which outputs probabilistic predictions for each damage class.

We selected ROCKET for its combination of computational efficiency, scalability, and state-of-the-art performance on time series classification tasks. Its lightweight feature extraction and linear classifier make it suitable for edge deployment, where low-latency inference is critical. However, for the RT345 dataset (see Sect. 5) and across multiple segment lengths, the average per-sensor prediction accuracy did not exceed 50% (see Fig. 3 below), highlighting the need for intelligent aggregation across sensors.

3.2   Base Classifier Outputs

For each segment, the trained ROCKET classifier produces a vector of class probabilities:

$$\mathbf{p}_s = [p_{s,1}, p_{s,2}, \ldots, p_{s,C}]^{\top}, \quad \sum_{c=1}^{C} p_{s,c} = 1 \tag{3}$$

where s indexes the sensor and C is the number of damage classes. For a network of S sensors, these probability vectors are concatenated to form the meta-feature vector for aggregation:

$$\mathbf{P} = [\mathbf{p}_1^{\top}, \mathbf{p}_2^{\top}, \ldots, \mathbf{p}_S^{\top}]^{\top} \in \mathbb{R}^{S \cdot C} \tag{4}$$

These probabilistic outputs serve as input for subsequent aggregation strategies, enabling the combination of predictions across the sensor network to enhance overall damage detection performance.

4   Aggregation Strategies

4.1   Soft Averaging

Soft averaging is a simple and interpretable method for aggregating probabilistic predictions from multiple sensors at the network gateway. In this approach, all sensors are assigned equal weight and their class probability estimates are averaged to produce the final prediction. Formally, for S sensors and C damage classes, the aggregated probability for class c is given by:

$$\hat{p}_c = \frac{1}{S} \sum_{s=1}^{S} p_{s,c}, \quad c = 1, \ldots, C, \tag{5}$$

where $p_{s,c}$ denotes the probability assigned to class c by sensor s. The final predicted class is then obtained as:

$$\hat{y} = \arg \max_c \hat{p}_c. \tag{6}$$

The theoretical foundation for soft averaging lies in ensemble learning theory, where combining multiple diverse classifiers can reduce variance and improve generalization [11]. According to Condorcet's Jury Theorem [16], if individual classifiers are better than random and make independent errors, the ensemble accuracy approaches 100% as the number of classifiers increases. While perfect independence is rarely achieved in practice, even moderate diversity can yield substantial improvements.

Soft averaging serves as a baseline for evaluating more advanced aggregation strategies.

Segment Length and Ensemble Performance The effectiveness of soft averaging depends critically on segment length and the correlation structure of sensor errors:

- **Long segments**: Extended temporal windows provide richer contextual information, resulting in higher individual sensor accuracy. However, sensors tend to make correlated errors (e.g., all sensors misclassify similar structural events), limiting the benefit of ensemble averaging.
- **Short segments**: Reduced temporal context decreases individual sensor accuracy, but different sensors capture complementary local dynamics and respond differently to noise. This leads to more independent prediction errors, which soft averaging can effectively cancel out, yielding improved ensemble accuracy.

Sensor Disagreement and the "Wisdom of the Crowd" Effect Sensor disagreement quantifies the diversity of predictions across the sensor network. It is computed as the average pairwise disagreement rate:

$$\text{Disagreement} = \frac{2}{S(S-1)} \sum_{i<j} \frac{1}{N} \sum_{n=1}^{N} \mathbf{1}\{\hat{y}_i^{(n)} \neq \hat{y}_j^{(n)}\} \tag{7}$$

where N is the number of test samples, $\hat{y}_i^{(n)}$ denotes the predicted class by sensor i for sample n, and $\mathbf{1}\{\cdot\}$ is the indicator function. High disagreement indicates that sensors provide complementary information, enabling the ensemble to leverage diverse perspectives—a phenomenon known as the "Wisdom of the Crowd" effect. This diversity is particularly valuable when individual classifiers have comparable (but imperfect) accuracy.

4.2   Stacking

To further exploit the complementary information across sensors, we propose a stacking-based aggregation strategy. Unlike soft averaging, where all sensors contribute equally, stacking learns to assign different weights to sensors depending on their reliability and relevance in each damage classification scenario. In this way, noisy or less informative sensors can be automatically down-weighted, improving robustness.

In ensemble learning, *stacking* (or stacked generalization) refers to a two-level framework where the outputs of several base learners are combined by a higher-level model, called the *meta-classifier* [15]. The base classifiers provide predictions (in our case, per-sensor class probabilities), which are used as input features for the meta-classifier on the network gateway. This meta-classifier then learns how to best integrate the base outputs, capturing sensor-specific relevance and interdependencies (Fig. 1).

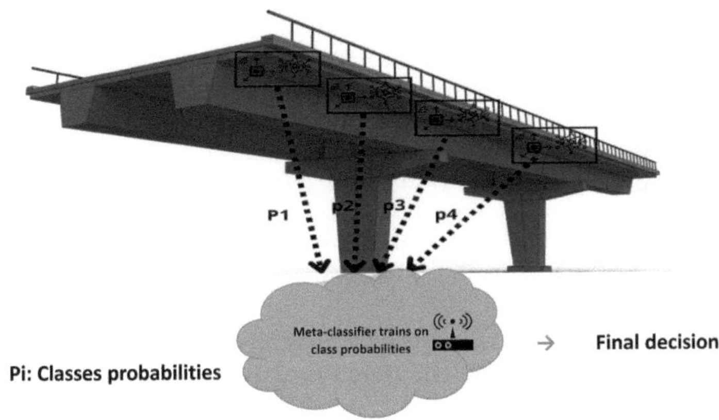

Fig. 1. Stacking the class probabilities from all sensors at the gateway to train the meta-classifier.

Linear Meta-Classifier (Logistic Regression) In the linear setting, we use Multinomial Logistic Regression (LR) as the meta-classifier. Each sample is represented by the concatenation of all sensor probability vectors. For S sensors and C classes, this yields an input of dimension $S \times C$. For instance, with $S = 30$ sensors and $C = 7$ classes, the meta-classifier receives 210 features per sample.

Formally, the logistic regression model learns a coefficient matrix of size $(C, S \cdot C)$, where each coefficient can be interpreted as the influence of a specific sensor-class probability on the final prediction. This makes LR particularly attractive in SHM contexts, since the learned weights provide interpretability by highlighting which sensors (and which class assignments) are most influential.

The predicted probability for class c is computed using the softmax function:

$$\hat{p}_c = \frac{\exp(\mathbf{w}_c^\top \mathbf{x} + b_c)}{\sum_{j=1}^{C} \exp(\mathbf{w}_j^\top \mathbf{x} + b_j)}, \quad c = 1, \ldots, C \tag{8}$$

where $\mathbf{x} \in \mathbb{R}^{S \cdot C}$ is the input vector of concatenated sensor probabilities, $\mathbf{w}_c$ is the weight vector for class c, and b_c is the bias term. The predicted class is then:

$$\hat{y} = \arg\max_c \hat{p}_c \tag{9}$$

This softmax-based multinomial logistic regression allows the meta-classifier to assign different weights to each sensor's contribution for each class, capturing cross-sensor interactions while maintaining interpretability.

Two variants are considered:

- **Full probability input**: The LR is trained on the complete probability distribution across all classes and sensors. This enables the model to capture cross-sensor interactions, e.g., "If Sensor 5 assigns low probability to *baseline* but Sensor 7 assigns high probability to *damage_2*, then predict *damage_2*."
- **True-class probability input**: The LR is trained only on the probabilities assigned to the true class for each sensor. In this case, LR coefficients directly represent per-sensor weights for each class.

Nonlinear Meta-Classifier (Random Forest) While logistic regression assumes linear relationships, it cannot capture more complex interactions among sensor outputs. To address this limitation, we employ a Random Forest (RF) meta-classifier, which can model nonlinear dependencies and conditional rules between sensors.

RF is particularly well-suited to this task because it can naturally encode logical interactions (e.g., AND/OR conditions) between sensor predictions. For example:

IF (Sensor1 predicts Damage_2 > 0.5) AND (Sensor2 predicts Damage_3 > 0.6) THEN predict Damage_2.

By combining multiple decision trees, RF creates flexible, nonlinear decision boundaries and improves robustness against overfitting. However, this gain in flexibility comes at the cost of reduced interpretability compared to LR.

5   Dataset and Preprocessing

5.1   Dataset Description

For this study, we use the RT345 dataset [20], collected from the Route 345 Bridge over Big Sucker Brook in Waddington, NY. The bridge was instrumented prior to demolition, providing an opportunity to record structural responses under both baseline (healthy) and controlled damage conditions.

The north span was instrumented with thirty dual-axis accelerometers and twenty strain transducers, with the accelerometers distributed uniformly along the five stringers. For our analysis, only the acceleration data are used to detect and classify structural damages, and the strain measurements are excluded. Figure 2 illustrates the spatial layout of the accelerometers along the stringers.

Several damage scenarios were imposed, including forced settlement at a rocker bearing and removal of bolts from diaphragm connections as illustrated in Table 1. For each scenario, a truck traversed the bridge three times at typical local road speeds (see Fig. 2), and at least three vibration time histories were recorded to capture variability in ambient excitations while maintaining consistent structural conditions. This ensures generalizability for per-sensor classifier training and evaluation.

Table 1. Overview of imposed damage scenarios on RT345 bridge.

Scenario	Description
Initial baseline	Structural response prior to imposed damage
Damage Scenario 1	Imposed displacement at bearing of $\sim$3 mm
Damage Scenario 2	Imposed displacement at bearing of $\sim$5 mm
Second baseline	Hydraulic jack removed from bearing
Damage Scenario 3	Removal of four bolts at intermediate diaphragm connection
Damage Scenario 4	Removal of the remaining two bolts at the diaphragm connection
Damage Scenario 5	Removal of all six bolts at intermediate diaphragm connection
Damage Scenario 6	Removal of all six bolts at the end diaphragm connection

5.2 Preprocessing and Segmentation

Before analysis, we preprocessed the dataset to ensure data quality and consistency:

- Missing data were handled, and we excluded the last damage scenario due to excessive missing values. Damage Scenario 6 contains numerous missing values across several time series due to sensor failures. To maintain the robustness of the proposed approach, this scenario has been excluded from the study.
- Outliers were clipped using a 4-standard deviation (z-score) threshold.
- Signals were segmented into fixed-length windows to capture sufficient temporal context.
- Each axis of each sensor was normalized to ensure fair per-sensor classifier training and consistent meta-learning aggregation.

These preprocessing steps enable robust training of per-sensor classifiers and effective aggregation at the network level, while maintaining generalizability across varying ambient excitations.

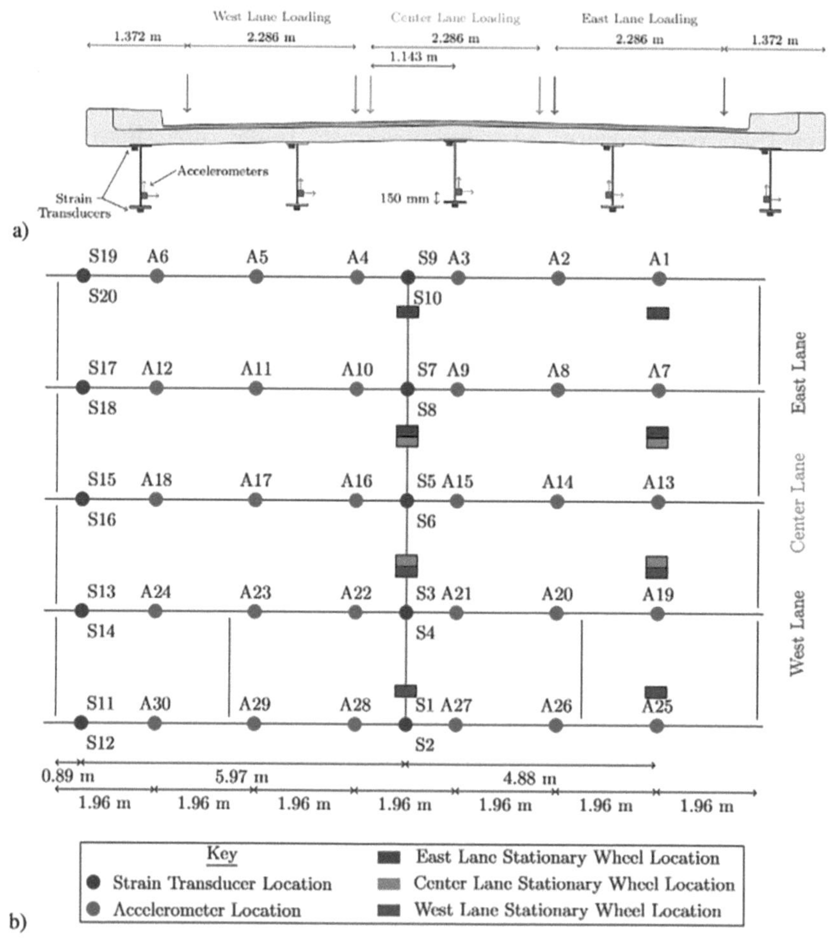

Fig. 2. Location of instrumentation and truck wheel positions in static load tests: a) cross section; b) framing plan [20].

6   Experimental Results and Evaluation

6.1   Results

Segment Length and Ensemble Performance The effectiveness of ensemble strategies strongly depends on the choice of segment length and the correlation of errors across sensors. Shorter segments tend to yield lower per-sensor accuracy but higher sensor disagreement, whereas longer segments improve single-sensor accuracy but reduce the diversity that ensembles can exploit.

To account for the limited dataset size and the inherent variability in train/test splits, we conducted 5-fold stratified cross-validation with a fixed random seed (42). We report mean accuracy across splits for both individual sensors and aggregated ensemble predictions. Table 2 summarizes the per-sensor accuracies, network-aggregated accuracies, and average disagreement across different segment lengths for the two base classifiers.

Figure 3 illustrates the trends for both ROCKET and STSF models.

- **Short segments**: Although individual sensor accuracy decreases, disagreement across sensors increases. This diversity enables ensembles to achieve substantial performance gains, sometimes approaching the accuracy of longer segments, but with reduced computational cost.
- **Long segments**: While per-sensor accuracy is higher, correlated errors limit the improvement obtainable through ensembling.

For the remainder of this study, we use ROCKET with the current configuration as the base classifier.

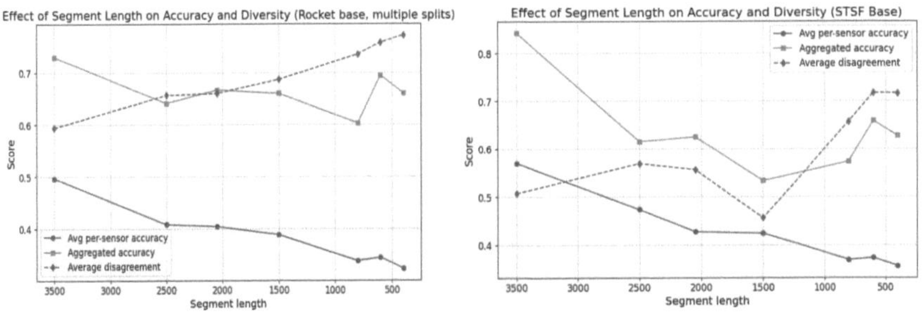

Fig. 3. Effects of segment length on individual sensor accuracy, sensor disagreement, and ensemble performance using soft averaging across multiple train/test splits: ROCKET (left) vs. STSF (right).

Meta-Classifier Weights and Interpretability To investigate how the linear meta-classifier combines sensor predictions, Figs. 4 and 5 visualize the learned weights. Figure 4 shows the logistic regression coefficients assigned to each sensor's probability of the actual class. The heatmap reveals that certain sensors consistently provide more discriminative information for specific damage classes. Noisy or ambiguous sensors are assigned lower weights, confirming that the linear meta-classifier effectively down-weights unreliable sources. For example, the meta-classifier heavily relies on sensor 11's probability estimate when predicting damage 2.

Figure 5 shows, interestingly, that contributions are not limited to the actual class probabilities: cross-class contributions are also observed. For instance, when

Table 2. Per-sensor, aggregated performance accuracies and average disagreement across segment lengths for ROCKET and STSF classifiers.

Model	Configuration	Segment	Avg. Per-Sensor	Aggregated	Avg. Disagreement
ROCKET	50 kernels LR max_iter=50, solver=lbfgs	3500	0.496	0.730	0.594
		2500	0.408	0.641	0.656
		2048	0.404	0.667	0.660
		1500	0.388	0.660	0.686
		800	0.338	0.603	0.735
		600	0.344	0.694	0.757
		400	0.323	0.660	0.771
STSF	50 estimators	3500	0.570	0.842	0.507
		2500	0.473	0.615	0.569
		2048	0.427	0.625	0.556
		1500	0.424	0.533	0.456
		800	0.369	0.573	0.657
		600	0.373	0.658	0.717
		400	0.356	0.627	0.716

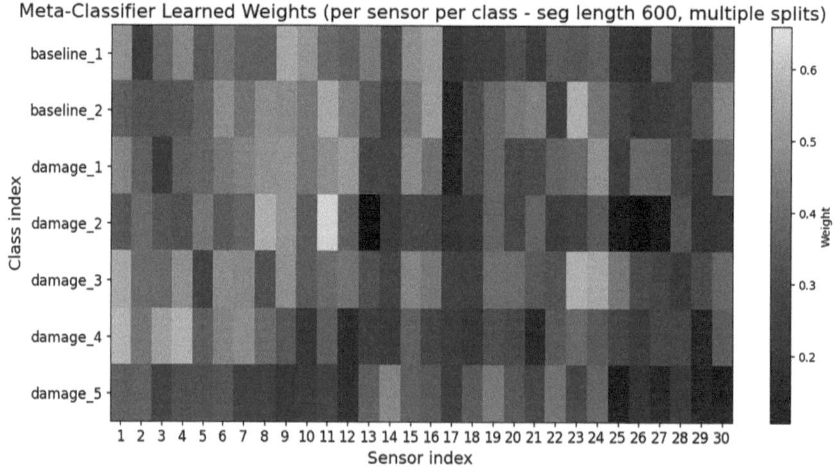

Fig. 4. Per-sensor weights learned by the logistic regression meta-classifier, highlighting the relative contribution of each sensor to ensemble decisions.

detecting damage 3, the classifier leverages information not only from the probability of class 3 but also from probabilities associated with classes 5 and 6. This reflects inter-sensor and inter-class relationships that naïve soft averaging cannot capture.

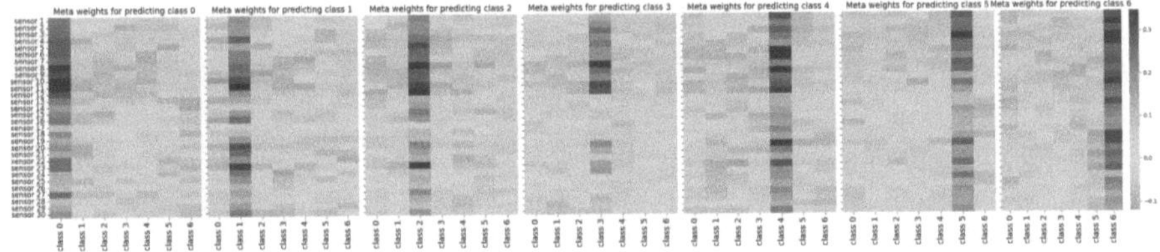

Fig. 5. Heatmap of all-class weights per sensor. Rows correspond to sensors, columns to class probabilities, showing how each contributes to predicting each damage class.

6.2   Comparison of Aggregation Strategies

Figures 6 and 8 illustrate the performance of the aggregation methods across different segment lengths: soft averaging, linear meta-classification (multinomial logistic regression with `max_iter=100` and `lbfgs` solver), and nonlinear meta-classification (random forest with 50 decision trees).

For this evaluation, we conducted 5 random stratified train/test splits using fixed seeds ($42 + i$, with $i = 0, \ldots, 4$) to ensure reproducibility. For each split, per-sensor ROCKET classifiers were trained independently, and their predictions were aggregated according to the selected method. The resulting accuracies, along with the average disagreements, are reported as mean $\pm$ standard deviation across splits in Table 3.

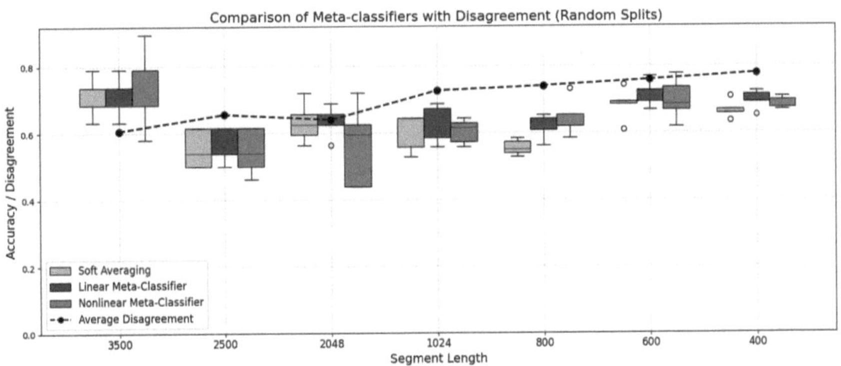

Fig. 6. Comparison of Soft, Linear, and Nonlinear Meta-Classifier accuracy versus segment length.

Figure 7 shows an example of the confusion matrix obtained after aggregation using the proposed Linear Meta-Classifier.

- **Linear meta-classifiers:** By applying logistic regression weights to the full class probability vectors, they consistently outperform soft averaging— particularly for short segments—by learning sensor-specific contributions that reflect both reliability and class relevance.

- **Nonlinear meta-classifiers**: Random forests capture higher-order dependencies between sensors and provide additional accuracy gains in certain complex scenarios. However, these gains come at the expense of interpretability and stability, as shown by larger performance variability.

To simulate bandwidth-constrained scenarios, we also evaluated the models using downsampled time series (factor 2). Results in Fig. 8 show that downsampling reduces computational and communication costs while having minimal impact on ensemble performance, especially when short segments are used.

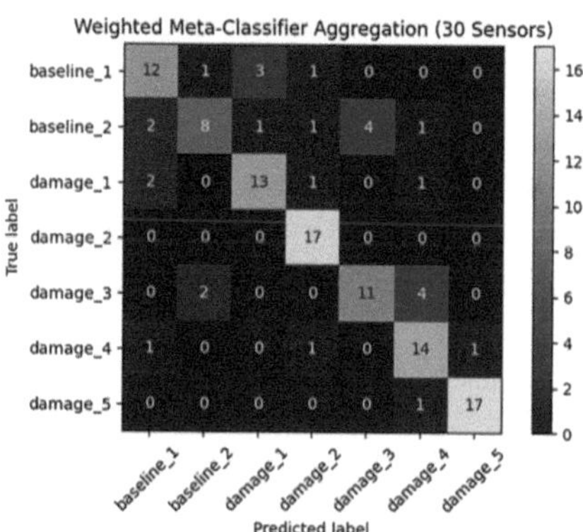

Fig. 7. Confusion matrix of the aggregated probabilities with the linear meta classifier.

6.3   Computational Considerations

Beyond prediction accuracy, computational efficiency is crucial for real-time SHM deployment, where multiple sensors require rapid inference under limited hardware and bandwidth constraints [3].

- **Prediction time**: LR prediction consists of a single matrixvector multiplication followed by a softmax operation, whereas RF requires traversing multiple decision paths across all trees, aggregating predictions, and performing majority voting or probability averaging [5].

  The computational complexity of LR per sample is $\mathcal{O}(n_{\text{features}} \times n_{\text{classes}}) = \mathcal{O}(S \cdot C^2)$, dominated by dense linear algebra operations. For the RF, each prediction requires $\mathcal{O}(n_{\text{trees}} \times d_{\text{avg}})$ operations, where d_{avg} denotes the average tree depth. Despite a similar order of magnitude in arithmetic operations, RF inference incurs substantially higher constant factors due to sequential branching, irregular memory access, and poor cache locality—making LR significantly faster and more suitable for real-time edge execution [5].

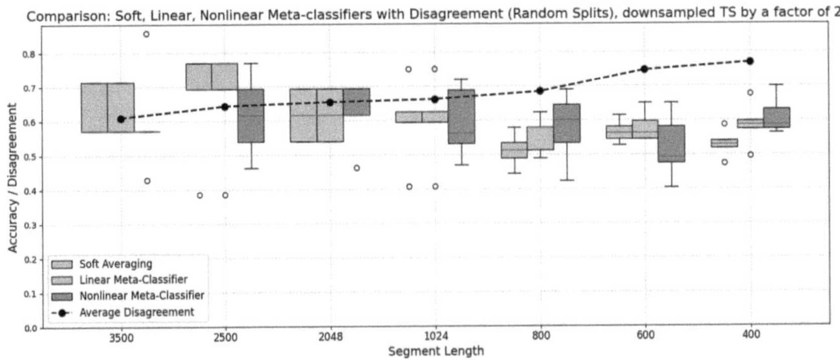

Fig. 8. Accuracy comparison of Soft, Linear, and Nonlinear Meta-Classifiers across segment lengths after downsampling time series by a factor of 2.

Table 3. Comparison of aggregation strategies across segment lengths. Values are mean ± standard deviation over 5 random splits.

Segment	Soft averaging	Linear	Nonlinear	Avg. Disagreement
3500	0.705 ± 0.054	0.705 ± 0.054	0.726 ± 0.107	0.606 ± 0.029
2500	0.554 ± 0.052	0.577 ± 0.049	0.546 ± 0.062	0.655 ± 0.028
2048	0.631 ± 0.054	0.637 ± 0.042	0.562 ± 0.110	0.639 ± 0.009
1024	0.586 ± 0.048	0.626 ± 0.049	0.603 ± 0.033	0.725 ± 0.010
800	0.555 ± 0.021	0.616 ± 0.031	0.647 ± 0.049	0.739 ± 0.009
600	0.682 ± 0.043	0.713 ± 0.034	0.695 ± 0.055	0.756 ± 0.008
400	0.666 ± 0.024	0.694 ± 0.025	0.687 ± 0.015	0.776 ± 0.003

– **Model size and memory footprint**: LR maintains a compact weight matrix of size $n_{\text{classes}} \times n_{\text{features}}$, with $n_{\text{features}} = S \times C$. For $S = 30$ and $C = 7$, this results in $7 \times 210 = 1{,}470$ parameters. In contrast, RF stores complete tree structures, including split thresholds, feature indices, and leaf values across all trees [5]. As a result, the serialized model size of LR remains nearly constant across segment lengths, while RF grows substantially for shorter segments because each tree stores more detailed splits to capture higher-resolution patterns.

Figure 9 illustrates the model size on disk for LR and RF meta-classifiers. LR consistently maintains a small footprint, whereas RF's size increases with shorter segment lengths, reaching up to ∼560 KB, yielding ratios of over 40× compared to LR.

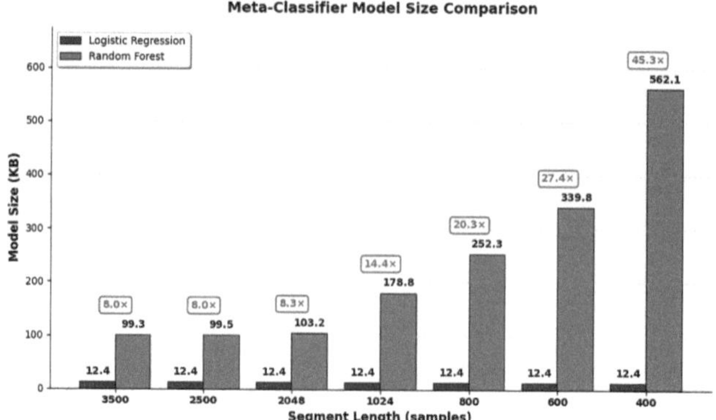

Fig. 9. Serialized model size on disk for LR and RF meta-classifiers across different segment lengths.

7   Time Features Representation for Damage Detection

Building on the demonstrated utility of aggregation strategies, we explored the use of time-domain features extracted from acceleration time series for damage detection in the SHM network. Unlike raw time series approaches, time-domain features provide a compact yet informative representation of the signal, preserving key discriminative information for classification while reducing computational complexity.

7.1   Feature Extraction

From each sensor segment, we extracted a comprehensive set of standard time-domain features, including:

- **Autocorrelation (ACF)** up to lag N, capturing repeating temporal patterns in the vibration signals.
- **Partial autocorrelation (PACF)** to quantify direct dependencies between time points.
- **Autoregressive (AR) coefficients** obtained from fitting an AR model of order p to each segment.
- **Scalar statistical features** such as mean, standard deviation, absolute sum of changes, change quantiles, and percentage of recurring values.

Feature extraction was performed in parallel using the `tsfresh` library [8] to enhance computational efficiency. This process generated a fixed-length feature vector for each segment and sensor, enabling the effective use of traditional classifiers, such as logistic regression and random forests.

7.2 Results

Using these time-domain features, we trained a baseline classifier (Multinomial Logistic Regression) for each sensor and evaluated the proposed ensemble strategies, including soft averaging, linear meta-classifiers, and nonlinear meta-classifiers.

Figure 10 summarizes the classification performance across different segment lengths.

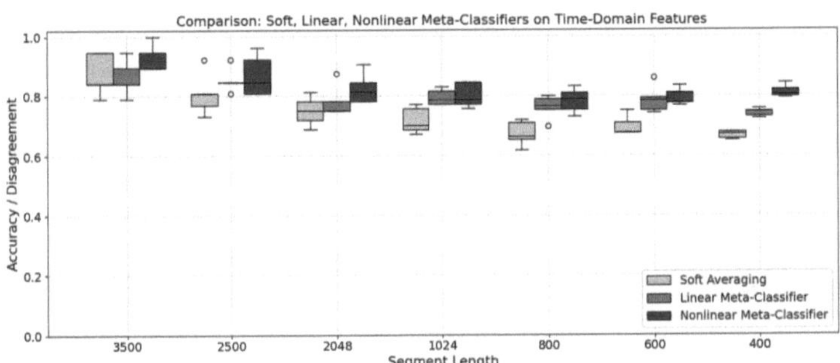

Fig. 10. Accuracy comparison of ensemble strategies using time-domain features across different segment lengths. Boxplots represent results over multiple random train/test splits.

Interestingly, carefully engineered time-domain features combined with a simple baseline classifier and intelligent aggregation strategies achieved significant improvements in aggregated accuracy across all segment lengths. This demonstrates that, even without complex deep learning models, the combination of meaningful features and sensor-level aggregation can yield robust and efficient damage detection in SHM networks.

8 Discussion and Conclusions

We considered a sensor network for Structural health monitoring and a decentralized approach (edge computing) in which each sensor hosts a lightweight classifier operating directly on its local time series. The aggregation of individual sensors' predictions enables improving accuracy and robustness [13]. In the present paper, we first focus on intelligent aggregation strategies for single-sensor classifiers in SHM networks, and secondly, consider alternative features for time series representations. We leverage acceleration time series data from a real instrumented structure, the RT345 bridge dataset, to detect and classify structural damages.

The results from both raw time series aggregation and time-domain feature-based approaches highlight the effectiveness of learned aggregation strategies in SHM networks. Key observations include:

- **Linear meta-classifiers (Logistic Regression)**: Provide a good trade-off between predictive performance, interpretability, and computational efficiency. The learned weights reveal the relative contribution of each sensor and class probability to the final ensemble prediction, enabling insights into the most informative sensors and damage-specific patterns. Linear aggregation consistently improves over naïve soft averaging, particularly for short segment lengths where sensor-level predictions are more variable.
- **Nonlinear meta-classifiers (Random Forests)**: Capture complex inter-sensor dependencies and nonlinear feature interactions, providing additional accuracy gains in challenging scenarios. However, this comes at the cost of interpretability, higher memory usage, and longer prediction times, which may limit deployment in resource-constrained SHM systems.
- **Time-domain feature representation**: Handcrafted features extracted from each sensor segment reduce the input dimensionality while preserving discriminative information. When combined with baseline classifiers and intelligent aggregation, time-domain features achieve competitive or superior aggregated accuracy compared to raw time series models, especially for shorter segments. This demonstrates that feature engineering remains a viable and computationally efficient alternative to deep learning for SHM tasks.
- **Edge deployment considerations**: Linear models trained on time-domain features are lightweight, enable real-time inference with sub-millisecond latency, and can run on memory- and power-constrained devices such as IoT gateways (e.g. Raspberry Pi systems). This makes them highly suitable for wireless sensor networks where energy efficiency and low-latency decisions are critical.
- **Sensor disagreement and reliability**: Across all approaches, sensors producing noisy or ambiguous predictions are automatically down-weighted by the aggregation strategies, highlighting the benefit of learned combination over naïve averaging. This enhances robustness to sensor variability and failure.

Overall, this paper demonstrates that combining single-sensor classifiers with learned aggregation strategies—linear or nonlinear—significantly enhances network-level SHM performance. Importantly, these results confirm that careful feature engineering combined with intelligent sensor fusion can match or even surpass the performance of more complex deep learning approaches, providing both practical and theoretical insights for SHM system design. Futur work should focus on exploring alternative base classifiers, compact yet richer time series representation from many domains to further enhance robustness and scalability.

References

1. Anaissi, A., Suleiman, B., Alyassine, W.: Personalised federated learning framework for damage detection in structural health monitoring. J. Civ. Struct. Heal. Monit. **13**(2), 295–308 (2023)

2. Asghari, A., Ghodrati Amiri, G., Darvishan, E., Asghari, A.: A novel approach for structural damage detection using multi-headed stacked deep ensemble learning. J. Vib. Eng. & Technol. **12**(3), 4209–4224 (2024)
3. Avci, O., et al.: A review of vibration-based damage detection in civil structures: from traditional methods to machine learning and deep learning applications. Mech. Syst. Signal Process. **147**, 107077 (2021)
4. Bhatta, S., Dang, J.: Use of IoT for structural health monitoring of civil engineering structures: a state-of-the-art review. Urban Lifeline **2**(1), 17 (2024). https://doi.org/10.1007/s44285-024-00031-2
5. Breiman, L.: Random forests. Mach. Learn. **45**, 5–32 (2001)
6. Buckley, T., Ghosh, B., Pakrashi, V.: Edge structural health monitoring (e-shm) using low-power wireless sensing. Sensors **21**(20), 6760 (2021)
7. Cheema, M.A., Sarwar, M.Z., Cantero, D., Rossi, P.S.: Clustered federated learning for population-based structural health monitoring. IEEE Internet Things J. (2025)
8. Christ, M., Braun, N., Neuffer, J., Kempa-Liehr, A.W.: Time series feature extraction on basis of scalable hypothesis tests (tsfresh-a python package). Neurocomputing **307**, 72–77 (2018)
9. Dabbous, A., Berta, R., Fresta, M., Ballout, H., Lazzaroni, L., Bellotti, F.: Bringing intelligence to the edge for structural health monitoring: the case study of the Z24 bridge. IEEE Open J. Ind. Electron. Soc. **5**, 781–794 (2024). https://doi.org/10.1109/OJIES.2024.3434341. https://ieeexplore.ieee.org/document/10612214
10. Dempster, A., Petitjean, F., Webb, G.I.: Rocket: exceptionally fast and accurate time series classification using random convolutional kernels. Data Min. Knowl. Disc. **34**(5), 1454–1495 (2020)
11. Dietterich, T.G.: Ensemble methods in machine learning, pp. 1–15 (2000)
12. Farrar, C.R., Dervilis, N., Worden, K.: The past, present and future of structural health monitoring: an overview of three ages. Strain **61**(1), e12495 (2025). https://doi.org/10.1111/str.12495. https://onlinelibrary.wiley.com/doi/abs/10.1111/str.12495
13. Fidma, M.A., Schmidt, F., Bercher, J.F.: Low-complexity approach to intelligent shm by combining machine learning models using single-sensor data. In: Chang, F.K., Guemes, A. (eds.) 15th International Workshop on Structural Health Monitoring. pp. 983–990. DEStech Publications (2025)
14. Hackmann, G., Sun, F., Castaneda, N., Lu, C., Dyke, S.: A holistic approach to decentralized structural damage localization using wireless sensor networks. Comput. Commun. **36**(1), 29–41 (2012)
15. Kuncheva, L.I.: Combining Pattern Classifiers: Methods and Algorithms. John Wiley & Sons (2014)
16. Ladha, K.K.: The condorcet jury theorem, free speech, and correlated votes. Am. J. Polit. Sci. 617–634 (1992)
17. Madani, E., Fiouz, A., Abdollahzadeh, D., Aminnejad, B.: A stacking learning-based method for identifying the structural damage in structures. In: Structures, vol. 70, p. 107864. Elsevier (2024)
18. Moallemi, A., Burrello, A., Brunelli, D., Benini, L.: Exploring scalable, distributed real-time anomaly detection for bridge health monitoring. IEEE Internet Things J. **9**(18), 17660–17674 (2022). https://doi.org/10.1109/JIOT.2022.3157532. https://ieeexplore.ieee.org/document/9729869
19. Pham, N.L., Ta, Q.B., Huynh, T.C., Kim, J.T.: Cnn federated learning for vibration-based damage identification of submerged structure-foundation system. J. Civ. Struct. Health Monit. 1–26 (2025)

20. Whelan, M.J., Gangone, M.V., Janoyan, K.D.: Data set from ambient vibration monitoring and static loading of a steel stringer bridge subject to imposed damage for structural health monitoring and damage detection. J. Bridg. Eng. **30**(7), 04725001 (2025)
21. Yang, Y., Lin, H., Qian, G., Hu, Z., Todd, M.D.: A privacy-preserving framework using federated learning for structural health monitoring with miter gates application. Struct. Health Monit. **2025**, (2025)

Enhancing the Assessment of the Quality of Explanations for AI-Based Network IDS

Audrey Fongue[(⊠)], Jerry Lonlac, Patrick Sondi, and Ahmed Meddahi

Centre for Digital Systems, IMT Nord Europe, Institut Mines-Télécom, Lille, France
{audrey.fongue,jerry.lonlac,patrick.sondi,
ahmed.meddahi}@imt-nord-europe.fr

Abstract. The rise of cyber threats makes Intrusion Dectection Systems (IDS) essential for network security. With the development of machine learning, these IDS have been significantly improved even if the trade-off between performance and interpretability remains an issue. In recent years, several authors have proposed white-box IDS systems to enhance trust and confidence of security analysts. However, only few of these works provide a systematic evaluation of the proposed explainable AI (XAI) techniques. In this paper, we propose a thorough analysis of LIME and SHAP explainers on a high performance ensemble-based IDS. The proposed IDS is trained on the publicly available datasets Edge-IIoTset, N-BaIot and CIC-IDS2017 with AGRU and XGBoost, and the results show that XGBoost classifies better with an accuracy of 1 on two datasets compared to 0.99 for AGRU. We then assessed the performance of the explainers under three metrics (stability, fidelity and sparsity) on XGBoost predictions. The results revealed that SHAP was more stable (stability > 80%) for various noise values in the feature values and more faithful (Fid+ > 60%) on N-BaIoT dataset, while it achieved the highest sparsity for the classes of the CIC-IDS2017 dataset.

Keywords: XAI · Network IDS · ITS · 5G CN · VNF

1 Introduction

Intrusion detection systems (IDS) play a vital role in cybersecurity by monitoring networks and systems to identify suspicious or malicious activity. Traditionally, these systems relied on signature-based or static rule-based methods, which are effective at detecting known attacks. However, with cyber threats evolving rapidly, these traditional approaches are showing their limitations. Among the research topics most addressed in the literature, there is a need for solutions that can detect rapidly intrusion attempts even in presence of big amount of data traffic. In addition, solutions capable of detecting innovative attacks are mandatory against the increasing number of intrusion attempts. The introduction of artificial intelligence (AI), particularly machine learning (ML) and deep

S. Boumerdassi et al. (Eds.): MLN 2025, LNCS 16424, pp. 99–120, 2026.
https://doi.org/10.1007/978-3-032-18494-8_8

learning (DL), has revolutionized intrusion detection. These techniques enable IDS to learn normal and abnormal behavior from data, providing an increased ability to detect unknown attacks and adapt to new types of threats. In the context of the fifth generation (5G) networks, AI-based N-IDS (Network IDS) have been proposed as virtualized network functions (VNF) or as part of the solutions securing protocols such as the session initiation protocol (SIP) [13].

Despite these advances, several challenges remain. Indeed, complex models, such as deep neural networks, are often considered "black boxes", thus making it difficult to understand the decisions made by the IDS based on these approaches. Particularly, in critical applications such as Intelligent Transportation Systems (ITS), the inferences made by AI-based N-IDS may have serious consequences, thus explaining the hesitation about the adoption of such approaches. Increasingly, researchers are now proposing intrusion detection systems that promote better understanding and transparency of AI-based model's decisions by introducing XAI (eXplainable artificial intelligence) techniques. However, despite the efforts made in using XAI tools in AI-based IDS proposals' evaluations, there is still a need for enhancing the assessment of the explanations provided by such tools in order to improve the confidence of the practitioners, e.g. Security Operations Center (SOC) analysts in this case. Existing work focuses either on predictive performance by leveraging Machine Learning, Deep Learning, Reinforcement Learning or on explainability, but few methods effectively combine high performance with robust and verifiable interpretability.

In this paper we precisely address this issue by proposing and illustrating an approach aiming to enhance the evaluation of the quality of explanations provided by XAI-based Network-IDS. Our main contributions are as follows:

- We provide a performant IDS based on AGRU and XGBoost models for attacks classification
- We demonstrate the effectiveness of the selected model on CIC-IDS2017, Edge-IIoTset, N-BaIoT witch shows improvements over reference methods with an explanation on using SHAP and LIME at both the global and local levels
- We evaluate the stability, sparsity and fidelity of explanations in relation to data perturbations.

In order to present our approach, the remaining of this paper is organized as follows. After an overview of the related work in Sect. 2, the workflow of our approach as well as the AI and XAI tools used in this work are presented in Sect. 3. The experimental setup and datasets are described in Sect. 4, and the results are presented and discussed in Sect. 5 before we deliver our conclusions.

2   Related Work

Several surveys in the literature address different aspects related to our proposal [14,18]. In the paper [21], the authors propose accuracy, completeness, efficiency and robustness as criteria to compare and evaluate LRP, LIME, LEMNA,

Gradients, IG and SHAP for vulnerability discovery, malware and malicious pdf files detection in four security systems namely DAMD, VulDeePecker, Drebin+ and Mimicus+ using MLP, CNN and RNN. They found that the methods LRP and IG comply best with all their criteria and resemble general-purpose techniques for security systems and that LIME is the best black-box option in the absence of white-box access. The authors of [7] propose a Domain Knowledge aided XAI for the detection of unknown attacks in a security system based on ANN, SVM, RF, Extra Trees and Naive baiyes on the CIC-IDS2017 dataset. For explainability, they made an infusion of popular domain knowledge (CIA principles) by converting related features into three features and compared the effectiveness of their models according to different sets of features (all, selected, based on domain knowledge, or highly generalized). The results showed that Random Forest performs best overall, especially with all features. The explainability part of this work is related to the value added to the features, not by using an explainability model. Shoukat et al. [17] present a framework for the intrusion detection problem including XAI. To classify attacks, they constructed an ensemble model based on an LSTM-AE and an Attention Gated reccurent Unit (AGRU) combined with softmax. They used three datasets including Edge-IIoTSet N-BaIoT and CIC-IDS2017 for their experiments. The results showed an accuracy of 99.79%, 99,49% and 98,57% for respectively N-BaIoT, Edge-IIoTset and CIC-IDS2017 datasets for the classification. They made global explainability and local explainability with SHAP for some random instances to identify the driving factors behind the model's decisions. Even if their proposition showed good results in attacks classification, the explainability part of their work lack an evaluation of the proposed explanations. Ashan et al. [1] present an ML based IDS for software-defined ad-hoc vehicle networks. They used an Ensemble model that combines Random Forest and Catboost as the main investigators and logistic regression as the final decision maker for the classification with a preselection of the 10 best features with the Chi-square test. They used SHAP to explain the model's decisions. Their tests, made on the VeReMi dataset achieved accuracy values of 99.68% and 98.11% for binary classification and multiclass classification respectively. No evaluation is done here. This paper [6] addresses the problem of the lack of systematic evaluation of several explanations methods used in IoT systems for anomaly detection by proposing a DNN framework to evaluate different white-box XAI strategies where they consider descriptive accuracy, efficiency, sparsity, robustness, stability and completeness as evaluation metrics. DeepSHAP, IG and LRP were used for the explainability part on N-BaIoT and MEMS datasets. They deduce from their results that white-box XAI provide good explanations but are limited by their dependence on DNNs, their instability and slowness complicating their use in IoT. White-box methods dominate in sparsity and efficiency, black-box methods in robustness. Paltun et al. [11] use XAI to evaluate how adversarial attacks impact the decisions of ML models by identifying and hiliting features modified by the attackers. They characterize normal behavior pattern of the data through the distribution of shap importance values. Their IDS is developed with auto-encoders and unsupervised neural networks with the ORAN infrastructure as the test setup. They used SHAP and compared with other feature importance methods such as LIME and permutation importance and the results showed that SHAP is the most effective for all the metrics with an accuracy of 0.92 and F1-score of 0.86. Kalakoti et al. [8] proposed an explainability framework for a N-IDS alert classification based on an LSTM where LIME, SHAP, DeepLIFT and IG were used. They assessed their explanations with four metrics: complexity, robustness, reliability and faithfulness on a dataset from Taltech in Estonia on which the classification gave an accuracy of 99%. Their analysis showed that DeepLift stands out with better performance in faithfulness, max sensitivity, RMA and RRA. EI-XIDS is an explainable ensemble learning (DNN + RL) based IDS framework proposed by the work of Xu et al. [22]. The RL process learns how to weight the XAI methods such as LIME, SHAP, LEMNA, DEEP-PAID and xNIDS to generate optimal counterfactuals explanations which generates security rules on NSL-KDD and UNSW-NB15 datasets. Their explanation framework achieved 97% and 96% on NSL-KDD and UNSW-NB15 witch outperformed other individual explanation methods even in terms of sparsity and robustness and LIME was the least effective. Another work [16] proposed an IDS approach based on DNN and CNN tested over the NSL-KDD and UNSW-NB15 datasets. They used filter-based method to reduce the number of features and reduce the computational cost. The DNN outperformed on the two datasets and they leveraged SHAP and LIME to foster transparency of their model but no evaluation was provided. Kumar et al. [5] addressed the security risk in interconnected vehicles by proposing a Deep Learning approach based on Federated Learning for Advanced Persistent Threats(APT) detection with a privacy preservation technique and SHAP for explainability. Experiments on Edge-IIoTset, CSE-CIC-IDS2018 and UNSW-NB15 datasets with and without privacy-preserving yielded best results of classification without privacy preserving. In this paper [20], the authors addressed the issue of upgrading IDS by resolving the problem with adversarial attacks. They proposed to leverage conventional ML-based IDS with an integration of XAI. They implemented the IDS with the Random Forest as primary and secondary classifiers and a Module to evaluate the credibility and transparency of the predicted outputs which leverages the predicted probability vector and the Shapley values array. The output of the module is then passed through the secondary classifier to get the final prediction. They assessed the framework on the test dataset with adversarial examples and compared with other ML-based IDS(SVM,RF and KNN) where they had the highest accuracy over all class attacks on the CSE-IDS2018 dataset. This background shows that the issue of evaluating explanations arises in this field, but there is still a lot of work that is limited to interpreting the explanations provided without evaluating their quality using appropriate metrics. In this paper, we mainly propose evaluating the fidelity, stability and sparsity of explanations in intrusion detection while high performances attacks detection. Evaluating explanations is crucial to support SOC analysts in interpreting model decisions, increasing trust, and ensuring actionable insights in operational environments.

3   A Framework for Assessing the Quality of Explanations

In this section, we present a comprehensive description of our proposed methodology, which includes the workflow, the AI and XAI tools used in our framework.

3.1   Workflow

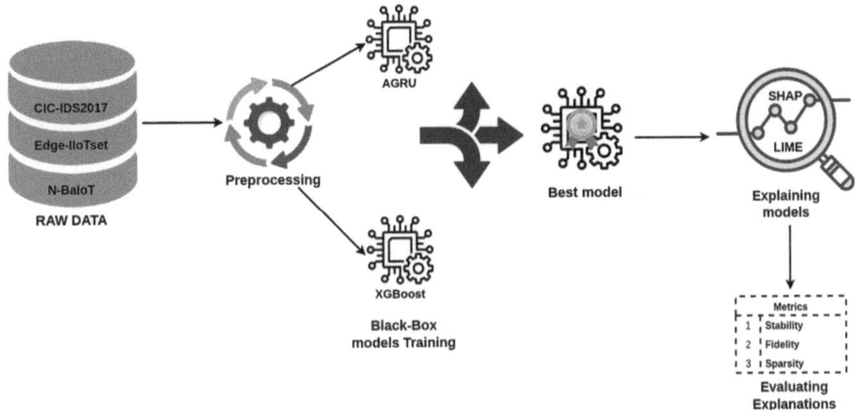

Fig. 1. A workflow for explanations evaluation.

The framework consists of several steps as illustrated in Fig. 1 which includes gathering data (CIC-IDS2017, Edge-IIoTset, N-BaIoT), preprocessing the data according to the models archictectures, then, these data are trained using an ensemble model(XGBoost) and a reccurent neural network (AGRU) to detect malicious traffic. The model with the best performances is used to explain local and global predictions using LIME [12] and SHAP [9] by interpreting the top contributing features. The last step consists in evaluating the explainers in terms of Stability, Fidelity and Sparsity. The goal is to enhance trust and confidence of practitioners in the provided explanations.

3.2   AI Algorithms

AGRU The capacity of attention mechanisms to dynamically prioritize relevant components of the input has led to substantial advancements in task performance, particularly within the field of Natural Language Processing (NLP). Gated Reccurent Unit (GRU) has proven its effectiveness in several studies compared to RNNs. AGRU is a Gated Reccurent Unit [3] with an Attention layer [17]. The Gated Recurrent Unit reduces the gating signals to two from the LSTM model to address the vanishing gradient issue. These two gates are the update gate(z_t) and the reset gate(r_t) and decide which information to transmit to the output. The GRU can be represented with this equation:

$$h_t = (1 - z_t) \odot h_{t-1} + z_t \odot \tilde{h}_t \tag{1}$$

where $\tilde{h}_t = g(W_h x_t + U_h(r_t \odot h_{t-1}) + b_h)$. The two gates are presented as follows: $z_t = \sigma(W_z x_t + U_z h_{t-1} + b_z)$ and $r_t = \sigma(W_r x_t + U_r h_{t-1} + b_r)$. The weights corresponding to these gates are also updated using the backpropagation through time stochastic gradient descent. The attention mechanism to make the model more efficient in threat detection is defined as follows [17]:

$$\mathcal{ATN}_{ij} = \text{softmax}\left(\mathcal{F}_{atn}(H_i, S_j)\right) \tag{2}$$

$$\mathcal{F}_{atn}(H_i, S_j) = v_a^\top \tanh\left([W_a H_i, W_a S_j]\right) \tag{3}$$

$$\text{Context}_i = \sum_j \mathcal{ATN}_{ij} H_j \tag{4}$$

XGBoost XGBoost [2] is a machine learning algorithm based on gradient boosting tree which supports multiple objectives (classification, Regression, ranking). It offers an optimal compromise between performance, training time and interpretability. The algorithm's empirical success on tabular data, demonstrated across numerous studies and competitive benchmarks, makes it a widely trusted choice. It builds a set of trees in an additive manner following this equation:

$$\hat{y}_i = \phi(x_i) = \sum_{k=1}^{K} f_k(x_i)$$

. Every tree f_k is sequentially added to correct the errors of the previous ones. In each iteration t, The gradient is calculated (gradient of first order and second order respectively):

$$g_i = \frac{\partial L}{\partial \hat{y}^{(t-1)}}, \qquad h_i = \frac{\partial^2 L}{\partial \hat{y}^{(t-1)}};$$

The objective is simplified:

$$\tilde{L}^{(t)} = \sum_i \left[g_i \cdot f_t(x_i) + \tfrac{1}{2} h_i \cdot f_t^2(x_i)\right] + \Omega(f_t)$$

and the optimal tree is constructed. The tree is constructed by doing the following steps for each node:

- Calculate the quality score for the actual/current structure
- Evaluate candidate splits with respect to the gain
- Select the best split which maximizes the gain
- Compute optimal weights for the leaf nodes.

For each split, the algorithm tests the two directions for missing values, scans only non-missing values and automatically learns the best direction by default. Each example passes through each tree until it reaches a leaf, and the scores of the leaves reached are added together.

3.3   XAI Methods

When a neural network makes a prediction for a given input, an explanation method seeks to understand why this choice was made. Feature attribution methods assign a relevance score to each feature of the input, indicating those that had the greatest influence on the model's decision. In this paper we use LIME and SHAP.

SHAP (SHapley Additive Explanations) SHAP [9] is a popular explainable AI (XAI) tool that is used to decode the overall model response (global explanation) and each prediction (local explanations) in terms of features contribution.

Its implementation is based on a method for estimating Shapley values issued from the cooperative game theory that involves distributing gains and costs fairly among several actors working in coalition. Game theory is often referred to when several actors or factors are involved in a strategy aimed at achieving a desired outcome or gain. SHAP transposes this theory in machine learning such that the game is to explain the prediction, the players are the input features and the total benefit is the prediction. Therefore, the shapley value of a given variable is its contribution to the prediction. For a given instance, the shapley value for a variable(or many variables) is its contribution to the difference between the value predicted by the model and the average of the predictions of all the instances. Given a set of features F, $S \cup F$, SHAP retrains the model on each subset S. To compute the effect of each feature i, the model f is trained with $(f_{S \cup \{i\}})$ and without the feature (f_S). Predictions for the two models are then compared to the input we want to explain such that: $f_{S \cup \{i\}}((x_{S \cup \{i\}}) - f_S(x_S)$. The following equation is used to compute feature attributions:

$$\phi_i = \Sigma_{S \subseteq F \setminus \{i\}} \frac{|S|!(|F| - |S| - 1)!}{|F|!} [f_{S \cup \{i\}}(x_{S \cup \{i\}}) - f_S(x_S)]$$

LIME (Local Interpretable Model-Agnostic Explanations) LIME [12] is a local model that aim to explain the prediction of an individual(instance) by analysing his neigborhood. It provides a qualitative comprehension between input features and the ouput value and is agnostic as SHAP meaning that it is capable to explain any type of machine learning model. Its process can be divided into two main steps. Step 1) Generate new entries in a neighborhood close to the instance to explain. Step 2) LIME then train a transparent model on the complex black-box model's predictions that we are trying to interpret. It learns through a simple model and thus interpretable(linear regression or decision tree for example). The transparent model acts as a substitute model for interpreting the results of the original complex model.

The explanation of an instance x is obtained by minimizing the following equation: $Explanation(x) = \arg\min_{g \in G} L(f, g, \pi_x) + \Omega(g)$ where f is the model to explain, g is the substitution model that will be used to explain f, $\Omega(g)$ is a measure of complexity of the explanation g, it penalises the complexity of g, π_x is a proximity measure between an instance z to x $(\pi_x(z))$ in order to define locality around x , G is the class of linear models. L is the locally weighted square loss that is minimized to ensure local fidelity and interpretability while having $\omega(g)$ low enough to be interpretable by humans. It is a measure of how unfaithfull g is in approximating f in the locality defined by π_x.

In a security system, the generated explanations must be trustworthy. This means that the important features should not be influenced by random fluctuations and the number of features must be as small as possible to facilitate the interpretation for SOC analysts. Explainability methods can be evaluated through several metrics. In this paper, we leverage Stability, Fidelity and Sparsity.

Definition 1. (*Stability*) An explanation method is stable if the generated explanations do not vary between multiple runs or do not vary a lot with small fluctuations. The Jaccard similarity is a measure used to compare two (or more) sets based on their intersection and union.

$$J(S_1, S_2, \ldots, S_n) = \frac{|S_1 \cap S_2 \cap \cdots \cap S_n|}{|S_1 \cup S_2 \cup \cdots \cup S_n|}$$

If we repeat the explanation several times using the same data or slightly pertubed, we obtain a set of important features each time. Jaccard tells us the extent to which these sets overlap. If $Jaccard \approx 1$ the explanations are stable, if $Jaccard \approx 0$, explanations are unstable (the features change significantly). In this work, we compute jaccard similarity to measure the stability [19].

Definition 2. (*Fidelity*) Fidelity captures how much is good an interpretable model in the mimic of the behavior of a black-box.

The following formula are proposed by [23] to assess the fidelity. Fid^+ evaluates if the identified features are necessary for the prediction and Fid^- evaluates if the identified features are sufficient to achieve the same results.

$$\mathrm{Fid}^+(\psi) = \frac{1}{|T|} \sum_{(x_i, y_i) \in T} \left[\mathbf{1}(y_i = f(x_i)) - \mathbf{1}(y_i = f(x_i - x_i \odot m_i)) \right]$$

$$\mathrm{Fid}^-(\psi) = \frac{1}{|T|} \sum_{(x_i, y_i) \in T} \left[\mathbf{1}(y_i = f(x_i)) - \mathbf{1}(y_i = f(x_i \odot m_i)) \right]$$

where $mi = \psi(xi)$ is the explanation corresponding to x_i produced by the explainer $\psi(\cdot)$, T is the dataset used to evaluate the performance of the explainer, $\mathbf{1}$: indicator function (1 if true, 0 otherwise). The higher $Fid+$, the better the explanation (removing important features significantly changes the prediction). The lower $Fid-$, the better the explanation (keeping only important features maintains the correct prediction).

Definition 3. (*Descriptive sparsity*) Sparsity is the limited number of features that can be processed by a human analyst and that is sufficient to explain a prediction. In [21], descriptive sparsity is measured by scaling the relevance values to the range $[-1, 1]$, computing a normalized histogram h of them and calculating the mass around zero (MAZ) defined by

$$\mathrm{MAZ}(r) \;=\; \int_{-r}^{r} h(x)\,dx, \quad r \in [0, 1].$$

The MAZ measures how relevance values accumulate within a symmetric window around 0, expanding along the x-axis. Sparse explanations show a steep rise near 0 (few relevant features), while dense explanations rise more gradually, meaning that methods with MAZ peaking at 0 are generally preferred.

4 Experiments

4.1 Experimental Setup

The experiments were carried out on a 64 bits Ubuntu 22.04.5 LTS, an Intel$^{®}$ Core^{TM} Ultra 7 165H $\times$ 22 processor with 1To DD and 32 Gio memory space. We used the Jupyter Notebook IDE for the experiments with Python 3.10.12, Keras, Tensorflow, Scikit-learn to fit the black-box models, LIME and SHAP librairies.

4.2 Datasets

Description In this work, we used three publicly available network security and intrusion detection datasets namely N-BaIoT, Edge-IIoTset and CIC-IDS2017 like in the work of [17].

- Edge-IIoTset [4]: is a comprehensive realistic cyber security dataset of IoT and IIoT applications. They identify and analyze 14 attacks related to IoT and IIoT connectivity protocols, which are categorized into five threats, including, DoS/DDoS attacks, Information gathering, Man in the middle attacks, Injection attacks, and Malware attacks with (63 features). The dataset contains 15 classes: Normal, MITM, Uploading, Ransomware, SQL_injection, DDoS_HTTP, DDoS_TCP, Password, Port_Scanning, Vulnerability_scanner, Backdoor, XSS, Fingerprinting, DDoS_UDP, DDoS_ICMP and keep the eight ones that are most frequent in the industry [17]: SQL_injection, DDoS_HTTP, DDoS_TCP, Vulnerability_scanner, Backdoor, DDoS_UDP and DDoS_ICMP.
- N-BaIoT [10]: This dataset addresses the lack of public botnet datasets, especially for the IoT. It suggests real traffic data, gathered from 9 commercial IoT devices authentically infected by Mirai and BASHLITE. The dataset contains 11 classes, 10 attacks divided in two catagories(Mirai, Gafgyt) and 1 benign class. In our experiments, we choosed the data files from the 1st, 2nd, 3rd and 7th IoT devices witch contain these classes: benign, gafgyt_combo, gafgyt_junk', gafgyt_scan, mirai_ack, mirai_scan, mirai_syn, mirai_udp with 115 features.

108   A. Fongue et al.

- CIC-IDS2017 [15]: The dataset is captured within 5 days from Monday july 3rd at 9:00 AM to Friday July 7th at 5:00 PM and is available in 8 csv files. The dataset contains 14 attacks types: Infiltration, Heartbleed, Web Attack Brute Force, Web Attack XSS, Web Attack Sql Injection, Bot, DDoS, DoS GoldenEye, DoS Hulk, DoS Slowhttptest, DoS slowloris, FTP-Patator, PortScan and SSH-Patator which can be categorized into 6 attacks profiles: Brute Force, HeartBleed, Botnet , Dos and DDos, Web and Infiltration. In our experiments we deleted Heartbleed and Infiltration instances because they contain few samples(36 and 11) than the other attacks and we grouped all web attack classes into one class (Web attack) and end up with 11 attacks with 78 features.

Preprocessing In our preprocessing pipeline, we leveraged several common techniques to enhance model performances:

- Checking and removing rows with missing values
- Removing duplicated rows
- We manually convert categorial class label to integer labels
- We used Standardscaler of the scikit-learn library to rescale the datasets in order to ensure that each feature contributes proportionally to the model's learning process.
- For Edge-IIoTset, we deleted some object columns and converted the remaining ones into numeric values using LabelEncoder from scikit-learn and end up with 46 features.
- One-Hot encoding was used on feature labels for the AGRU model
- We divided the datasets in a ratio of $70-30$ for training and testing. Tables (1, 2 and 3) provide the details on the number of training and testing instances for each class of the three datasets.

Table 1. Distribution of classes for training and testing sets in Edge-IIoTset

	Normal	SQL_injection	DDOS_HTTP	DDOS_TCP	Vulnerability_scanner	Backdoor	DDOS_UDP	DDOS_ICMP
Train	1004220	35545	35060	35136	34993	16855	84875	47585
Test	430303	15426	14777	14926	15033	7176	36692	20354
Total	1848956		Test	554687			Train	1294269

4.3   Evaluation Metrics

AI Models Metrics To assess the performances of the models used in our pipeline, we use the following metrics:

Table 2. Distribution of classes for training and testing sets in CIC-IDS2017

	Benign	Bot	DDOS	DOS_GoldenEye	Dos_Hulk	Dos_slowhttptest	DOS_slowloris	FTP-Patator	Portscan	SSH-Patator	Web Attack
Train	1466151	1370	89440	7301	121270	3670	3772	4113	63702	2239	14975
Test	628906	578	38574	2985	51576	1558	1613	1818	26992	980	646
Total	2520751		Test	756226						Train	1575525

Table 3. Distribution of classes for training and testing sets in N-BaIoT

	benign	gafgyt_combo	gafgyt_junk	gafgyt_scan	mirai_ack	mirai_scan	mirai_syn	mirai_udp
Train	96752	42083	21697	20852	150795	105800	167456	272318
Test	41723	17643	9290	9010	64685	45077	71924	116828
Total	125393		Test	376180			Train	877753

Accuracy: is the total number of correct classifications (benign or attack) on the whole datasets.

$$Accuracy = \frac{TP + TN}{TP + FP + FN + TN}$$

Precision: is the number of instances correctly classified as positive among all the examples classified as positive.

$$Precicion = \frac{TP}{TP + FP}$$

Recall: is the proportion of examples correctly classified as positive(attacks) over the total number of attacks in the dataset.

$$Recall : \frac{TP}{TP + FN}$$

F1-score: is an harmonic mean of precision and recall

$$F1\text{-score} = 2 * \frac{Precision * Recall}{Precision + Recall}$$

where:

- True Positive (TP) represents instances predicted as attacks are really attacks.
- True Negative (TN) are instances predicted as Benign are really benign.
- False Positive (FP) represents instances predicted as attacks that are normally benign.
- False Negative (FN) are attacks that are predicted as benign instances

Model Parameters The parameters for the AGRU are the same as in the work of [17] unless for the input layer because we didn't use the LSTM-AE.

The input layer dimension for the AGRU here equals to the number of features of the dataset. For XGBoost, the objective is multi:softmax, the num_class is 11, 8 and 8 for CIC-IDS2017, Edge-IIOTset and N-BaIot respectively, the n_estimators is 100, the eval_metric is the mlogloss, the learning_rate is 0.3. We set the early_stoping_rounds parameter to 10. the subsample to 0.85 with colsample_bytree, colsample_bylevel and colsample_bynode to 0.85 and the evaluation_set representing 30% of the training set.

5   Results and Discussion

In this section, we provide the results of the classification, the explanations with corresponding interpretations and the evaluation of the XAI models (Tables 4, 5 and 6).

5.1   Classification

Table 4. Performance comparison of XGBoost and AGRU on Edge-IIoTset

Class	XGBoost				AGRU			
	Precision	Recall	F1-score	Accuracy	Precision	Recall	F1-score	Accuracy
Normal	1	1	1	–	1	1	1	–
SQL_injection	0.99	1	0.99	–	0.99	1	0.99	–
DDOS_HTTP	0.99	0.99	0.99	–	0.99	0.99	0.99	–
DDOS_TCP	1	1	1	–	0.99	1	1	–
Vulnerability_scanner	1	0.99	0.99	–	0.99	0.99	0.99	–
Backdoor	1	0.99	0.99	–	1	0.99	0.99	–
DDOS_UDP	1	0.99	0.99	–	0.99	1	0.99	–
DDOS_ICMP	0.99	1	0.99	–	1	0.99	0.99	–
Macro Avg	0.99	0.99	0.99	–	0.99	0.99	0.99	–
Micro Avg	1	1	1	–	0.99	0.99	0.99	–
Accuracy	–	–	–	1	–	–	–	0.99

The classification results show that XGBoost outperformed AGRU, even in terms of execution speed so we used it to understand why some instances are predicted as attacks.

5.2   Explanations Interpretation

Here are the Summary plots on the test sets of each dataset. The summary plot is used to summarise the importance and effect of features on a model's predictions, it shows which features have the greatest influence (negative or positive)

Table 5. Performance Comparison of XGBoost and AGRU on CIC-IDS2017

Class	XGBoost				AGRU			
	Precision	Recall	F1-score	Accuracy	Precision	Recall	F1-score	Accuracy
Benign	0.99	0.99	0.99	–	0.99	0.99	0.99	–
Bot	0.89	0.76	0.82	–	0.94	0.35	0.51	–
DDoS	0.99	0.99	0.99	–	0.99	0.99	0.99	–
DoS GoldenEye	0.99	0.99	0.99	–	0.97	0.97	0.97	–
DoS Hulk	0.99	0.99	0.99	–	0.98	0.97	0.98	–
DoS Slow-httptest	0.99	0.99	0.99	–	0.87	0.88	0.88	–
DoS slowloris	0.99	0.99	0.99	–	0.92	0.98	0.95	–
FTP-Patator	1	0.99	0.99	–	0.99	0.98	0.98	–
PortScan	0.98	0.99	0.99	–	0.98	0.99	0.99	–
SSH-Patator	0.99	0.99	0.99	–	1	0.91	0.95	–
Web Attack	0.98	0.98	0.98	–	1	0.08	0.15	–
Macro Avg	0.98	0.97	0.98	–	0.97	0.83	0.85	–
Micro Avg	0.99	0.99	0.99	–	0.99	0.99	0.99	–
Accuracy	–	–	–	0.99	–	–	–	0.99

Table 6. Performance Comparison of XGBoost and AGRU on N-BaIoT

Class	XGBoost				AGRU			
	Precision	Recall	F1-score	Accuracy	Precision	Recall	F1-score	Accuracy
Benign	1	1	1	–	0.99	0.99	0.99	–
Gafgyt_combo	0.99	0.99	0.99	–	0.99	0.96	0.97	–
Gafgyt_junk	0.99	0.99	0.99	–	0.93	0.98	0.96	–
Gafgyt_scan	0.99	1	0.99	–	0.99	0.99	0.99	–
mirai_ack	1	1	1	–	0.99	0.99	0.99	–
mirai_scan	1	1	1	–	0.99	0.99	0.99	–
mirai_syn	1	1	1	–	1	0.99	0.99	–
mirai_udp	1	1	1	–	0.99	0.99	0.99	–
Macro Avg	0.99	0.99	0.99	–	0.99	0.99	0.99	–
Micro Avg	1	1	1	–	0.99	0.99	0.99	–
Accuracy	–	–	–	1	–	–	–	0.99

on predictions, ranking them by average importance. We used the TreeSHAP implementation of SHAP for the experimentations.

The SHAP waterfall plot is used to explain the prediction of an individual instance in detail. It illustrates how each feature contributes to shifting the prediction from the baseline value (expected value) to the final prediction.

A decision plot with SHAP is used to visualize how each feature contributes to the final prediction for an instance or group of instances. Here we plot the

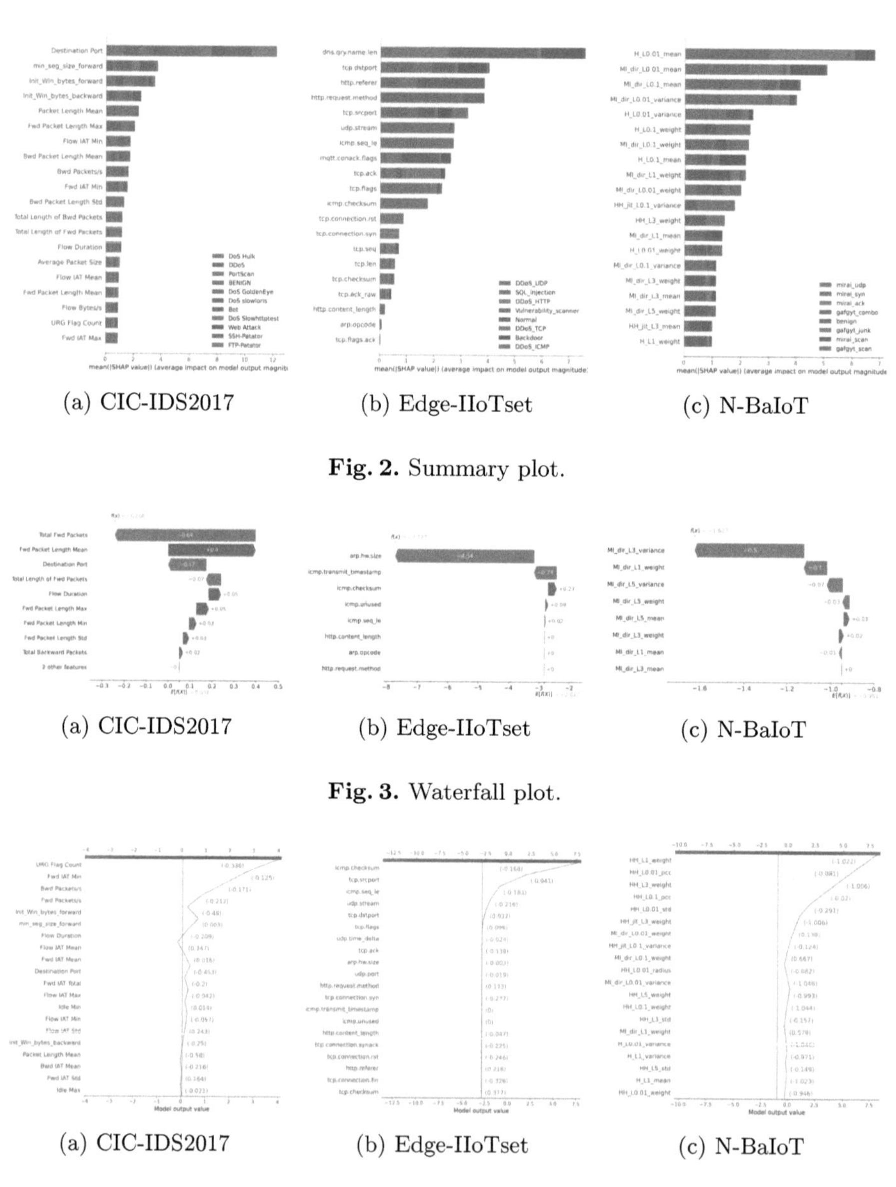

(a) CIC-IDS2017   (b) Edge-IIoTset   (c) N-BaIoT

Fig. 2. Summary plot.

(a) CIC-IDS2017   (b) Edge-IIoTset   (c) N-BaIoT

Fig. 3. Waterfall plot.

(a) CIC-IDS2017   (b) Edge-IIoTset   (c) N-BaIoT

Fig. 4. Decision plot.

the decision for single instances. Each feature is represented by a line or segment showing how it changes the prediction relative to the baseline. Positive features shift the prediction to the right and increase the probability of the class while negative features shift the prediction to the left and reduce the probability of the class. The value around the red line correspond to the cumulative effect of the features on the prediction.

LIME was also used to evaluate the influence of the features (the top 10) on the selected instances. Figure 2 provides the summary plots of the tree datasets while Figs. 3 and 4 provide the SHAP waterfall plots and decision plots for the 4th instance of each dataset, which corresponds to classes Dos_Hulk, Dos_ICMP and gafgyt_combo for respectively CIC-IDS2017, Edge-IIoTset and N-BaIoT datasets. Destination Port is the most influential feature of CIC-IDS2017 followed by ming_seg_size_forward, int_win_bytes_forward, Init_win_bytes_backward, Packet length mean, Fwd Packet length Max, Flow IAT min, Bwd Packets, Fwd IAT min, etc. which contributes the most in increasing or decreasing the prediction for each class, with the magnitude represented by the color length on the bar for each feature. For Edge-IIoTset, the most influential feature is dns.gry.name_len followed by tcp.dst port, http.referer, http.request.method, tcp.srcport, udp.stream, icmp.sed_le,

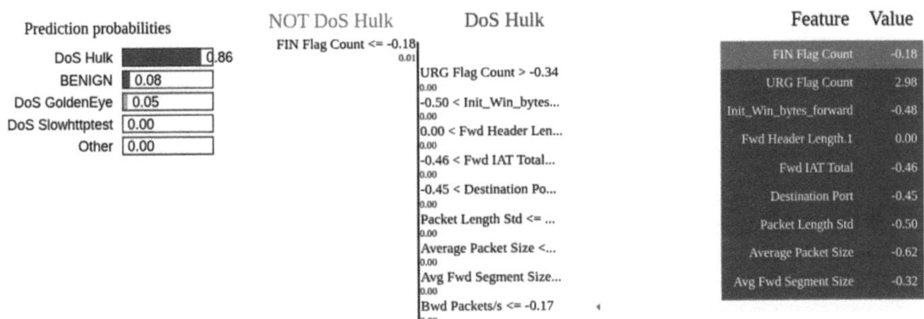

Fig. 5. CIC-IDS2017.

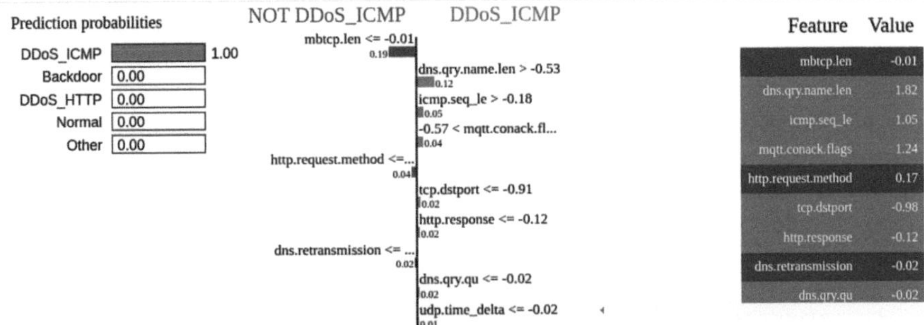

Fig. 6. Edge-IIoTset.

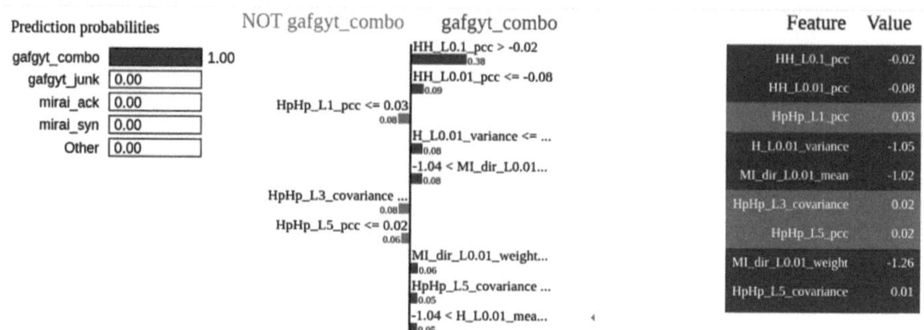

Fig. 7. N-BaIoT.

mqtt.conack.flags, tcp.ack, tcp.flags, etc. The features with the highest influence in N-BaIoT are H_L0_01.mean, MLdir_L0.1.mean, MLdir_L0.1_weight, H_L0.1.weight, H_L0.1.mean, MLdir_L1, weight etc.

In Fig. 3a, we have the explanation for an intance of CIC-IDS2017 which is predicted as Dos_Hulk, the plot shows that Fwd Packet Length Mean contributed the most(0,4) in predicting this class, followed by Flow Duration, Fwd Packet Length Max, Fwd Packet Length Min, Fwd Packet Length Std and Total Backward Packets, while Total Fwd packets, Destination Port and Total Length of Fwd packets tend to push the prediction to another class. Figure 3b shows that icmp.checksum, icmp.unused and icmp.leq_le contribute in predicting the instance of Edge-IIoTset to Dos_ICMP, while arp.hw.size and icmp.transmit_timestamp push the prediction to another class, http.content_length, arp.opcode and http.request.method are ignored by the model for this instance. In Fig. 3c, we can see that Ml_dir_L5_mean, Ml_dir_L3_weight push the prediction to the class gafgyt_combo while ML_dir_L3_variance, Ml_dir_L1_weight, ML_dir_L5_variance, ML_dir_L5_weight and ML_dir_L1_mean decreases the prediction, Only two minor features slightly increase the probability of this class but the model choosed the final class despite the majority of features reducing its probability, suggesting that other classes have even lower logits. In Fig. 4, We can see that for CIC-IDS2017 (Fig. 4a), the last four features push the prediction to the oher classes with URG Flag Count, Init_in_bytes_forward, Flow IAT Mean, Flow IAT Total and Idle Mean, the rest of the features put the prediction to the predicted class (Dos_Hulk). Figure 4b shows that almost all the features push the prediction to the right class unless icmp.checksum. In Fig. 4c, we see that the negatives feature contributions have less impact on the prediction especially HH_L5_Std, ML_dir_L1_weight, H_L0.01_variance, Ml_dir_H_L0.01_variance, HH_L0.01_radius, HH_L0.01_pcc and HH_L1_weight. On the other hand, Fig. 7 shows the explanations of LIME for the tree datasets. For CIC-IDS2017, on the left, we see that the model predicted the instance to the class Dos_Hulk with a probability of 0.86, 0.08 for the BENIGN and 0.05 for GoldenEye, in the middle, we have the range of values associated with each feature that influence the prediction, we see that FIN Flag Count with values (≤ -0.18) will push the prediction to the other classes while features in the right side conduct the prediction to the outputed class. On the right side of the figure, the table indicates the original values of the instance for each feature. For, Edge-IIoTset, the model predicted the instance to DDOS_ICMP with a probability of 1, and features that influence the most the prediction are dns.qry.name.len(the predicted class) and mbtcp.len(the other classes). LIME also explained the instance of N-BaIoT with a probability of 1, showing the range values of HH_L0.01_pcc, HH_L0.1_pcc, H_L0.01_variance, Ml_dir_H_L0.01_variance, Ml_dir_H_L0.01_weight, H_L0.01_mean and HpHp_L5_covariance that push the prediction to gafgyt_combo.

In short,the explanations provided by LIME and SHAP have almost the same influencial features, the difference is in the direction of the influence which is enforced by the fact that LIME provide different explanations for the same instance for several runs the majority of time (Figs. 5, 6, 8 and 9).

5.3 Evaluation of the Explainers

We evaluated the stability of the explainers (Fig. 10) on the three datasets with a budget of 200 samples, 10 perturbations and k = 10 for the top important features under several gaussian noise values. We also assessed the sparsity (Fig. 12) per class and the fidelity (Fig. 11) of the explainers with different k values for 200 samples for Dos_Hulk, Dos_ICMP and gafgyt_combo classes of the three datasets.

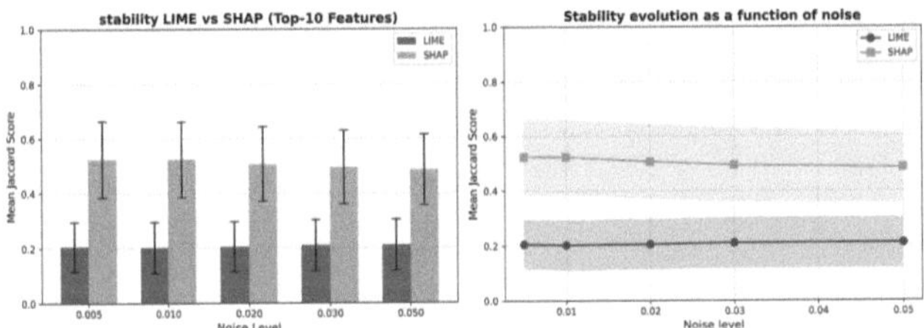

Fig. 8. Stability evaluated with CIC-IDS2017 dataset.

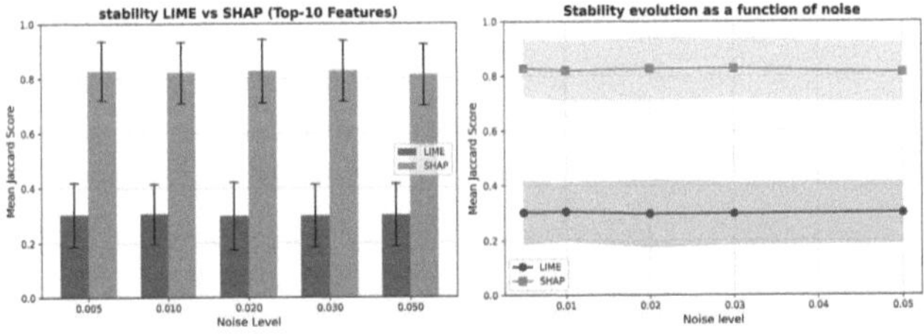

Fig. 9. Stability evaluated with Edge-IIoTset dataset.

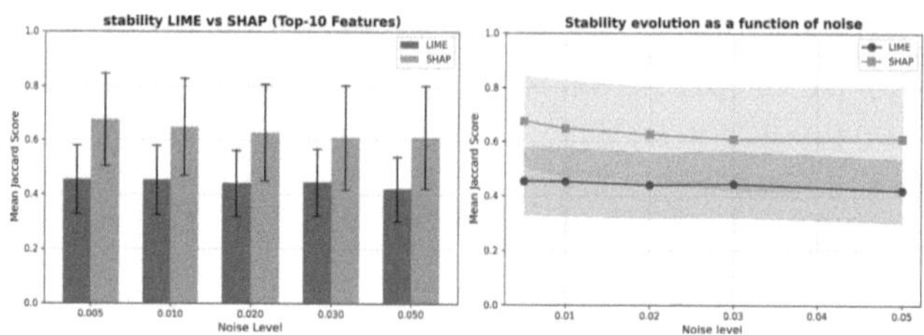

Fig. 10. Stability evaluated with N-BaIoT dataset.

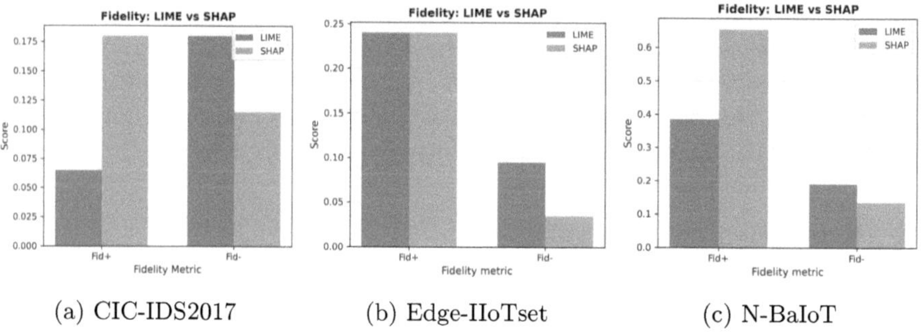

(a) CIC-IDS2017   (b) Edge-IIoTset   (c) N-BaIoT

Fig. 11. Fidelity with the top 10 features.

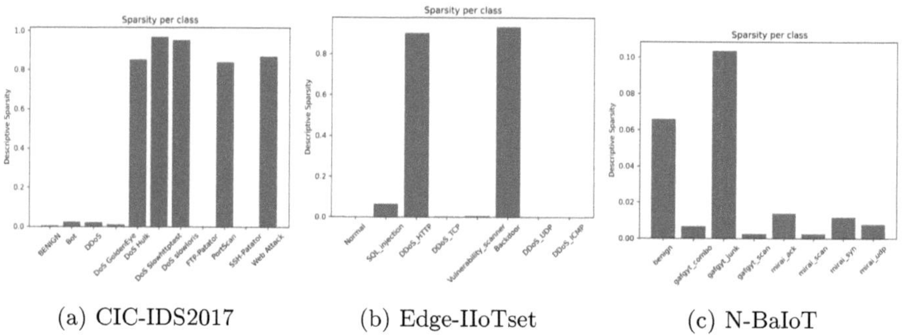

(a) CIC-IDS2017   (b) Edge-IIoTset   (c) N-BaIoT

Fig. 12. Descriptive sparsity of SHAP per class with r = 0.1.

Figure 10 shows the evaluation results of the stability of LIME and SHAP on the datasets. For CIC-IDS2017, for the noise values of 0.005 and 0.01 with k = 10, we observe a stability of above 50% that starts decreasing from the noise of 0.02 where it is almost 50%. This means that only slightly more than half of the features deemed important remain the same from one pertubation to the next. The instability of LIME is demonstrated by the 20% for each noise value. For Edge-IIoTset, the stability of SHAP is greater than 80% for all noise values showing that less than 20% of the important features change among the different pertubations, LIME stability is 30%. On N-BaIoT, the stability is almost 70%

for the noise of 0.005, it means that more than 30% of important features change among the pertubations. For all the other noise values even 0.05, the explanations are more than 60% stable with SHAP and more than 40% with LIME.

The fidelity of the explainers has also been assessed for k = 10 (Fig. 11). For CIC-IDS2017, Fid+ = 0.180 and Fid- = 0.115 for SHAP, Fid+ = 0.050 and Fid- = 0.180. SHAP Fid+ is very low and as stated in definition 3.3, Fid+ evaluates if the important features are necessary and the result shows that even without these features, the model can still achieve the same result, it thus shows that these features are not independent for the prediction of this class. The fidelity of LIME is comprehensible because each time it provides a different explanation. In terms of Fid-, the results shows that training the model with only the k features is sufficient to achieve the same prediction. For Edge-IIoTset, Fid+ and Fid- for SHAP are 0.240 and 0.035 meaning that the model is not independent of the top 10 features for the prediction of Dos_ICMP attack and Fid- value means that the model has 0.035 chance to predict another class when training with the top 10 features. Fid+ for LIME is the same as for SHAP and Fid- = 0.095, which is the probability for the model to predict another class. For N-BaIoT, Fid+ and Fid- with SHAP are 0.655 and 0.135 showing that the removing features changes the prediction for the class gafgyt_combo in 60% of cases, and training the model with only the 10 features has 13,5% of chance to change. Regarding sparsity, for CIC-IDS2017 (Fig. 12a), the explanations of 5 classes(Dos GoldenEye, Dos_Hulk , Dos Slowhttptest, PortScan and Web Attack) among the eleven are sparse. For Dos_Hulk for example, the sparsity is 0.96 meaning that 96% of the importance is concentrated near zero(around the radius of 0.1 we used), in other words the majority of features make virtually no contribution, the model relies on only a small number of important features. For Edge-IIoTset (Fig. 4b), only Vulnerability_scanner and DDOS_HTTP are sparse, for the class DOS_ICMP, the sparsity is $2.94 * 10^{-6}$, it means that many features of the dataset are required for the prediction. For N-BaIot (Fig. 4c), there are only two sparse classes: benign and gafgyt_junk and the sparsity for gafgyt_combo is 0.006 meaning that the decision is more diffuse because many features contribute significantly. The interpretations of Fid- in our experiments can sometimes be contrary with sparsity of the class, but the sparsity has been calculated for all the instances of the test set while the fidelity is evaluated only on 200 samples of the test set with different classes. Fidelity (Fid+) allowed to see that the most important features in N-BaIoT are common for almost all the classes in the dataset, which is not the case for the other datasets where the fidelity shows that the most important features are different from one class to another. The results of sparsity highlights the fact that some classes need more features to be identified. We also found that measuring the fidelity on the test set containing only instances of a specific class leads to the highest fidelity (Fid+ = 1, Fid- = 0).

6   Conclusion

In this paper, we addressed the lack of assessment of the quality of explanations of AI based decisions in the network and information security domains, particularly regarding the Intrusion Detection Systems. We propose a thourough analysis of two popular Explainable algorithms SHAP and LIME on three security datasets namely CIC-IDS2017, Edge-IIoTset and N-BaIoT for the predictions of a tree-based ensemble model (XGBoost) using three metrics: Stability, Fidelity and Sparsity. The experimental results show that SHAP was stable with the highest percentage on CIC-IDS2017 among the tree datasets (more than 80% for several noise values) showing that the explanations do not vary too much with the noises. The highest fidelity was also achieved by SHAP on N-BaIoT (Fid+ = 0.655) showing how common are the most important features for the different attack classes. However, CIC-IDS2017 dataset has more sparse classes than the other two datasets. Providing detailed analysis, such as those developed in this paper, to a SOC analyst can help understanding deeply the features that have the highest impacts, the minimum set of features that characterize certain attack types, and even the particular values of some features that are most determinant. However, there is still a need for fundamental work to be done regarding XAI methods in order to improve the accuracy based on these metrics. In our future work, we aim to stabilize the explanations provided by LIME and improve the accuracy of both methods, before extending and evaluating our approach to other explainability models.

Acknowledgment. This work was supported by the framework of the TRAVEL Project, through the French National Research Agency (ANR) under Grant ANR-24-IAS1-0003.

References

1. Ahsan, S.I., Legg, P., Alam, S.I.: An explainable ensemble-based intrusion detection system for software-defined vehicle ad-hoc networks. Cyber Secur. Appl. **3**, 100090 (2025)
2. Chen, T., Guestrin, C.: Xgboost: a scalable tree boosting system. In: Proceedings of the 22nd ACM SIGKDD International Conference on Knowledge Discovery and Data Mining, pp. 785–794 (2016)
3. Dey, R., Salem, F.M.: Gate-variants of gated recurrent unit (GRU) neural networks. In: 2017 IEEE 60th International Midwest Symposium on Circuits and Systems (MWSCAS), pp. 1597–1600. IEEE (2017)
4. Ferrag, M.A., Friha, O., Hamouda, D., Maglaras, L., Janicke, H.: Edge-iioTset: a new comprehensive realistic cyber security dataset of IoT and IIoT applications for centralized and federated learning. IEEe Access **10**, 40281–40306 (2022)
5. GK, S.K., Muniyal, B., Rajarajan, M., et al.: Explainable federated framework for enhanced security and privacy in connected vehicles against advanced persistent threats. IEEE Open J. Veh. Technol. (2025)

6. Gummadi, A.N., Arreche, O., Abdallah, M.: A systematic evaluation of white-box explainable ai methods for anomaly detection in IoT systems. Internet Things **30**, 101505 (2025)

7. Islam, S.R., Eberle, W., Ghafoor, S.K., Siraj, A., Rogers, M.: Domain knowledge aided explainable artificial intelligence for intrusion detection and response. In: Martin, A., Hinkelmann, K., Fill, H., Gerber, A., Lenat, D., Stolle, R., van Harmelen, F. (eds.) Proceedings of the AAAI 2020 Spring Symposium on Combining Machine Learning and Knowledge Engineering in Practice, AAAI-MAKE 2020, USA, Volume I. CEUR Workshop Proceedings, vol. 2600. CEUR-WS.org (2020)

8. Kalakoti, R., Vaarandi, R., Bahsi, H., Nõmm, S.: Evaluating explainable AI for deep learning-based network intrusion detection system alert classification (2025). arXiv:2506.07882

9. Lundberg, S.M., Lee, S.: A unified approach to interpreting model predictions. In: Guyon, I., von Luxburg, U., Bengio, S., Wallach, H.M., Fergus, R., Vishwanathan, S.V.N., Garnett, R. (eds.) Advances in Neural Information Processing Systems 30: Annual Conference on Neural Information Processing Systems 2017, December 4–9, 2017, Long Beach, CA, USA, pp. 4765–4774 (2017)

10. Meidan, Y., Bohadana, M., Mathov, Y., Mirsky, Y., Shabtai, A., Breitenbacher, D., Elovici, Y.: N-baiot–network-based detection of iot botnet attacks using deep autoencoders. IEEE Pervasive Comput. **17**(3), 12–22 (2018)

11. Paltun, B.G., Fuladi, R., El Malki, R.: Robust intrusion detection system with explainable artificial intelligence. In: 2025 Joint European Conference on Networks and Communications & 6G Summit, pp. 145–150. IEEE (2025)

12. Ribeiro, M.T., Singh, S., Guestrin, C.: "Why should I trust you?": explaining the predictions of any classifier. In: Krishnapuram, B., Shah, M., Smola, A.J., Aggarwal, C.C., Shen, D., Rastogi, R. (eds.) Proceedings of the 22nd ACM SIGKDD International Conference on Knowledge Discovery and Data Mining, San Francisco, CA, USA, August 13–17, 2016, pp. 1135–1144. ACM (2016)

13. Sbai, O., Allaert, B., Sondi, P., Meddahi, A.: SIP-DDoS: Sip framework for DDoS intrusion detection based on recurrent neural networks. In: Renault, É., Boumerdassi, S., Mühlethaler, P. (eds.) Machine Learning for Networking, pp. 72–89. Springer Nature Switzerland, Cham (2024)

14. Senevirathna, T., La, V.H., Marchal, S., Siniarski, B., Liyanage, M., Wang, S.: A survey on XAI for 5g and beyond security: technical aspects, challenges and research directions. IEEE Commun. Surv. Tutorials **27**(2), 941–973 (2025)

15. Sharafaldin, I., Lashkari, A.H., Ghorbani, A.A., et al.: Toward generating a new intrusion detection dataset and intrusion traffic characterization. ICISSp **1**(2018), 108–116 (2018)

16. Sharma, B., Sharma, L., Lal, C., Roy, S.: Explainable artificial intelligence for intrusion detection in IoT networks: a deep learning based approach. Expert Syst. Appl. **238**, 121751 (2024)

17. Shoukat, S., Gao, T., Javeed, D., Saeed, M.S., Adil, M.: Trust my IDS: an explainable AI integrated deep learning-based transparent threat detection system for industrial networks. Comput. Secur. **149**, 104191 (2025)

18. Sun, H., Liu, Y., Al-Tahmeesschi, A., Nag, A., Soleimanpour-Moghadam, M., Canberk, B., Arslan, H., Ahmadi, H.: Advancing 6g: survey for explainable ai on communications and network slicing. IEEE Open J. Commun. Soc. (2025)

19. Swamy, V., Du, S., Marras, M., Kaser, T.: Trusting the explainers: teacher validation of explainable artificial intelligence for course design. In: LAK23: 13th International Learning Analytics and Knowledge Conference, pp. 345–356 (2023)

20. Wali, S., Farrukh, Y.A., Khan, I.: Explainable AI and random forest based reliable intrusion detection system. Comput. Secur. 104542 (2025)
21. Warnecke, A., Arp, D., Wressnegger, C., Rieck, K.: Evaluating explanation methods for deep learning in security. In: IEEE European Symposium on Security and Privacy, EuroS&P 2020, Genoa, Italy, pp. 158–174. IEEE (2020)
22. Xu, Y., Li, C., Zhang, K., Xia, H., Tu, B.: EI-XIDS: an explainable intrusion detection system based on integration framework. In: 2024 27th International Conference on Computer Supported Cooperative Work in Design (CSCWD), pp. 2680–2685. IEEE (2024)
23. Zheng, X., Shirani, F., Chen, Z., Lin, C., Cheng, W., Guo, W., Luo, D.: F-fidelity: a robust framework for faithfulness evaluation of explainable ai (2024). arXiv:2410.02970

An Availability Management Framework for Microservices Based Safety-Critical CIoT Systems

Hassaan Siddiqui[1,2] and Ferhat Khendek[2(✉)]

[1] Tecsys Inc., Montreal, Canada
`hassaan.siddiqui@mail.concordia.ca`
[2] ECE, Concordia University, Montreal, Canada
`ferhat.khendek@concordia.ca`

Abstract. Safety-critical Cellular Internet of Things (CIoT) systems demand a high degree of availability to ensure safe and uninterrupted operations. Given the distributed and heterogeneous nature of these systems, spanning IoT devices, edge nodes, on-premises servers, and cloud platforms, traditional monolithic software architectures are inadequate in delivering the necessary flexibility, scalability, and reliability. In contrast, the Microservices Architecture (MA) offers a promising alternative by promoting decentralization, modularity, and dynamic scalability. However, despite its advantages and some improvements for availability, MA does not necessarily meet high-availability requirements, particularly in safety-critical settings. Advanced availability management mechanisms tailored to the unique demands of safety-critical CIoT systems are required to enhance their availability. In this work, we propose an availability management framework for MA based safety-critical CIoT systems, integrating machine learning based anomaly detection to enable proactive fault-tolerance as reactive mechanisms often fail meeting availability requirements. Our framework aims not only at detecting and recovering from failures, but also predicts potential failures before they manifest, thereby avoiding/minimizing downtime and enhancing the availability of the system.

Keywords: Microservices · Cellular IoT (CIoT) · Availability management · Safety-critical systems · Kubernetes · Machine learning

1 Introduction

Ensuring high-availability in software systems has long been a significant challenge, particularly in monolithic architecture where all components of an application are tightly coupled and deployed as a single unit. In such systems, a failure in one component often necessitates the restart or redeployment of the entire application, leading to extended downtime and increased operational complexity. The monolithic architecture limits fault isolation, scalability, and rapid recovery, which are all essential for availability and reliability. The challenge becomes even more pronounced in safety-critical Cellular Internet of Things (CIoT) systems [1], where availability is not just a performance requirement

S. Boumerdassi et al. (Eds.): MLN 2025, LNCS 16424, pp. 121–134, 2026.
https://doi.org/10.1007/978-3-032-18494-8_9

but a safety imperative. These systems are often deployed across a wide range of platforms, including IoT devices, edge nodes, on-premises servers, cloud environments, and are used in contexts where service disruption can lead to life-threatening consequences, damage to critical infrastructure, or loss of data [2, 3]. Hence, ensuring continuous operation and availability is paramount.

Microservices Architecture (MA) has emerged as a promising alternative [4–7]. MA decomposes applications into independent, loosely coupled services that can be deployed, scaled, and managed individually [8]. This architecture enables better fault isolation, improved scalability, and faster recovery, thereby enhancing overall system reliability and availability. However, MA also introduces new complexities and challenges. With multiple services running across distributed environments, the number of potential failure points increases significantly. Issues such as service dependency failures, network latency, and resource contention become more prevalent. Furthermore, managing availability in such dynamic systems requires intelligent orchestration and real-time Fault-tolerance (FT).

Our previous research investigated the use of MA coupled with the Kubernetes (K8s) Container Orchestrator (CO) for safety-critical CIoT systems [1, 9]. While Kubernetes provides support for service orchestration, scaling, and recovery, our evaluations revealed that it fails to meet the stringent availability requirements of safety-critical applications. These shortcomings highlight the need for more proactive and advanced availability management approaches. To address these challenges, we propose a Machine Learning (ML) [10] based Availability Management Framework (AMF) tailored for safety-critical CIoT systems. This framework is designed to augment the existing orchestration mechanisms by incorporating predictive analytics and anomaly detection techniques that allow for early identification of potential failures before they lead to service disruptions. The goal is to achieve proactive FT, thereby avoiding/minimizing downtime, reducing the impact of failures, and ensuring that availability requirements are consistently met in safety-critical environments.

The rest of the paper is organized as follows: Sect. 2 reviews related work. Section 3 presents the proposed AMF. We conclude in Sect. 4.

2 Related Work

MA organizes distributed applications into a set of small, modular services that are loosely coupled and independently deployable, with each microservice handling a distinct business function. This architecture improves scalability, flexibility, and maintainability by allowing individual microservices to be updated, scaled, or redeployed without impacting the overall application [11]. Containerization works together with MA by encapsulating each service, along with its necessary dependencies and runtime environment, into lightweight, portable containers. These containers promote environment consistency across development, testing, and production stages, streamlining deployment processes and minimizing configuration issues.

To manage the operational complexity of large-scale containerized systems, COs are employed. Among them, K8s is a leading CO platform that automates essential operations such as load balancing, scaling, and fault recovery by continuously monitoring container health and automatically replacing failed units. The integration of MA with CO technologies like K8s establishes a resilient and scalable framework [12], particularly well-suited for the demands of distributed, safety-critical CIoT systems. In our previous research [6], we reviewed existing literature on the application of MA to IoT systems and found that MA shows considerable promise in addressing the inherent challenges of heterogeneous and dynamic IoT environments [4, 5, 7, 13–17]. However, despite its architectural advantages, maintaining high-availability in MA based containerized applications remains a challenge due to the inherent complexity of MA. In such systems, each microservice typically runs in its own isolated container, resulting in numerous potential failure points. These failures may stem from various issues, such as pod or container crashes, depleted system resources, network disruptions, or memory-related leaks and excessive consumption. While microservices are designed to function independently, their interdependencies can cause the failure of one service to degrade or disrupt the End-to-End (E2E) availability of the overall system. Furthermore, K8s primarily employs standard recovery mechanisms, such as restarting or rescheduling failed containers, which often fall short in addressing the root causes of more intricate faults. Consequently, the processes of fault detection, isolation, and recovery in these environments are both essential and non-trivial. In our previous studies [1, 9], we analyzed the service availability of a safety-critical CIoT system built on MA and K8s, and found that this combination does not meet the stringent availability requirements demanded by such systems.

To achieve high-availability, there are reactive FT mechanisms that detect a failure after it has happened and then recover the affected service or system. Nevertheless, a failure can also be predicted before it happens through proactive FT. Proactive FT provides better availability as it prevents the failure from happening and can trigger service recovery mechanisms proactively, thus there is no or minimal impact on service or system availability [18]. Researchers have been exploring ML based anomaly detection mechanisms for proactive FT of MA based systems. Tran et al. [18] proposed a proactive stateful FT mechanism for K8s containerized services. Their proposed framework utilizes a recurrent neural network based failure prediction mechanism and a service migration mechanism for service recovery. Jin et al. [19] proposed an anomaly detection mechanism to detect root cause in MA based systems. Their proposed framework utilizes robust principal component analysis and single indicator anomaly detection algorithm. Raeiszadeh et al. [20] proposed distributed tracing based FT technique that combines graph neural network and positive-unlabeled learning for detecting anomalies in MA based systems. Jia et al. [21] also noted that the traditional FT mechanisms for MA could not meet the real-time requirements. They proposed microservices logging caching strategy and distributed checkpoint algorithm based FT mechanism for IIoT Edge. Their proposed recovery mechanism uses causal logging to record the non-deterministic events of microservices, and completes the state recovery of microservices by loading checkpoint and replaying log records. They also conducted a few experiments to evaluate the proposed FT mechanism by integration it with K8s and concluded that the proposed FT mechanism has less impact on service performance compared with other FT mechanisms.

While recent studies have shown that incorporating ML based anomaly detection into MA can significantly enhance the availability of individual services, these efforts have primarily focused on isolated service-level metrics. The existing body of work tends to emphasize detecting and mitigating failures within single microservices or containers, leveraging resource utilization patterns, behavior modeling, or log analysis. These approaches fall short in addressing the availability of E2E services, which is particularly crucial in safety-critical CIoT systems. In such systems, service delivery often spans across multiple distributed components running on heterogeneous platforms including edge, cloud, and IoT devices. A disruption in any single microservice, even when detected early, can cascade and compromise the availability of the complete E2E service chain. Thus, ensuring high-availability in safety-critical CIoT systems demands a holistic anomaly detection and mitigation framework that accounts not only for individual microservice failures but also for their interdependencies and collective impact on E2E service delivery. This highlights the need for advanced, context-aware availability management strategies that can meet the stringent availability and reliability requirements of such systems.

3 Availability Management Framework

In this section we present the overall architecture of our proposed framework, discuss its different modules, and its deployment.

3.1 Overall Picture

Our proposed AMF is designed to enhance the resilience of MA based safety-critical CIoT systems by taking into account the distributed and complex nature of such systems and the limitations of MA coupled with CO (K8s). It covers both reactive and proactive aspects of fault management. On one hand, it facilitates recovery from unforeseen failures by leveraging orchestration mechanisms to restore failed microservices promptly. On the other hand, it incorporates predictive capabilities through anomaly detection techniques, enabling the system to anticipate potential failures based on observed behavioral patterns. By identifying early warning signs of faults, the framework can proactively trigger switchover strategies, thereby preventing service disruption before it occurs. This dual capability ensures continuous service availability and aligns with the stringent reliability requirements of safety-critical environments. The proposed AMF consists of three modules as shown in Fig. 1, the monitoring module, the prediction module and the recovery module.

3.2 Monitoring Module

The monitoring module has two components, i.e., a healthcheck and a resource monitor. The healthcheck component does a periodic check on all microservices at set intervals to see if the microservice is healthy. This healthcheck component is different than K8s default check, as K8s default check only checks if pod is healthy, whereas this healthcheck component also checks that the services/code running inside the pod are working as expected. As in some conditions, it is possible that the pod is up and running, but some part of code or service within the pod is not running as expected which could impact the service provided by that microservice. The notification flow for the healthcheck component is shown in Fig. 2. If a microservice exhibits unexpected behavior or fails to function as expected, its healthcheck will fail. This failure will alert the recovery module, which will subsequently initiate the appropriate failover mechanism to restore the affected microservice.

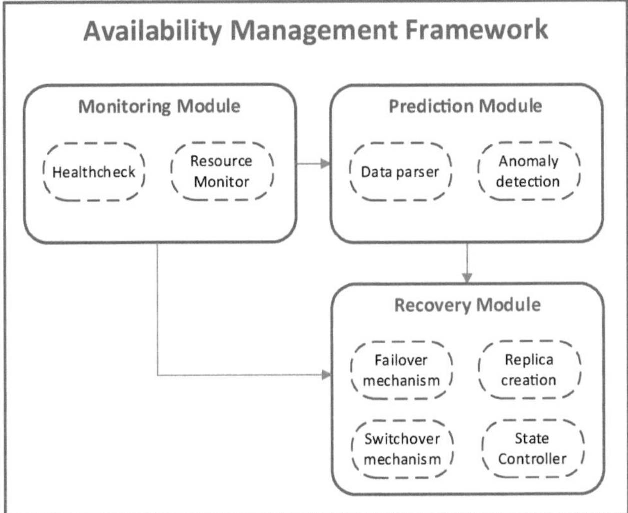

Fig. 1. AMF architecture

The second component of the monitoring module, resource monitor, performs two tasks. First, it periodically checks the resource utilization for each microservice including memory and CPU utilization and saves all data in an internal database. The data from the resource monitor database is used to train ML model to detect anomalies. Second, after each periodic check, it notifies the prediction module of the current resource utilization, which then can detect if there is any anomaly, as shown in Fig. 3. For the resource monitor, we have used Prometheus [22], an open-source monitoring tool for K8s, which stores all data as time series. It scrapes the memory and CPU utilization of all microservices at one sec interval, and saves it in its internal database.

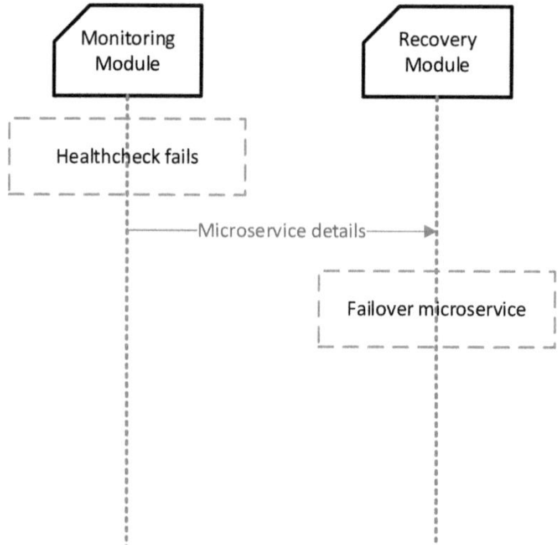

Fig. 2. Notification flow for healthcheck

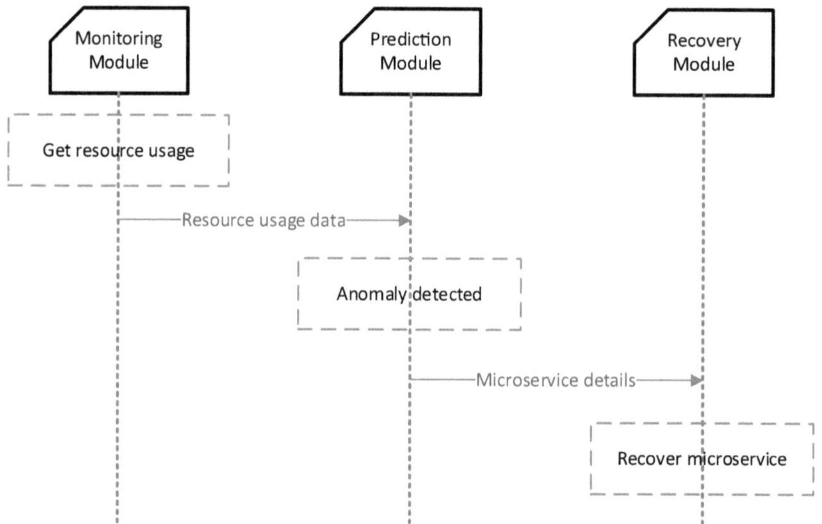

Fig. 3. Data flow between AMF modules

3.3 Prediction Module

The prediction module has two components, the data parser and the anomaly detector. The data parser component collects data from resource monitor database and parses it to be ready for the ML model. The anomaly detector component employs an ML model following the conventional paradigm of offline training followed by online prediction, as shown in Fig. 4. The ML model is trained offline on the data from the CIoT system to detect anomalies online. During the offline training phase, historical data is collected, parsed to be presented to the ML model and then labeled properly. A suitable learning algorithm is then trained on the labeled data, validated against unseen samples to assess performance, and packaged for deployment. Given the computational demands, this phase is conducted in a controlled environment offline. Once the ML model deployed, the online prediction phase operates in real-time, ingesting live system data to perform inference without further training. The model continuously analyzes incoming streams to detect potential faults, enabling the system to flag anomalies. Furthermore, during the offline training phase, selecting the right ML model, and training this model to detect anomalies accurately and precisely is a challenge. This involves understanding the nature of the data, the type of anomalies to be detected, and the performance requirements of the model. In this research, our focus is to detect anomalies related to high memory and high CPU usage. These anomalies can indicate potential issues such as memory leaks, inefficient code, etc. For these types of anomalies, both supervised learning techniques and unsupervised learning techniques are suitable. If these types of anomalies are considered as a classification problem, where the goal is to classify each instance as either normal or anomalous, then supervised learning techniques like DecisionTree classifier or RandomForest classifier can be used. This approach involves training a model offline on a labeled dataset, where the input data is paired with the correct output, which means having a dataset where normal and anomalous states are clearly labeled. DecisionTree classifier splits the data into subsets based on feature values, creating a tree-like structure [23] whereas RandomForest classifier builds multiple decision trees and merges their results to improve accuracy [24]. Nonetheless, unsupervised (clustering) techniques can also be suitable for detecting memory or CPU utilization anomalies. Unsupervised learning approach does not require labeled data. Instead, it identifies patterns and structures in the data to detect anomalies by grouping similar data points together, and then anomalies are detected as data points that do not fit well into any cluster. Some examples of clustering techniques include K-Means clustering which partitions data into K-clusters based on feature similarity, or Fuzzy c-means clustering. Both supervised and unsupervised learning techniques have their merits and can be suitable for detecting anomalies in high memory and CPU usage. The choice depends on the availability of labeled data and the specific requirements of the anomaly detection task.

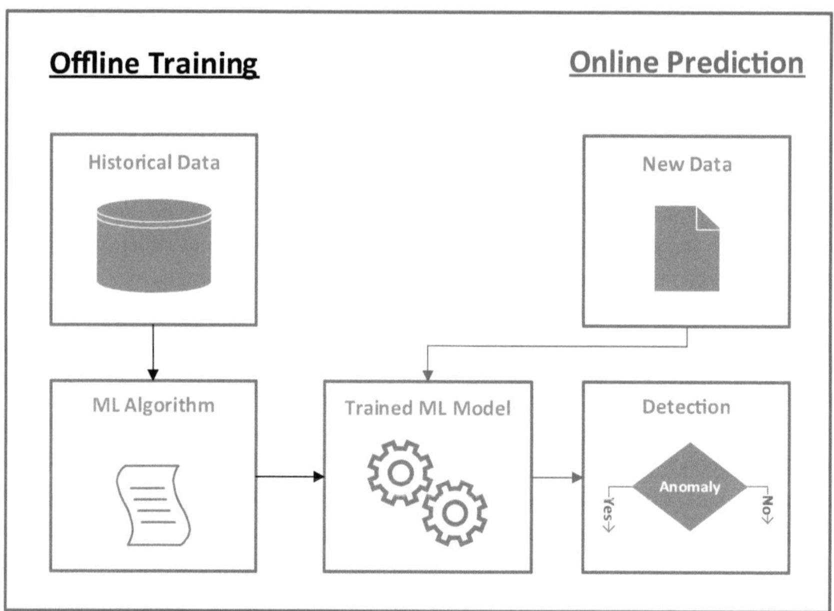

Fig. 4. ML model training vs prediction

In our AMF implementation, the data parser is implemented in Python, and it fetches data from a Prometheus database over REST API call, and then parses the data to feed it to the ML model. For ML model, we are using supervised learning with RandomForest classifier.

3.4 Recovery Module

The third module of the proposed AMF is the recovery module which is responsible for maintaining service continuity by managing microservice recovery in response to either detected anomalies or actual failures. The recovery module has four components, failover mechanisms, switchover mechanisms, replica creation and state controller. When a microservice experiences a failure, the system can immediately trigger failover by redirecting its workload to a pre-existing redundant replica, thereby minimizing downtime. Alternatively, if the anomaly detection module identifies abnormal behavior indicating a potential failure, the recovery module can proactively create a redundant replica of the affected microservice. It can then seamlessly switch the operation to this healthy replica before an actual failure occurs, thus avoiding service interruption altogether. The choice of failover/switchover strategy, whether cold standby, hot standby, or dynamic replica creation, can be customized based on the specific requirements of the safety-critical CIoT system, the availability of system resources and the type of microservice, i.e., stateful or stateless. This modular and adaptive recovery design ensures that the framework can provide robust fault-tolerance while remaining flexible to different deployment constraints and operational priorities.

3.5 Stateful vs. Stateless Microservices

In the AMF, both stateful and stateless microservices are managed through the integration of K8s' native controllers and recovery module's state controller to ensure resilient and consistent service availability. For stateless microservices, the AMF utilizes the K8s deployment controller, which simplifies scaling and recovery by allowing multiple replicas of a microservice to operate interchangeably while sharing access to a common Persistent Volume (PV). This is ideal for services that do not retain internal state across sessions.

In contrast, stateful microservices, which maintain service-specific data or context over time, are managed using the K8s StatefulSet controller. Each replica in a StatefulSet is associated with a dedicated PV, ensuring that state information is preserved even if the pod is restarted or relocated. This setup is crucial for consistency and data integrity in stateful workloads. However, as the replica pod and the original pod do not share the same PV, the state stored in the original pod's PV is not replicated to a replica pod's PV by default, which could cause loss of state in event of the original pod's failure or switchover to a replica pod. To tackle this problem, the proposed AMF adopts the State Controller (SC) proposed by [12], which replicates the state of the original pod into the PV of the replica pod periodically to ensure that the state of the original pod is in parity with the state of replica pod. The SC [12] interacts with the K8s API server, continuously monitoring cluster events and responding accordingly. It assigns high-availability states to active pods and enables active pods to replicate their state data to designated standby pods. It can automatically create multiple state replication services as needed. Pods are organized into active-standby pairs, with the standby pod labeled as a "peer" and linked to the corresponding active pod's name. The state replication is helpful in both cases, i.e., sudden failure or detected anomaly. In case of sudden failure, the recovery module initiates a failover mechanism, whereas in case when the AMF's prediction module detects an anomaly in a stateful microservice, the recovery module proactively initiates switchover mechanism. This involves redirecting traffic to a healthy replica of the affected microservice. This dual-action approach not only mitigates service disruption but also ensures that the new instance resumes operation with minimal loss of context or functionality. By integrating K8s controllers with intelligent recovery logic, the AMF provides a robust foundation for maintaining high-availability across both stateless and stateful components in safety-critical CIoT systems. In case of pod's CPU or memory related anomalies, the replica can be created on the same node, whereas in case of a node related anomalies, the replica can be created on another node, as shown in Fig. 5.

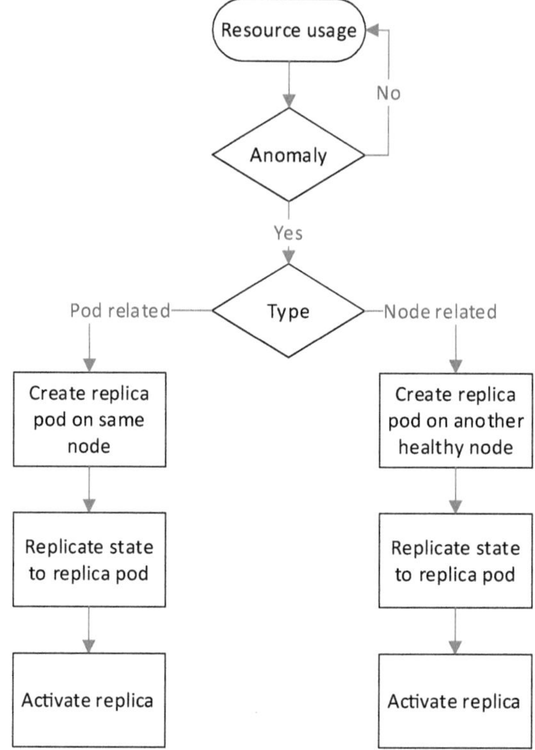

Fig. 5. State management flow for the anomaly detection case

Furthermore, the proposed AMF incorporates a configurable redundancy model that allows system designers and operators to tailor redundancy levels for each microservice according to its specific availability requirements and criticality within the overall system. This flexibility is particularly valuable in safety-critical CIoT environments, where not all microservices contribute equally to the operational safety and reliability. For instance, in an autonomous vehicle, the vehicle control application, that is responsible for functions such as steering, braking, and acceleration, must maintain high-availability to ensure passenger safety and prevent hazardous situations. As such, the AMF could be configured to maintain multiple hot-standby replicas and proactive state synchronization, for this service. In contrast, a vehicle entertainment system does not pose immediate safety risks if interrupted, so its availability requirements are considerably lower. For such non-critical services, the AMF could allocate fewer replicas, rely on cold-standby recovery strategies, and reduce state synchronization frequency to optimize resource utilization. This granular, service-specific redundancy configuration enables operators to balance fault-tolerance with cost and resource efficiency, ensuring that critical services receive the highest protection while avoiding unnecessary overhead for less essential components. Ultimately, this approach aligns the system's fault-tolerance strategy with the operational priorities and constraints of the target safety-critical CIoT deployment.

3.6 AMF Deployment Architecture

As CIoT systems are generally distributed, it is recommended that the monitoring module is deployed on each node to monitor the health and resource utilization of each microservice in real-time.

The deployment of prediction module is challenging as it contains the trained ML model and there are pros and cons of either having a centralized ML model or training multiple ML models on each node. Therefore, a careful trade-off must be considered. ML model could be placed on cloud, but it might impact the latency of detected anomalies, which is crucial for safety-critical systems. In 5G based CIoT systems, Multi-Access Edge Compute (MEC) is available which can help minimize the latency, however MEC has lower resources than cloud nodes and ML algorithms are resource intensive. For our AMF, we recommend to deploy prediction module on edge node as it will provide prediction to all nodes with minimal latency.

The deployment of recovery module depends on the deployment strategy for the application and Cloud-native Network Functions (CNFs). For instance, if microservices are deployed on a CO platform, like K8s, then deployment strategy for recovery module should match the K8s cluster configuration. If K8s is configured as a single multi-node cluster hosting the whole CIoT E2E system, then recovery module can be placed centrally on K8s control-plane. Whereas if the K8s is configured as multiple single-node clusters, then recovery module should be placed on each node and integrated with K8s.

For illustration purpose, Fig. 6 shows a potential deployment of the proposed AMF. The AMF is integrated with our MA based safety-critical CIoT testbed [1], which implements a prototype of Tele-operated Driving (ToD) use case [25], a safety-critical CIoT system that has an availability requirement of five nines (5-9s), i.e. 99.999%. This ToD system is a distributed application that has multiple microservices deployed on four nodes i.e., On-Board Unit (OBU), edge node, cloud node, and Remote Driving Station (RDS). Each node has a single-node K8s cluster, and all applications are microservices based and are deployed on a K8s deployment. More details on the ToD testbed are available in [1]. From Fig. 6, it can be observed that the monitoring module is deployed on all four nodes whereas the prediction module is deployed centrally only on the edge node. Moreover, the recovery module is deployed on all four nodes as this ToD system has a single-node K8s cluster on each of the four nodes.

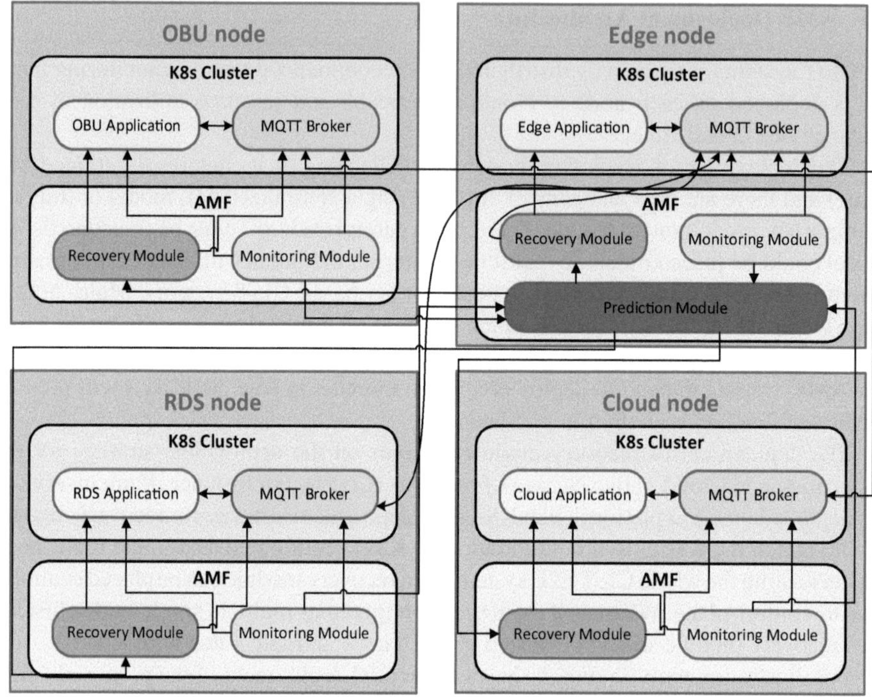

Fig. 6. Potential deployment of AMF for the ToD case study

4 Conclusions and Future Work

We previously demonstrated that although MA enhances modularity, scalability, and flexibility, which are the essential Non-Functional Requirements for managing the complexity of safety-critical CIoT systems, it also introduces considerable challenges in maintaining system availability and fault-tolerance which makes MA insufficient for safety-critical environments. These challenges arise from the distributed, loosely coupled nature of microservices, where failures in individual components, such as memory leaks or container crashes, can propagate and disrupt E2E service availability. Traditional recovery mechanisms, such as those provided by Kubernetes, are largely reactive and generic, often failing to address the root causes of such failures effectively, especially in safety-critical contexts where even short service outages can have severe consequences. To overcome these limitations, this paper proposed a ML based Availability Management Framework tailored for MA based safety-critical CIoT systems. The framework integrates proactive anomaly detection mechanisms capable of identifying early signs of failure, such as abnormal resource usage patterns, before they escalate into system-wide disruptions. By predicting and responding to issues in advance, the framework enhances fault-tolerance and ensures higher service availability. In conclusion, the proposed framework fills a critical gap in current availability management strategies for MA based safety-critical CIoT systems. By combining the adaptability of MA with the predictive power of ML, it lays the foundation for building more dependable and resilient safety-critical CIoT infrastructures capable of sustaining uninterrupted operations across diverse and dynamic environments.

In future work, we aim to conduct a comprehensive validation of the proposed framework across multiple dimensions to ensure its practical effectiveness in real-world safety-critical CIoT systems. This will include the validation of the deployment architecture, assessing how different architectural configurations affect the responsiveness and reliability of the framework under diverse network and system conditions. We will look into ML model selection to determine which models best suit the anomaly detection needs of heterogeneous microservice-based CIoT systems. A rigorous ML model evaluation will be performed using metrics such as precision, recall, and F1-score to ensure timely and accurate anomaly detection without introducing computational overhead that could degrade system performance. Finally, we will analyze the impact of the proposed framework on end-to-end service availability, quantifying improvements in fault-tolerance under various failure scenarios. This multifaceted validation will help solidify the framework's viability and guide further refinements for deployment in safety-critical CIoT environments.

Acknowledgments. This work has been partially supported by the Natural Sciences and Engineering Research Council (NSERC) of Canada.

Disclosure of Interests..   The authors have no competing interests to declare that are relevant to the content of this article.

References

1. Siddiqui, H., Khendek, F.: Microservices for reliable safety-critical cellular IoT systems— a case study. In: GLOBECOM 2024—2024 IEEE Global Communications Conference, pp. 1455–1460 (2024). https://doi.org/10.1109/GLOBECOM52923.2024.10901455
2. Knight, J.C.: Safety critical systems: challenges and directions. In: Proceedings of the 24th International Conference on Software Engineering. Association for Computing Machinery, New York, NY, USA (2002)
3. Laplante, P.A., DeFranco, J.F.: Software engineering of safety-critical systems: themes from practitioners. IEEE Trans. Reliab. **66**(3), 825–836 (2017)
4. Mena, M., Criado, J., Iribarne, L., Corral, A., Chbeir, R., Manolopoulos, Y.: Towards high-availability cyber-physical systems using a microservice architecture. Computing (2023)
5. Power, A., Kotonya, G.: A microservices architecture for reactive and proactive fault tolerance in IoT systems. In: 2018 IEEE 19th International Symposium on "A World of Wireless, Mobile and Multimedia Networks" (WoWMoM) (2018)
6. Siddiqui, H., Khendek, F., Toeroe, M.: Microservices based architectures for IoT systems— State-of-the-art review. Internet Things Elsevier, p. 100854 (2023)
7. Santana, C., Andrade, L., Delicato, F.C., Prazeres, C.: Increasing the availability of IoT applications with reactive microservices. Serv. Oriented Comput. Appl. (2020). https://doi.org/10.1007/s11761-020-00308-8
8. Lewis, J., Fowler, M.: Microservices. https://martinfowler.com/articles/microservices.html
9. Siddiqui, H., Khendek, F.: Memory failures in microservices based Cellular IoT systems—An experimental evaluation of service availability. In: 2025 IEEE 102th Vehicular Technology Conference (VTC2025-Fall), Chengdu, China. In press (2025)

10. Tu, J., Yang, L., Cao, J.: Distributed machine learning in edge computing: challenges, solutions and future directions. ACM Comput. Surv. **57**(5), 132:1–132:37 (2025). https://doi.org/10.1145/3708495

11. Microservices Pattern: Microservice Architecture pattern: microservices.io. http://microservices.io/patterns/microservices.html

12. Vayghan, L.A., Saied, M.A., Toeroe, M., Khendek, F.: A Kubernetes controller for managing the availability of elastic microservice based stateful applications. J. Syst. Softw. **175**, 110924 (2021). https://doi.org/10.1016/j.jss.2021.110924

13. Vresk, T., Čavrak, I.: Architecture of an interoperable IoT platform based on microservices. In: 2016 39th International Convention on Information and Communication Technology, Electronics and Microelectronics (MIPRO), pp. 1196–1201 (2016)

14. Santana, C., Alencar, B., Prazeres, C.: Microservices: a mapping study for internet of things solutions. In: 2018 IEEE 17th International Symposium on Network Computing and Applications (NCA), pp. 1–4 (2018). https://doi.org/10.1109/NCA.2018.8548331

15. Campeanu, G.: A mapping study on microservice architectures of Internet of Things and cloud computing solutions. In: 2018 7th Mediterranean Conference on Embedded Computing (MECO), pp. 1–4 (2018)

16. Falas, Ł., Świątek, P., Schauer, P., Trzaska, R.: Practical implementation of internet of things service systems architecture. In: Proceedings—25th International Conference on Systems Engineering, ICSEng 2017, pp. 291–298 (2017)

17. Celesti, A., Carnevale, L., Galletta, A., Fazio, M., Villari, M.: A watchdog service making container-based microservices reliable in IoT clouds. In: Proceedings—2017 IEEE 5th International Conference on Future Internet of Things and Cloud, FiCloud 2017 (2017)

18. Tran, M.-N., Vu, X.T., Kim, Y.: Proactive stateful fault-tolerant system for Kubernetes containerized services. IEEE Access **10**, 102181–102194 (2022). https://doi.org/10.1109/ACCESS.2022.3209257

19. Jin, M., et al.: An anomaly detection algorithm for microservice architecture based on robust principal component analysis. IEEE Access **8**, 226397–226408 (2020). https://doi.org/10.1109/ACCESS.2020.3044610

20. Raeiszadeh, M., Ebrahimzadeh, A., Saleem, A., Glitho, R.H., Eker, J., Mini, R.A.F.: Real-time anomaly detection using distributed tracing in microservice cloud applications. In: 2023 IEEE 12th International Conference on Cloud Networking (CloudNet), pp. 36–44 (2023). https://doi.org/10.1109/CloudNet59005.2023.10490038

21. Jia, Y., Wang, T., Qiu, T., Zhang, X., Wang, R., Wo, T.: Fault tolerance of stateful microservices for industrial edge scenarios. In: 2023 IEEE International Conference on Joint Cloud Computing (JCC), pp. 50–56 (2023). https://doi.org/10.1109/JCC59055.2023.00013

22. Prometheus—Monitoring system & time series database. https://prometheus.io/

23. Decision Trees: scikit-learn. https://scikit-learn.org/stable/modules/tree.html

24. Random forests: scikit-learn. https://scikit-learn.org/stable/modules/ensemble.html

25. C-V2X Use Cases Volume II: Examples and Service Level Requirements: 5G Automotive Association, White Paper (2020). http://5gaa.org/news/c-v2x-use-cases-volume-ii-examples-and-service-level-requirements/

Dataflow for Predicting Stone Degradation in Built Heritage up to 2100

Diyane David Nonon Saa[1](✉), Cyril Rabat[1], Céline Schneider[2],
Patricia Vazquez[2], and Hacène Fouchal[1]

[1] Lab-I*, Université de Reims Champagne-Ardenne, Reims, France
diyane-david-dissoclima.nonon-saa@univ-reims.fr
[2] GEGENA, Université de Reims Champagne-Ardenne, Reims, France

Abstract. Natural stone used in built heritage is affected by weathering due to outdoors exposure. In the context of climate change, it is crucial to assess how kinetics of this weathering will evolve. This paper proposes a complete dataflow to project the evolution of humidity and temperature, with the aim of anticipating the microclimates to which monuments will be exposed from now until 2100. The study takes the Saint-Remi Basilica in Reims (France) as a case study and relies on three main sources: (i) in situ measurements collected on the monument between 2018 and 2019 using sensors recording temperature and humidity, (ii) ERA5 reanalysis data used as local climate data for the area surrounding the monument, and (iii) climate projections provided by the DRIAS platform (Météo-France), covering different climate scenarios up to 2100. The proposed dataflow constitutes a reproducible workflow linking data acquisition and preprocessing, the selection of prediction algorithms, the integration of climate scenarios, and the identification of microclimates. This allows for the systematic assessment of environmental dynamics likely to affect the alteration of heritage materials. This dataflow focuses on temperature and humidity, as these are the variables recorded by the sensors deployed on the monument. These two factors are the most critical for the deterioration of stones, as they directly influence moisture absorption, thermal expansion, and other physical and chemical mechanisms that lead to material alteration.

Keywords: Built heritage · Time-series analysis · Data collection · Data processing · Machine learning · Weather prediction · Stone preservation

1 Introduction

Built heritage is vulnerable to extreme events associated with climate change. According to the International Council on Monuments and Sites (ICOMOS), the exposure of monuments and cultural landscapes to climate-related risks has reached an alarming scale [1]. In France, climate projections estimate an increase

© The Author(s), under exclusive license to Springer Nature Switzerland AG 2026
S. Boumerdassi et al. (Eds.): MLN 2025, LNCS 16424, pp. 135–150, 2026.
https://doi.org/10.1007/978-3-032-18494-8_10

temperature from 2.5° to 8.6° by 2100 [2] according to different scenarios. Anticipating local climatic scenarios has therefore become crucial to adapting heritage conservation strategies.

Stone-built monuments are sensitive to fluctuations in temperature and humidity, which accelerate material degradation [3]. Solar radiation induces thermal gradients within the stone, generating stresses at grain boundaries that may lead to disintegration [4]. Furthermore, moisture absorbed by the stone can freeze during cold periods: freeze-thaw cycles progressively weaken the material through ice pressure, creating cracks and promoting granular disintegration [5]. Repeated exposure to these processes ultimately reduces the mechanical integrity of the stone.

These deterioration mechanisms are strongly influenced by local microclimates. For example, the Saint-Remi Basilica in Reims (UNESCO World Heritage Site) was instrumented in 2017 with a network of temperature and humidity sensors. Measurements collected over two full years (2018–2019) enabled a detailed characterization of its microclimatic conditions [6]. Results showed that sun-exposed facades (south/west orientations) exhibited higher mean temperatures than shaded facades (north/east) [6] which are more subject to sub-zero temperatures, freeze cycles and rain. Stone decay is not uniform across facades, as variations in orientation and exposure create local differences in environmental stress. These contrasts highlight how microclimates generated heterogenous weathering within the same monument. Restoration should therefore prioritize the most vulnerable areas rather than treating the monument as a uniform whole. Continuous monitoring of climate parameters across the entire building is thus essential for identifying its most sensitive zones.

This study proposes an initial approach to predict microclimatic parameters at the building scale and to support preventive conservation. Three main data sources were used:

- **In situ measurements:** temperature and humidity data were collected hourly at the basilica between 2018 and 2019.
- **ERA5 reanalysis data:** local climatic variables derived from the Copernicus ERA5 global reanalysis, providing hourly data since 1940.[1]
- **DRIAS climate projections:** regional scenarios provided by Météo-France, covering multiple emission pathways up to 2100.[2]

The main contributions of our study are:

- To develop a reproducible data-processing workflow linking data acquisition, preprocessing, predictive modeling, and climate scenario integration.
- To implement and evaluate AI-based algorithms for bias correction and downscaling of climate projections, enabling consistent multi-scale datasets.

---

[1] https://cds.climate.copernicus.eu/datasets/reanalysis-era5-single-levels?
   tab=overview.
[2] https://www.drias-climat.fr/.

- To produce localized projections of temperature and humidity up to 2100, focusing on the identification of microclimates that influence stone decay in cultural heritage monuments.

These two climatic variables are considered the most critical factors driving stone degradation. By modeling their long-term evolution under different exposure conditions, this study aims to provide a prospective tool to support the preventive conservation of built heritage.

2   Related Work

This literature review begins with the work of Huby et al. [4,6], focusing on microclimatic monitoring to evaluate potential stone weathering in monuments. In particular, the work on microclimatic monitoring was used to assess potential stone weathering on a monument. This study provided a detailed climatic characterization of the Saint-Remi Basilica in Reims, identifying distinct microclimates and "typical day" weather events (sunny, cloudy, rainy, and frost days) which were subsequently reproduced in laboratory conditions. Although this foundational work did not employ machine learning, it demonstrated how temperature and humidity fluctuations induce thermo-hydric strains in limestone materials, highlighting differences in behavior between stones under realistic climate conditions. Building on such insights, Petit et al. [7] explored data-driven approaches to predict weathering risks. Their work applied machine learning techniques to model the behavior of historical building materials subjected to climatic constraints, thereby offering a complementary perspective to experimental studies.

Similar to climate-focused research, automated visual inspection of stone facades using AI particularly deep learning has advanced rapidly. Boutet [8] reviews the integration of new technologies for pathology detection in built heritage and concludes that convolutional neural networks play a central role in identifying surface damage (e.g., cracks, biocolonization) on historical materials. While this synthesis highlights the maturity of image-based diagnostics, it remains descriptive and does not address how climatic drivers influence deterioration processes over time.

Similarly, Hatir et al. [9] introduced a vision-based workflow that periodically assesses stone decay in a large rock-cut monastery using Mask R-CNN to map cracks, scaling, missing fragments, and biological growth. Trained on more than 1,700 annotated images, their model reports high performance ($mAP \approx 98\%$) and enables efficient large-scale condition mapping. However, the approach remains inherently retrospective: it documents existing damage but does not integrate environmental drivers (e.g., solar exposure, temperature–humidity cycles) or predict how degradation will evolve.

Karimi et al. [10] presented a YOLO-based detector for defects on Portuguese azulejo facades, trained on more than 5,000 annotated images. The model achieves high precision for glaze loss and cracks with real-time inference but remains purely diagnostic: it neither accounts for solar load or temperature–humidity cycles nor forecast deterioration, and its transferability to heterogeneous stone masonry is uncertain. Ying et al. [11] coupled YOLO with the Segment Anything Model (SAM) to detect stone decay and project detections onto 3D models, improving class generalization and spatial mapping. However, the pipeline still depends on annotated imagery, neglects microclimatic drivers, and lacks facade-scale based on future risk.

Boesgaard et al. [12] developed an ensemble model (XGBoost) to predict variations in indoor relative humidity (RH) 24 h in advance. The model was trained on temperature and humidity time series and performed well in a warehouse environment but showed reduced accuracy in a church. It demonstrate the potential for short-term preventive control; however, relative to our objective, it remains limited to short-term forecasting. Hernandez-Gil et al. [13] estimated limestone retreat under different climate change scenarios by correlating photogrammetric erosion with temperature and precipitation forecasts. Although this approach considers future climate scenarios, it remains purely empirical and does not employ modern machine learning techniques.

Overall, the literature demonstrates a strong convergence between heritage science and machine learning, yet also reveals a clear methodological gap. Most existing studies apply ML to diagnostic or imaging tasks – for example, detecting cracks or classifying decay on facades using CNNs and other deep architectures. In contrast, only a few effort have focused on prognostic modeling of material degradation over time. As highlighted in the recent review by Karimi et al. [10], few studies have quantitatively modeled damage progression in cultural heritage using AI, and long-term risk prediction remains rare. This gap underscores the innovative contribution of our work. By developing temporal ML models (such as LSTM recurrent networks) trained on coupled climate projections and sensor data, a forecasting approach is developed to predict the medium- and long-term deterioration of stone façades under changing environmental conditions. In doing so, the application of AI in heritage conservation is extended from immediate visual diagnostics to forward-looking risk assessment, an approach that remains largely unexplored and has the potential to significantly enhance preservation strategies in the context of climate change.

3   Methodology

The methodological workflow developed in this study provides a reproducible process that connects data acquisition, preprocessing, predictive modeling, and the integration of climate scenarios. The workflow is structured into three main steps: (1) converting daily climate data into hourly series using ERA5 reanalysis, (2) bias-correction DRIAS climate projections with LSTM neural networks, and (3) generating localized climate projections up to 2100 under different climate scenarios. Although the Basilica of Saint-Remi in Reims is used as a case study, the workflow is generic and can be applied to other monuments.

3.1 Data Collection and Processing

Data Collection Three types of data are used: experimental data, local observation data, and climate projection data.

Experimental data: For experimental data, our case study focuses on the Basilica of Saint-Remi in Reims, a historic monument built in the 11th century and listed as a UNESCO World Heritage Site. Representative of the regional architectural heritage, the basilica is primarily constructed from Courville limestone, used since the Middle Ages, and Savonnières limestone, employed from the 19th century for both construction and restoration. Access to the monument allowed the installation of a sensor network on the two towers of the western facade. To characterize the basilica's microclimates, temperature sensors and combined temperature–humidity sensors were deployed on the towers. Openings located approximately 25 and 30 m above ground facilitated sensor placement, enabling orientations toward the south, east, north, and west. At the first level of the north tower, east- and south-facing sensors could not be installed due to inaccessible openings. In total, four temperature sensors were positioned on the north tower and two on the south tower at the first level, while four combined temperature–humidity sensors were installed on each tower at the second level. Altogether, six temperature sensors and eight combined temperature–humidity sensors were deployed on the Basilica of Saint-Remi [4,6] (Fig. 1).

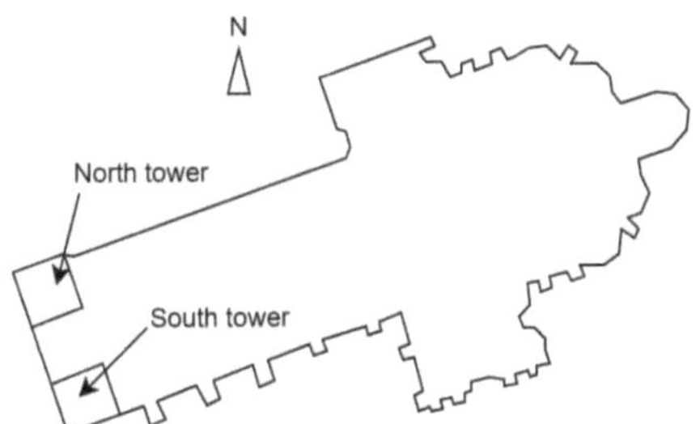

(a) Orientation of the towers of the basilica.

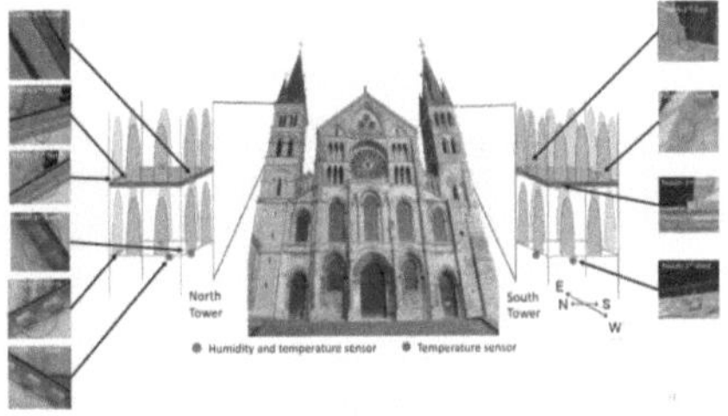

(b) Network of sensors installed on the basilica (Source: from Emilie Huby, 2021).

Fig. 1. Orientation of the towers and network of sensors installed on the Saint-Remi Basilica.

Local observation data: For observational data, the ERA5 reanalysis dataset is used. This dataset was produced by the European Centre for Medium-Range Weather Forecasts (ECMWF) for the Copernicus Climate Change Service (C3S). ERA5 represents the fifth generation of global atmospheric reanalyses and provides a consistent reconstruction of the Earths climate from 1940 to the present. It combines extensive historical observations–including ground stations, aircraft, and satellite measurements–with advanced numerical weather prediction models using state-of-the-art data assimilation techniques, producing a homogeneous and reliable dataset independent of real-time forecasting. ERA5 delivers hourly estimates of numerous atmospheric, land-surface, and oceanic variables, such as temperature, wind, humidity, soil moisture, snow cover, and surface wave conditions, on a global grid with 31 km horizontal resolution and 137 vertical levels extending up to 80 km altitude. Each variable includes ensemble-based uncertainty estimates, while pre-computed daily and monthly averages facilitate long-term analyses. The dataset is continuously updated with a latency of approximately five days, ensuring near real-time availability alongside more than eight decades of historical records. Owing to its comprehensive temporal coverage and high spatio-temporal resolution, ERA5 has become a cornerstone for climate-related research, from global climate variability studies and model validation to regional and local assessments of environmental risks such as heatwaves, heavy precipitation events, or hydrological stress. In this study, ERA5 provides local climatic information around the Basilica of Saint-Remi, forming a robust basis for analyzing past and present climatic conditions and their potential impacts on cultural heritage [14].

Climate projection data: The DRIAS platform is a French initiative coordinated by Météo-France, CERFACS, and IPSL, providing regionalized climate projections for France. These projections are derived from global climate models and downscaled to national and regional scales, covering the period up to 2100. DRIAS provides climate data under three greenhouse gas emission scenarios corresponding to different Representative Concentration Pathways (RCPs): RCP2.6, a low-emission scenario aiming for strong mitigation; RCP4.5, an intermediate stabilization scenario; and RCP8.5, a high-emission scenario representing the most pessimistic trajectory. In this study, DRIAS outputs were used to obtain projected climate data in the vicinity of the Basilica of Saint-Remi.

Figure 2 presents the datasets and their respective periods of coverage.

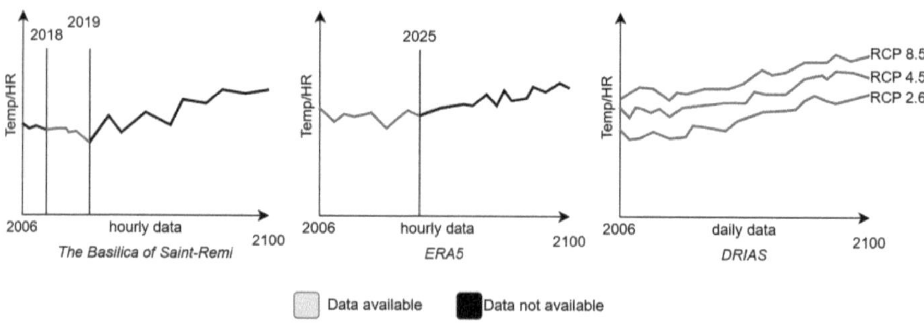

Fig. 2. Summary table of the datasets: The Basilica of Saint-Remi, ERA5, and DRIAS (with the three scenarios RCP 2.6, RCP 4.6, and RCP 8.6).

Data Processing Data cleaning is a crucial preprocessing step prior to training machine learning models. The objective of this study is to explore algorithms capable of automatically detecting anomalous or inconsistent data.

The processing of sensor data was carried out using two unsupervised learning algorithms: **DBSCAN** and **Isolation Forest**. **DBSCAN** (Density-Based Spatial Clustering of Applications with Noise) groups data points into clusters based on their density, using two key parameters: ε (neighborhood radius) and $MinPts$ (minimum number of points within a neighborhood). A point x_i is considered a core point if:

$$|N_\varepsilon(x_i)| \geq MinPts,$$

where

$$N_\varepsilon(x_i) = \{x_j \mid \text{distance}(x_i, x_j) \leq \varepsilon\}.$$

Points that do not belong to any dense cluster are classified as noise or anomalies. In parallel, the **Isolation Forest** algorithm detects unusual observations by recursively partitioning the feature space using random binary trees. Each point x_i is isolated by randomly selecting a feature q and a split value p, and the average path length $h(x_i)$ required to isolate x_i is then used to compute its anomaly score:

$$s(x_i, n) = 2^{-\frac{h(x_i)}{c(n)}},$$

where $c(n)$ represents the average path length for a sample of size n. A score close to 1 indicates a high likelihood that the point is anomalous. The combined use of these two methods ensured robust data preprocessing by detecting both density-based outliers and statistically isolated observations, thereby providing a comprehensive analysis of irregularities in the sensor measurements.

After applying both algorithms to the measurements recorded at the Basilica of Saint-Remi, outliers–defined as data points that significantly deviate from the overall trend–were identified.

In this study, the outliers identified in the dataset were replaced through linear interpolation using the `interpolate(method='linear')` function from the `pandas` library. This method estimates anomalous values by linearly interpolating between the nearest valid neighboring data points. Formally, the interpolated value $\hat{y}(x)$ at a given position x is defined as:

$$\hat{y}(x) = (1 - \alpha)\, y_i + \alpha\, y_{i+1}, \quad \alpha \in [0, 1],$$

where y_i and y_{i+1} denote the nearest valid observations surrounding x, and α represents the relative distance of x between x_i and x_{i+1}, defined as:

$$\alpha = \frac{x - x_i}{x_{i+1} - x_i}.$$

3.2 Time-Series Modeling LSTM (Long Short Term Memory)

The Long Short-Term Memory (LSTM) model was selected as the approach for long-term forecasting, with the objective of predicting stone degradation by identifying microclimates that may affect the material. Prior to this selection, several time-series models were tested on sensor data collected from the Basilica of Saint-Remi during 2017–2018, including ARIMA, SARIMA, Prophet, and AutoARIMA. Among these methods, the LSTM – a recurrent neural network (RNN) architecture–produced the most promising results, effectively capturing both global trends and localized fluctuations. This ability to reveal microclimatic patterns makes it particularly relevant for assessing stone weathering risks and supporting the preservation of cultural heritage sites.

LSTM (Long Short-Term Memory) The Long Short-Term Memory (LSTM) network is an enhanced variant of recurrent neural networks (RNNs) specifically designed to overcome the short-term memory limitations inherent in conventional RNNs. Its architecture includes a memory cell and three types of gates–input, forget, and output–that dynamically control the storage, removal, and propagation of information over time. This gating mechanism enables the network to retain relevant dependencies across long sequences, effectively mitigating the vanishing gradient problem and making LSTMs particularly suitable for complex time-series forecasting tasks.

Hyperparameters. The main hyperparameters considered in the LSTM architecture are:

- **Number of layers** (L): depth of the network.
- **Hidden units** (h): number of neurons per layer.
- **Learning rate** (η): step size for weight updates.
- **Batch size** (B): number of samples per training batch.
- **Dropout rate** (p): probability of deactivating neurons during training to prevent overfitting.
- **Activation functions** (e.g., tanh, σ): functions used within the LSTM gates.
- **Number of epochs** (E): total passes over the training dataset.
- **Optimizer** (e.g., Adam, SGD): algorithm used to update network weights.

3.3 Long-Term Forecasting of Experimental Temperature and Humidity Data

This methodology is structured around three main steps (Fig. 3):

1. **Translation from daily to hourly data using the ERA5 reanalysis dataset:** The ERA5, DRIAS, and experimental sensor datasets differ in temporal resolution: while DRIAS climate projections are available on a daily basis, ERA5 reanalysis data and experimental measurements provide hourly observations.

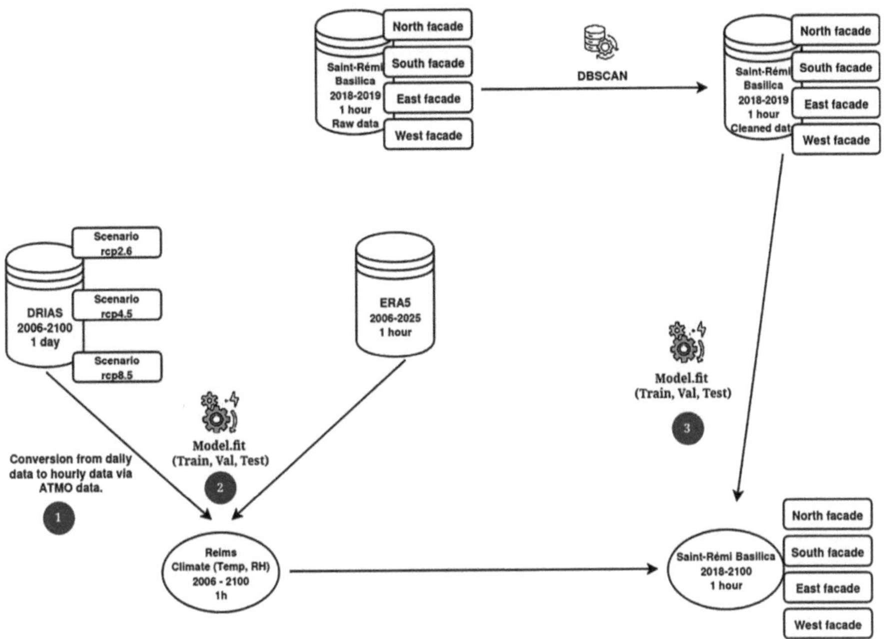

Fig. 3. Workflow for projecting data for the Basilica of Saint Remi until 2100

Since DRIAS provides only daily climate projections, whereas this study requires an hourly resolution, a sequential downscaling model was developed. The input variables X consist of daily features derived from ERA5–namely mean, minimum, and maximum temperatures–while the output variables y correspond to the 24 hourly temperature values associated with each day. The model was trained on ERA5 data for the period 2006–2025 using paired samples (X, y). Once calibrated and validated, it was applied to the daily DRIAS projections (2006–2100) to generate temporally consistent hourly time series.

The detailed architecture of our sequential model is presented below

- **Preprocessing:**
  - *Cyclical encoding of temporal features:* the day of the year and the month are transformed into sine and cosine components (sin, cos) to represent their periodic nature. This avoids artificial discontinuities (e.g., between day 365 and day 1) and enables the model to capture seasonal and annual cycles.
  - *Target reshaping:* transformed into a 2D matrix (days $\times$ 24 h).
  - *Feature scaling:*
    * For input variables X: Standardization is always applied to normalize daily features (mean, min, max temperatures and temporal encodings).

* For output variables y:
  · Temperature prediction: Standardization.
  · Humidity prediction: MinMax scaling.
- **Input Shape:**
  • Temperature projection: `temperature_min`, `temperature_max`, `temperature_mean`, `day_sin`, `day_cos`, `month_sin`, `month_cos`.
  • Humidity projection: `RH_mean`, `temperature_min`, `temperature_max`, `temperature_mean`, `precipitation_mean`, `day_sin`, `day_cos`, `month_sin`, `month_cos`.
- **Architecture:**
  • Dense layer with 256 units, ReLU activation, He-normal initialization, and L2 regularization.
  • Batch Normalization + Dropout layer (rate = 0.3).
  • Dense layer with 128 units, ReLU activation, L2 regularization.
  • Batch Normalization + Dropout layer (rate = 0.2).
  • Dense layer with 64 units, ReLU activation.
  • Final Dense output layer with 24 units (representing hourly values).
  • For humidity prediction: custom `TanhRange` layer constraining outputs to $[0, 100]$.
- **Training:**
  • Optimizer: Adam with learning rate = 0.001 and gradient clipping (`clipvalue=0.5`).
  • Loss function: Mean Squared Error (MSE).
  • Metric: Mean Absolute Error (MAE).
  • Callbacks: Early stopping (patience = 10, restore best weights) and learning rate reduction on plateau (factor 0.5, patience = 5, minimum LR = 1e-6).
  • Maximum epochs = 100, batch size = 16.
- **Validation Strategy:**
  • TimeSeriesSplit with 5 folds, ensuring chronological separation between training and validation sets.
  • Best model selected based on the lowest validation loss across folds.

2. **Bias Correction of Climate Projections Using LSTM Neural Networks:** The DRIAS provides climate projections for France covering the period 2006–2100, offering valuable scenarios for assessing future climate change. However, these simulations often exhibit systematic biases when compared to local observational records, which can undermine the reliability of impact studies at regional or city scales. To address this issue, a data-driven approach based on Long Short-Term Memory (LSTM) networks was proposed. These networks are particularly well suited to capturing temporal dependencies and seasonal variability in climate time series. In our framework, the input variables (X) correspond to temperature and humidity data from DRIAS, while the target variables (y) are the corresponding local observations. By learning the nonlinear relationships between the simulated and observed data, the model generates bias-corrected series that more accurately represent local climatic conditions.

The detailed architecture of our sequential model is presented below:

- **Input Shape:**
  - Each input sequence has length `sequence_length` and contains features.
  - The data are formatted as three-dimensional tensors: (`samples, sequence_length, features`).
- **Architecture:**
  - LSTM layer with 256 units, `tanh` activation, and `return_sequences=True` to allow stacking.
  - LSTM layer with 128 units and `tanh` activation, producing the final sequence representation.
  - Dense output layer with 1 unit, corresponding to the predicted target variable (e.g., temperature or humidity).
- **Training:**
  - Optimizer: Adam with default learning rate.
  - Loss function: Mean Squared Error (MSE).
  - Callback: Early stopping (patience = 10, restore best weights) to avoid overfitting.
  - Maximum epochs = 30, batch size = 32.
- **Validation Strategy:**
  - A temporal split is applied between training and test sets to ensure chronological separation.
  - Model performance is assessed using validation loss on the held-out dataset.

3. **Climate Projections up to 2100 for Heritage Monuments: A Case Study of the Basilica of Saint-Remi**:
   The methodology begins with the conversion of daily climate data into hourly series using the ERA5 reanalysis dataset, in order to capture the fine-scale temporal variability required for heritage impact studies. This is followed by the bias correction of DRIAS climate projections using LSTM neural networks, which ensures consistency between simulated data and local observations. Based on these corrected datasets, a sequential model was implemented, where the input variables correspond to the corrected DRIAS climate data and the target variables represent the conditions observed at the monument. This approach enables the generation of localized climate projections at the scale of the Basilica, extending up to the year 2100 under different climate scenarios.

The detailed architecture of our sequential model is presented below:

- **Architecture:**
  - LSTM layer with 256 units, `tanh` activation, and `return_sequences=True` to allow stacking.

- LSTM layer with 128 units and `tanh` activation, producing the final sequential representation.
- Dense output layer with 1 unit corresponding to the predicted target variable (e.g., temperature or humidity).
  - **Training:**
    - Optimizer: `Adam` with default learning rate.
    - Loss function: Mean Squared Error (MSE).
    - Callback: Early stopping (`patience` = 10, `restore_best_weights` = True) to prevent overfitting.
    - Training configuration: maximum of 30 epochs and batch size of 32.
  - **Validation Strategy:**
    - Temporal split between training and test sets to ensure chronological consistency.
    - Model performance evaluated using validation loss on the held-out dataset.

4   Results

The analysis first focused on the conversion of daily climate data into hourly series using the ERA5 reanalysis dataset. The performance of the bias correction applied to climate projections was evaluated using LSTM neural networks.

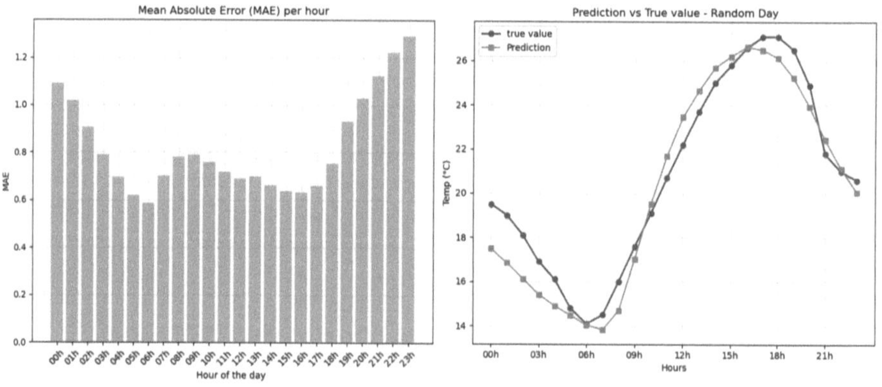

Fig. 4. Translation of DRIAS daily temperature data into hourly series using the ERA5 reanalysis dataset as a reference.

1. **Translation from daily data to hourly data via ERA5 reanalysis dataset:**
   Figure 4 (left), the Mean Absolute Error (MAE) varied throughout the day. The lowest errors ($\tilde{0}.6$ (°C) occurred between 06:00 and 18:00, indicating

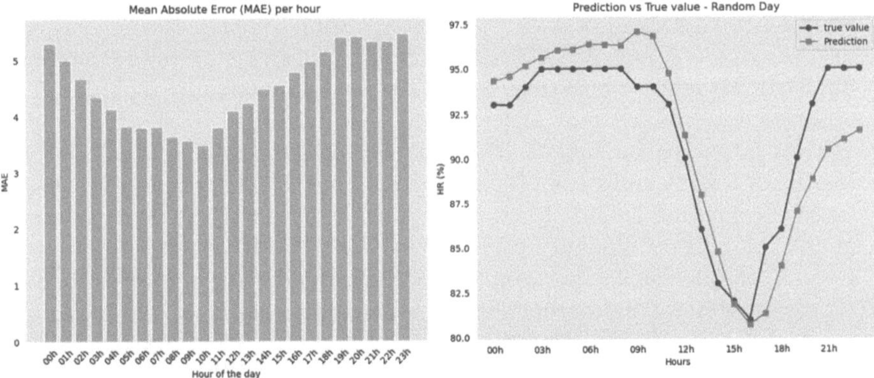

Fig. 5. Conversion of DRIAS daily humidity data into hourly series using the ERA5 reanalysis dataset as a reference.

better predictive accuracy during daytime, while the highest errors ($> 1°C$) appeared at night and late evening (00:00–02:00 and 20:00–23:00), where the model struggled more to capture variations.

Figure 4 (right), predictions are compared to real values for a day chosen randomly. The model follows the cycle well, reproducing the morning increase and afternoon peak, but slightly underestimates temperatures during early morning and late evening.

Figure 5 (left), the Mean Absolute Error (MAE) of relative humidity varied throughout the day. The lowest errors (3.5%) were observed in the morning (08:00–11:00), while the highest errors ($> 5\%$) occurred at night and late evening (00:00–02:00 and 19:00–23:00), indicating that the conversion was less accurate during these periods.

Figure 5 (right), the translated hourly series was compared with the true values for a random day. The method reproduced the cycle of relative humidity well, with high values at night, a pronounced decrease during the day, and a recovery in the evening. However, it tended to slightly overestimate high humidity levels at night and underestimated some evening variations.

2. **Bias Correction of Climate Projections Using LSTM Neural Networks**:

   Figures 6 and 7, compared The bias-corrected temperature and relative humidity series generated by the LSTM model were compared with the corresponding local observational records over the validation period. The results present that the model captured the temporal dynamics and seasonal variability of the observed data, reproducing both short-term fluctuations and broader trends.

   For temperature, the LSTM-based correction effectively reduced the systematic biases present in the original DRIAS projections, resulting in a significantly improved agreement with the observed data. As shown in Table 1, the model achieved a Mean Absolute Error (MAE) of **3.42 °C** and a Root Mean

Square Error (RMSE) of **4.29** °**C**, demonstrating a substantial enhancement in predictive accuracy after bias correction.

Similarly, for relative humidity, the LSTM model successfully reproduced the observed seasonal patterns and variability, as evidenced by the performance metrics presented in Table 2. The model obtained a Mean Absolute Error (MAE) of **5.21%** and a Root Mean Square Error (RMSE) of **6.48 %**. Despite these encouraging results, some discrepancies remained, particularly during periods of extreme humidity values.

Overall, the agreement between the corrected and observed series for both temperature and humidity highlights the capability of the LSTM-based approach to improve the realism of climate projections. These findings demonstrate the potential of the method to provide more reliable bias-corrected climatic variables for impact studies at a local scale.

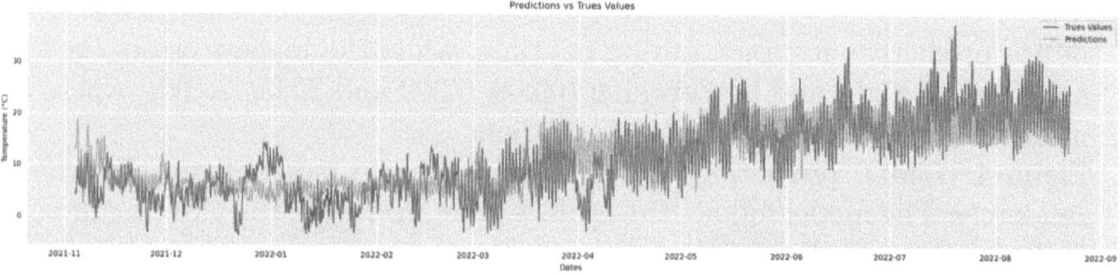

Fig. 6. Bias correction of climate temperature projections using an LSTM neural network.

Table 1. Performance evaluation of the LSTM model after bias correction of climate temperature projections.

Indicator	Value (°C)
MAE	3.42
RMSE	4.29

MAE (Mean Absolute Error)
RMSE (Root Mean Square Error)

5   Conclusion

The initial steps of a generic methodology for predicting the behavior of stones on historical monuments up to the year 2100 are presented in this work, depending on various climate change scenarios.

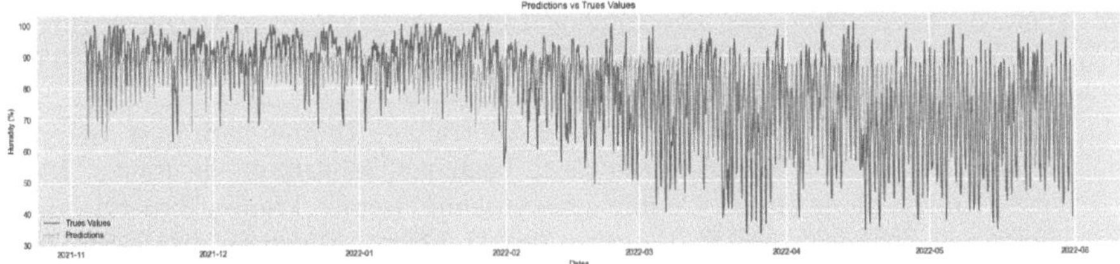

Fig. 7. Bias Correction of Climate Humidity Projections Using LSTM Neural Networks.

Table 2. Performance evaluation of the LSTM model after bias correction of climate humidity projections.

Indicator	Value (%)
MAE	5.21
RMSE	6.48

MAE (Mean Absolute Error)
RMSE (Root Mean Square Error)

It has been shown how past data collected by dedicated sensors (installed at various locations on monuments) can be utilized in a dataflow process to filter, analyze, and predict future behaviors.

Several AI-based algorithms were experimented with, and an LSTM (Long Short-Term Memory) model was selected for its superior performance observed during the testing phase.

This first attempt provided an overview of the entire methodology. As future work, the goal is to collect real data over the next two years and refine the prediction algorithms parameters. Monitoring has already been initiated on another historical monument located in a rural area. This additional dataset will be processed using the same methodology, which will allow for the analysis of the effect of the rural environment on the predictions.

References

1. Markham, A., Brabec, E., Burke, S. et al.: Future of Our Pasts: Engaging Cultural Heritage in Climate Action. International Council on Monuments and Sites (ICOMOS), Paris, France, 120 pp (2019). ISBN 978-2-918086-29-1. https://www.researchgate.net/publication/337900960_The_Future_of_Our_Pasts_Engaging_cultural_heritage_in_climate_action_-_outline_of_climate_change_and_cultural_heritageAvailable online
2. Terray, L., Boé, J.: Quantifying 21st-century France climate change and related uncertainties. Comptes Rendus Géoscience, **345**(3), 136–149 (2013). https://doi.org/10.1016/j.crte.2013.02.003

3. Koch, A., Siegesmund, S.: The combined effect of moisture and temperature on the anomalous expansion behaviour of marble. Environ. Geol. **46**(3–4), 350–363 (2004). https://doi.org/10.1007/s00254-004-1037-9

4. Huby, E.: Réponse de matériaux à des contraintes thermo-hydriques obtenues par suivi climatique: étude de cas de la basilique Saint-Remi de Reims. Ph.D. thesis, Université de Reims Champagne-Ardenne, Reims, France. Supervisors: C. Thomachot-Schneider and G. Fronteau (2021). https://theses.fr/2021REIMS018

5. Sesana, E., Gagnon, A. S., Ciantelli, C., Cassar, J., and Hughes, J. J. (2021). Climate change impacts on cultural heritage: a literature review. WIREs Climate Change **12**(4), e710. https://doi.org/10.1002/wcc.710

6. Huby, E., Thomachot-Schneider, C., Vázquez, P., Fronteau, G.: Use of micro-climatic monitoring to assess potential stone weathering on a monument: example of the Saint-Remi Basilica (Reims, France). Environ. Monitor. Assess. **192**(12), 796 (2020). https://doi.org/10.1007/s10661-020-08753-w

7. Petit, B., Huby, E., Schneider, C., Vazquez, P., Rabat, C., Fouchal, H.: Machine learning to model the risk of alteration of historical buildings. In: Renault, E., Boumerdassi, S., and Mühlethaler, P. (eds.) Machine Learning for Networking. Lecture Notes in Networks and Systems, vol. 1452, pp. 218–231. Springer Nature Switzerland, Cham (2024). https://doi.org/10.1007/978-3-031-59933-0_15

8. Boutet, S.: L'intégration des nouvelles technologies et de l'intelligence artificielle dans la conservation du patrimoine bâti pour détecter la présence de pathologies. Master's thesis, Université de Liège, Liège, Belgium (2025). https://matheo.uliege.be/handle/2268.2/22348

9. Hatir, M., Ince, I., Korkanç, M.: Intelligent detection of deterioration in cultural stone heritage. J. Build. Eng. **44**, 102690 (2021). https://doi.org/10.1016/j.jobe.2021.102690

10. Karimi, N., Mishra, M., Lourenço, P.B.: Deep learning-based automated tile defect detection system for Portuguese cultural heritage buildings. J. Cultural Heritage **68**, 86–98 (2024). https://doi.org/10.1016/j.culher.2024.05.009

11. Ying, W., Khoshelham, K., Kemp, J.: Assessment of rock and stone decay in heritage sites using machine learning. In: ISPRS Annals of the Photogrammetry, Remote Sensing and Spatial Information Sciences, Vol. X-G-2025, pp. 1019–1026. Copernicus GmbH (2025). https://doi.org/10.5194/isprs-annals-X-G-2025-1019-2025

12. Boesgaard, C., Hansen, B.V., Kejser, U.B., Mollerup, S.H., Ryhl-Svendsen, M., Torp-Smith, N.: Prediction of the indoor climate in cultural heritage buildings through machine learning: First results from two field tests. Heritage Sci. **10**(1), 176 (2022). https://doi.org/10.1186/s40494-022-00805-3

13. Hdz-Gil, L., Gil-Martín, L. M., Fernández, P., Hernández-Montes, E.: Predicting the influence of climate change on the deterioration of heritage building materials using photogrammetric observations. Appl. Sci. **15**(11), 6232 (2025). https://doi.org/10.3390/app15116232

14. Soci, C., Hersbach, H., Simmons, A., Poli, P., Bell, B., Berrisford, P., Horányi, A., Muñoz-Sabater, J., Nicolas, J., Radu, R., Schepers, D., Villaume, S., Haimberger, L., Woollen, J., Buontempo, C., Thépaut, J.-N.: The ERA5 global reanalysis from 1940 to 2022. Quart. J. Royal Meteorol. Soc. 150 Wiley (2024). https://doi.org/10.1002/qj.4803

Balancing Accuracy and Energy: An Empirical Study of Optimal Subset Size Selection

Oumayma Haddaji[✉], Olivier Brun, and Balakrishna Prabhu

LAAS-CNRS, Université de Toulouse, CNRS, INSA, Toulouse, France
{ohaddaji,brun,bjprabhu}@laas.fr

Abstract. This paper investigates the trade-off between model performance and energy efficiency in supervised learning by varying the size of the training data, motivated by the increasing energy consumption of machine learning models. We establish empirical energy scaling laws for neural network training and develop optimization frameworks for balancing accuracy (the percentage of correctly classified samples on the test set) and energy consumption through stratified random sampling. We demonstrate that energy consumption per training epoch scales linearly with dataset size for CNNs, with architecture-dependent coefficients ranging from 2.143×10^{-5} kJ/sample (MNIST) to 1.356×10^{-4} kJ/sample (CIFAR-10). Critically, we show that model complexity, not dataset characteristics, determines energy scaling patterns. Our comprehensive analysis across MNIST, Fashion-MNIST, and CIFAR-10 reveals optimal subset sizes for energy efficiency: 5% for MNIST and Fashion-MNIST and 24% for CIFAR-10 when maximizing accuracy per unit energy consumed. We extend these findings to federated learning with 20 clients, validating the framework's generalizability across distributed training scenarios. For practitioners targeting specific accuracy thresholds, we provide energy budgeting strategies—for example, achieving 80% accuracy on MNIST requires only 7.5% of the data while saving 82% energy. The derived energy models enable solving three classes of optimization problems: minimizing energy subject to accuracy constraints, maximizing accuracy within energy budgets, and optimizing efficiency metrics. This work provides actionable guidance for sustainable AI development and establishes a methodology for deriving energy scaling laws for new datasets and architectures.

Keywords: Energy-efficient machine learning · Neural network optimization · Sustainable AI · Random sampling · Energy scaling laws

1 Introduction

The rapid growth of machine learning (ML) has brought incredible advancements. However, it has also led to a significant and often overlooked problem:

S. Boumerdassi et al. (Eds.): MLN 2025, LNCS 16424, pp. 151–172, 2026.
https://doi.org/10.1007/978-3-032-18494-8_11

the increasing energy consumption of ML models. This has created a critical environmental concern, especially for large-scale deployments.

Developers constantly strive for higher accuracy in ML models. Meanwhile, even small improvements in accuracy often require a disproportionately large increase in computational resources and, consequently, energy. This creates a critical trade-off between model performance and energy efficiency that needs to be addressed.

One effective way to tackle this is through appropriate selection and pruning of the training data. Training ML models on entire, massive datasets is computationally intensive and can be energy-inefficient. Data summarization, which involves selecting a representative subset of the data for training, can significantly reduce computational overhead and energy consumption without severely compromising model accuracy [12,18]. The representative subset can be obtained using various techniques which can be either sophisticated and based on solving an optimization problem or can be as simple as random selection.

Among various data summarization techniques, stratified random sampling stands out. This method divides a dataset into homogeneous subgroups, which in an image classification problem–like CIFAR-10, Fashion-MNIST, or MNIST– would be the classes and then randomly samples from each. Research has shown that this approach can be highly effective. For example, a study [10] comparing optimization-based subset selection and random sampling found that stratified random sampling performed similarly to, and in some cases even better than, more complex optimization-based methods in terms of energy efficiency. This is because while sophisticated summarization techniques could select representative subsets, they did so at a high energy cost that outweighed any accuracy gains.

In this paper, we focus on stratified random sampling as a representative data summarization technique and conduct rigorous empirical measurements to establish how energy consumption depends on dataset size, model complexity, and architectural choices. Our objective is to provide various energy consumption curves based on measurements as well as accuracy curves based on experiments for training on benchmark datasets. Using these curves, one can then solve different optimization problems and determine the optimal subset size that they would like to use when training models on these datasets.

2   Motivation

In the context of supervised learning, where the goal is to train a model to make predictions based on labeled data, different optimization problems can be formulated for taking into account the energy and accuracy trade-off. For example, given an objective function f mapping energy consumption (e) and accuracy (a) into a real number, we can write

$$\min_{s,A} f(e, a) \tag{1}$$

where s is the subset size and A is the data summarization algorithm. Another possibility is to maximize the accuracy subject to energy constraint:

$$\max_{s,A} \quad a \tag{2}$$

$$\text{s.t. } e \leq \text{budget}, \tag{3}$$

and the complementary problem to minimize the energy subject to a constraint on accuracy:

$$\min_{s,A} \quad e \tag{4}$$

$$\text{s.t. } a \geq \text{requirement}, \tag{5}$$

To solve these problems, the first step is to determine how the accuracy and energy depend upon the subset size. One of the contributions of this paper is to obtain these dependencies (or functional curves) using measurements and experiments for stratified random sampling. Further, we illustrate how they can be used to compute optimal subset size for certain simple objective functions. We hope that curves obtained in this study can be used by researchers and practitioners who are working on these datasets to select the most efficient subset size to meet their specific energy and accuracy objectives by solving optimization problems like (1) and (3), and (5).

This paper is organized as follows. Section 3 reviews relevant literature. Section 4 describes our energy measurement strategy and theoretical foundations. Section 5 details the experimental setup including hardware infrastructure, datasets, and model architectures. Section 6 presents our empirical findings on energy scaling patterns. Section 7 demonstrates practical applications through optimization problems and Sect. 8 extends findings to federated learning scenarios. Finally, Sect. 9 summarizes the key contributions and implications for sustainable AI development.

3 Background and Related Work

3.1 Supervised Learning Fundamentals

In supervised learning, a model learns from labeled datasets of the form $\{(x^{(1)}, y^{(1)}), \ldots, (x^{(n)}, y^{(n)})\}$ where $x^{(i)}$ are feature vectors and $y^{(i)}$ are their labels, typically assumed to be i.i.d. samples [11]. The goal during training is to find optimal model parameters (θ^*) through empirical risk minimization, minimizing the average error across training examples using loss functions such as Mean Squared Error for regression or cross-entropy for classification tasks.

Neural networks process data through interconnected layers, with specialized architectures like Convolutional Neural Networks (CNNs) proving particularly effective for structured data through convolutional layers, pooling operations, and fully connected layers for predictions [9].

3.2   Energy-Efficient Machine Learning: A Broad Perspective

The rapid deployment of machine learning models has created significant energy consumption challenges, spurring extensive research into energy-efficient deep learning techniques [3,14]. The field has developed along several complementary directions, each addressing different aspects of the energy-performance trade-off.

Model Compression and Acceleration: A substantial body of work focuses on reducing model complexity through various compression techniques. Network pruning methods systematically remove redundant weights and connections [19], while quantization reduces numerical precision to decrease computational requirements [13]. Knowledge distillation transfers knowledge from large teacher networks to smaller student models, maintaining performance while reducing computational overhead [6]. These approaches typically achieve energy savings through reduced floating-point operations and memory access patterns.

Architectural Innovations: Hardware-aware neural architecture search and efficient network design have produced architectures optimized for specific energy constraints [15]. MobileNets [8], EfficientNets [16], and similar architectures demonstrate that carefully designed models can achieve competitive accuracy with significantly lower computational requirements. Energy estimation frameworks have been developed to predict consumption during the design phase [20], enabling architects to optimize for energy efficiency from the outset.

Hardware and System-Level Optimizations: Specialized hardware accelerators [5], optimized software frameworks [4], and dynamic voltage/frequency scaling [7] contribute to energy efficiency at the system level. These approaches focus on maximizing computational efficiency for given model architectures rather than modifying the models themselves.

3.3   Data-Centric Approaches to Energy Efficiency

While model-centric approaches dominate the literature, data-centric strategies for energy efficiency remain underexplored despite their potential for significant impact. Training on massive datasets is computationally intensive, and reducing data volume through intelligent selection can substantially decrease energy consumption without proportional accuracy loss.

Data Summarization Techniques: Various methods exist for selecting representative subsets from large datasets. Sophisticated approaches include core-set selection algorithms that solve optimization problems to identify the most informative samples [18] and gradient-based selection methods that identify samples contributing most to model updates [12].

Sampling Strategies: Simple random sampling provides a baseline approach, while stratified sampling ensures proportional representation across classes or strata. Importance sampling weights examples based on their contribution to the learning objective. Each approach presents different trade-offs between selection complexity and maintained model performance.

3.4   Energy Scaling Laws and Empirical Analysis

Recent work has begun establishing empirical relationships between dataset size, model complexity, and energy consumption. Tripp et al. [17] demonstrated nonlinear relationships between energy consumption and model parameters for fully-connected networks. While their work establishes linear energy scaling with dataset size for fully-connected architectures, fundamental questions remain about whether these scaling patterns hold for convolutional neural networks processing structured image data.

Existing energy studies provide measurements and high-level efficiency metrics but lack systematic frameworks that practitioners can directly apply to balance accuracy and energy constraints through data selection strategies.

3.5   Research Gaps and Contribution

Current literature exhibits several critical limitations. First, existing work lacks practical optimization frameworks based on empirical energy models that enable systematic trade-offs between accuracy and energy consumption. Second, the generalizability of energy-efficiency strategies to distributed learning scenarios like federated learning remains unexplored.

This study addresses these gaps by: (1) developing practical optimization frameworks for balancing accuracy and energy consumption through stratified random sampling and (2) validating these frameworks in both centralized and federated learning environments.

4   Energy Measurement Strategy and Estimation

To understand how energy consumption, accuracy, and subset size relate, one way is to measure them across a wide range of subset sizes. Due to limited access to specialized hardware for measuring energy (see details in Sect. 5), we measured per-epoch energy consumption for various subset sizes, assuming consistent energy use across epochs. The full training until convergence was then performed on a separate platform. For centralized setup, we calculated total energy by multiplying the measured per-epoch energy by the total number of epochs required for convergence, noting that the chosen subset size influences the number of epochs to convergence, but not the per-epoch energy consumption.

Before diving into experimental results, let's briefly look at the theory behind energy consumption and subset size. Training a neural network with gradient descent and backpropagation is computationally intensive. It involves a feedforward step, a backpropagation step, and weight and bias updates. For a training set of size s, with L layers and n neurons per layer, the total training time scales roughly as $O(sn^2L)$, indicating a direct, linear relationship with the size of the training data. The exact constants in this relationship are hardware-dependent and can be determined by empirical measurements.

5   Experimental Setup

This section describes the hardware infrastructure, datasets, model architectures, and energy measurement methodology employed to evaluate the energy consumption of data summarization techniques in machine learning training.

5.1   Hardware Infrastructure

All experiments were conducted on the Grid5000 platform [1], a large-scale distributed computing testbed designed for reproducible research. We utilized the paradoxe cluster located at the Rennes site, which provides homogeneous compute nodes with identical hardware configurations to ensure consistent energy measurements across experiments.

The detailed hardware specifications are presented in Table 1. Each node is equipped with dual Intel Xeon Gold 5320 processors (Ice Lake-SP architecture)

Table 1. Hardware specifications of the Grid5000 Rennes paradoxe cluster nodes used for energy measurements.

Property	Specification
Cluster Configuration	
Platform	Grid5000 Rennes site
Cluster Name	paradoxe
Node Model	HPE ProLiant DL360 Gen10+
Manufacturing Date	2023-05-27
Total Available Nodes	32
Total CPUs (cluster)	64
Total Cores (cluster)	1664
Per-Node Hardware Specifications	
CPU Model	Intel Xeon Gold 5320 (Ice Lake-SP)
CPU Architecture	x86_64
Base Clock Frequency	2.20 GHz
CPUs per Node	2
Cores per CPU	26
Total Cores per Node	52
Memory	384 GiB
Storage Configuration	
Primary Storage	1.92 TB SSD SATA HP MK001920GZXRC
Secondary Storage	1.92 TB SSD SATA HP MK001920GZXRC
Total Storage per Node	3.84 TB
Network Configuration	
Primary Interface	eth0/ens10f0np0, 25 Gbps Ethernet
Network Controller	Broadcom BCM57414 NetXtreme-E
Driver	bnxt_en
Energy Monitoring	
Monitoring Tool	Mojitos
Monitoring Level	Operating System (GNU/Linux)
Measurement Granularity	System-level energy and network usage
Sampling Method	Real-time OS-level monitoring

running at 2.20 GHz, providing 52 cores per node with a total of 384 GiB of memory. The nodes feature modern HPE ProLiant DL360 Gen10+ servers manufactured in 2023, ensuring contemporary hardware representative of current datacenter deployments. Storage is provided via dual 1.92 TB SSD drives per node, connected through high-speed 25 Gbps Ethernet networking.

5.2 Energy Measurement Methodology

Energy consumption was monitored using Mojitos [2], an open-source tool specifically designed for precise energy and network usage monitoring at the operating system level on GNU/Linux systems. This approach provides comprehensive system-level energy measurements that capture the complete computational overhead, including CPU, memory, and I/O operations during model training.

5.3 Datasets

We evaluated our approaches on three benchmark datasets that represent varying levels of complexity and computational requirements:

- **MNIST**: The classic handwritten digit recognition dataset containing 60,000 training samples and 10,000 test samples, each represented as 28×28 grayscale images across 10 classes.
- **Fashion-MNIST**: A more challenging dataset with the same structure as MNIST but containing fashion items instead of digits, maintaining identical data splits of 60,000 training and 10,000 test samples.
- **CIFAR-10**: A complex object recognition dataset comprising 50,000 training and 10,000 test samples of 32×32 color images across 10 object classes, requiring more sophisticated model architectures.

5.4 Model Architectures

We designed three distinct convolutional neural network architectures to systematically investigate the effects of model complexity across different datasets, as detailed in Table 2.

Simple-CNN: For MNIST and Fashion-MNIST datasets, we employed a lightweight architecture featuring two convolutional layers ($1 \rightarrow 6 \rightarrow 16$ channels) with ReLU activation functions, followed by max-pooling operations and a single fully connected output layer. This simple design with only 5,142 parameters serves as our baseline architecture.

CIFAR-CNN: Given the increased complexity of natural image classification in CIFAR-10, we implemented a deeper architecture with three convolutional layers ($3 \rightarrow 32 \rightarrow 64 \rightarrow 128$ channels), incorporating batch normalization for training stability, dropout layers for regularization, and five fully connected layers (1000 units each) for classification. This complex model contains over 5 million parameters.

Complex-CNN: To isolate the effects of model complexity from dataset characteristics, we trained a model with CIFAR-CNN complexity ($1{\to}32{\to}64{\to}128$ channels, 4 million parameters) on the simpler MNIST dataset. This architecture maintains the same depth and regularization techniques as CIFAR-CNN but uses single-channel input to match MNIST's grayscale format.

All models utilized the Adam optimization algorithm with cross-entropy loss for training.

6 Results

6.1 Energy Consumption per Epoch Analysis

To establish baseline energy consumption patterns, we first analyzed CNN training on standard computer vision datasets. We conducted 100 trials to estimate energy usage for single epochs on randomly chosen subsets of CIFAR-10, MNIST, and Fashion-MNIST.

Table 2. CNN architecture specifications showing parameter count differences across simple to complex architectures.

Complexity	Model	Conv Layers	FC Layers	Trainable Parameters
Simple	Simple-CNN	2	1	5,142
Complex	CIFAR-CNN	3	5	5,329,102
Complex	Complex-CNN	3	5	4,431,502

Simple-CNN: Lightweight architecture ($1{\to}6{\to}16$ channels) trained on MNIST and Fashion-MNIST.
CIFAR-CNN: Complex architecture ($3{\to}32{\to}64{\to}128$ channels) designed and trained on CIFAR-10.
Complex-CNN: Complex architecture ($1{\to}32{\to}64{\to}128$ channels) trained on MNIST to isolate model complexity effects.

Figure 1, shows the minimum, average, and maximum energy consumption recorded for a training epoch across a variety of subset sizes for the three datasets. It demonstrates that energy consumption exhibits a clear linear relationship with subset size across all datasets, with minimal variability between trials. This low variability confirms that subset composition has negligible impact on energy consumption–only subset size matters, making the mean a reliable estimator for optimization problems.

However, Fig. 1b shows that a baseline energy consumption of approximately 0.2 kJ is observed for subset sizes up to 5%, where the minimum, mean, and maximum values are nearly identical. This suggests an initial energy overhead for the computational processes, such as initializing hardware and software. The energy needed for these initial tasks is consumed before the subset size starts to have a noticeable impact, and it's this fixed overhead that accounts for the stable energy consumption observed at the lowest subset sizes.

The linear trend predicted in the theoretical analysis in Sect. 4 is evident in Fig. 1d . The exact coefficients of this linear trend for the three datasets are shown in Table 3 in which s is the number of training samples. We use the absolute number of samples instead of fraction to allow for direct comparison across datasets, as equivalent percentages (e.g., 10%) represent different sample counts (e.g., 6,000 for MNIST vs. 5,000 for CIFAR-10).

In addition to training dataset-appropriate architectures (Simple-CNN on MNIST and Fashion-MNIST, CIFAR-CNN on CIFAR-10), Table 3 includes a fourth experimental condition where a complex architecture equivalent to our

Table 3. Energy consumption models for different datasets and architectures, where s is the number of samples. CIFAR-10: $5000 \leq s \leq 50000$. MNIST and Fashion MNIST: $600 \leq s \leq 60000$.

Dataset	Model	Energy consumption in kJ (linear fit)
MNIST	Simple-CNN	$1.791 \times 10^{-1} + 2.143 \times 10^{-5} \times s$
Fashion MNIST	Simple-CNN	$1.144 \times 10^{-1} + 2.103 \times 10^{-5} \times s$
CIFAR-10	CIFAR-CNN	$8.120 \times 10^{-1} + 1.356 \times 10^{-4} \times s$
MNIST	Complex-CNN	$1.204 \times 10^{-1} + 1.484 \times 10^{-4} \times s$

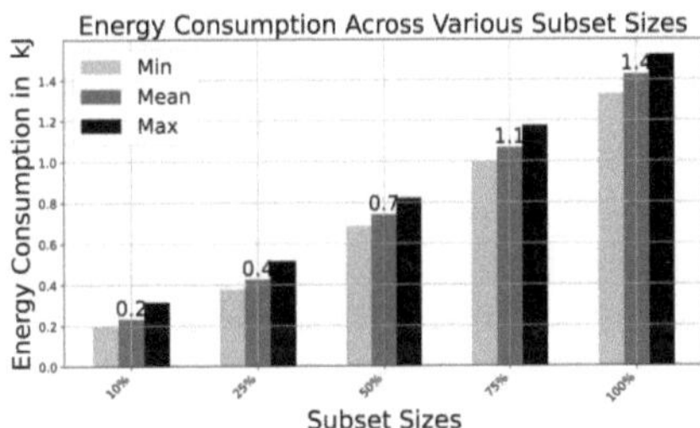

(a) Fashion-MNIST: energy statistics

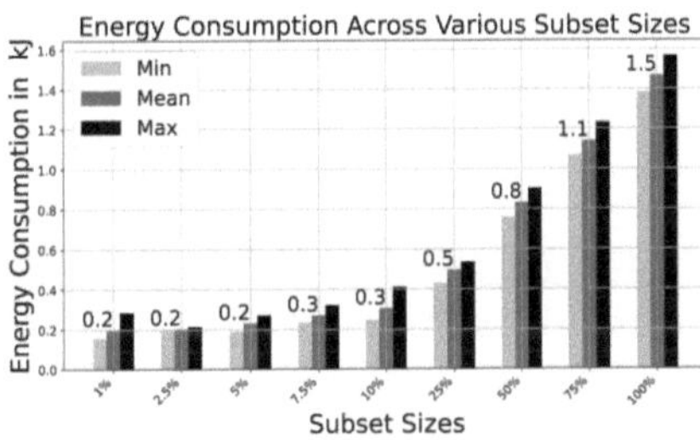

(b) MNIST: energy statistics

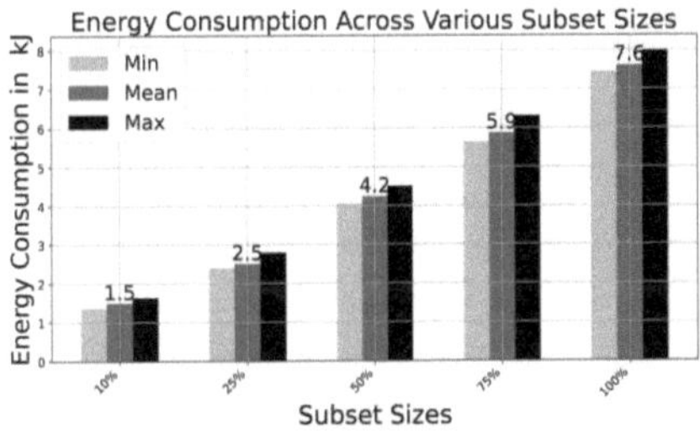

(c) CIFAR-10: Max, min, and mean energy consumption

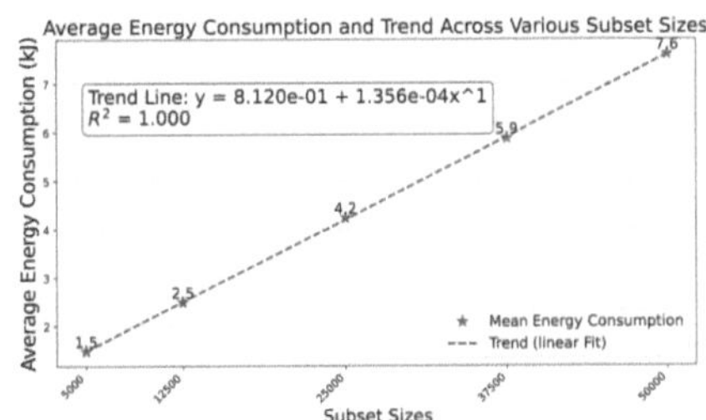

(d) CIFAR-10: Linear fit for mean energy consumption across subset sizes

Fig. 1. Energy consumption (kJ) of a training epoch for different subset sizes across Fashion-MNIST, MNIST, and CIFAR-10 datasets. Top row shows Fashion-MNIST and MNIST statistics, bottom row shows CIFAR-10 statistics and linear trend.

CIFAR-10 model (Complex-CNN) was trained on the simpler MNIST dataset. This controlled comparison isolates the effects of model complexity from dataset characteristics (see details in Sect. 5.4).

We observe that MNIST and Fashion MNIST datasets have similar fits since they are fed to the same model. This reinforces the hypothesis that the energy consumption is a function of the neural network and not the dataset on which it is trained. CIFAR-10 consumes significantly more energy due to the complexity of its model. Notably, when MNIST is trained on a CIFAR-10 level model (Complex-CNN), its energy consumption rate $(1.484e - 04)$ aligns more closely with CIFAR-10 than with MNIST trained on Simple-CNN model, confirming that model complexity is the primary driver of energy consumption rather than dataset characteristics. The constant term in the fit represents the base energy consumption when the subset size is minimal, with CIFAR-10 having significantly higher base energy consumption due to the complexity of its model.

6.2   Analysis of Subset Size on Training Convergence and Performance

After calculating the energy consumed per training epoch, the next crucial step involves determining the achievable accuracy and the total number of epochs required for convergence for each subset size. This heavily depends on the training's stopping criterion. In our experiments, training was terminated if the test accuracy did not improve by at least 0.5% for five consecutive epochs, or if the limit of 500 epochs was reached.

CIFAR-10 Dataset Analysis We first analyze the relationship between subset size and model performance on the CIFAR-10 dataset. Figure 2 presents the initial insights into this relationship, displaying both the average test accuracy achieved and the mean number of epochs required for convergence. A fitted sigmoid curve in Fig. 2a indicates that using a larger percentage of subset size generally leads to higher average accuracy, eventually reaching a plateau. This relationship is described by the equation:

$$y = \frac{563.5673}{1 + e^{-3.4905(x-(-2.1727))}} + (-562.7617) \tag{6}$$

where y represents average accuracy and x represents the subset size.

Conversely, Fig. 2b, with its hyperbolic fit, demonstrates that increasing the percentage of subset size significantly reduces the number of training epochs needed. This suggests that using a larger proportion of the training data provides more stable gradient estimates, which in turn accelerates the training process in terms of epoch count. The fitted hyperbolic curve for mean number of epochs is described by the following equation:

$$y = 34.55 + \frac{35.85}{x + 0.10} \tag{7}$$

where y represents mean number of epochs and x represents the subset size.

Overall, our analysis of CIFAR-10 training reveals that the size of the training data subset has a dual influence on model performance. Specifically, beyond a certain subset size, it is possible to achieve both a high level of accuracy and a reduced number of training epochs.

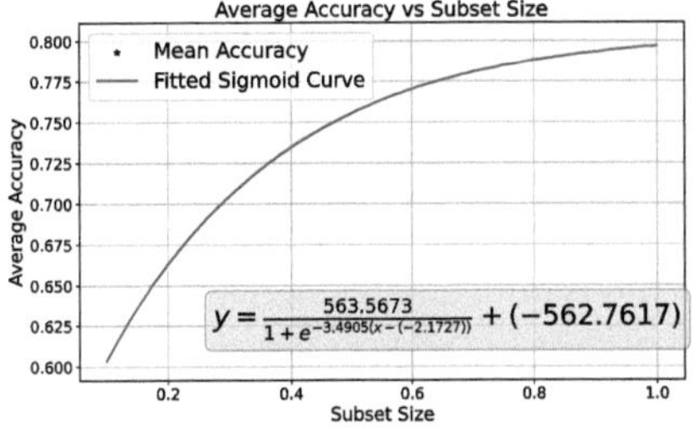

(a) The average test accuracy achieved by the model.

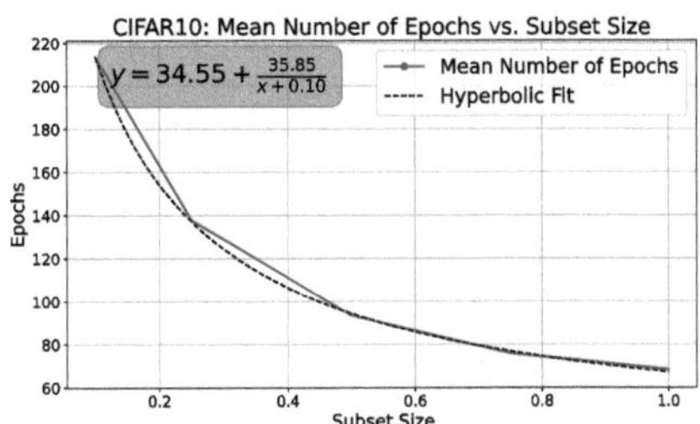

(b) The mean number of epochs required for convergence.

Fig. 2. Impact of Subset Size on Training Epochs and Model Accuracy for CIFAR-10.

MNIST and Fashion-MNIST Dataset Analysis To evaluate whether these relationships generalize across datasets of varying complexity, we conducted the same analysis on the MNIST and Fashion-MNIST datasets. The analysis on the MNIST and Fashion-MNIST datasets reveals a distinct trade-off between model performance and energy efficiency, similar to the CIFAR-10 results. Figure 3 illustrates how increasing the subset size of the training data affects both accuracy and the number of epochs required for convergence. A key observation is that the relationships for MNIST and Fashion-MNIST are notably different from that of CIFAR-10, suggesting that they are less complex problems. The curves show a much steeper initial slope, indicating a faster rate of change. This means that for these datasets, the model can achieve a high level of accuracy and converge more quickly, even with a smaller training data subset. This is reflected in the fitted sigmoid curves for average accuracy, described by the equations:

$$y = \frac{309.8610}{1 + e^{-23.1281(x+0.3483)}} + (-308.8808) \tag{8}$$

for MNIST, and

$$y = \frac{402.9150}{1 + e^{-16.7165(x+0.4810)}} + (-402.0371) \tag{9}$$

for Fashion-MNIST, where y represents average accuracy and x represents the subset size. Additionally, the mean number of epochs required for convergence is described by the hyperbolic fits:

$$y = 10.69 + \frac{0.52}{x + 0.002} \tag{10}$$

for MNIST, and

$$y = 20.04 + \frac{1.10}{x + 0.006} \tag{11}$$

for Fashion-MNIST, where y represents mean number of epochs and x represents the subset size.

Notably, Fashion-MNIST achieves lower average accuracy (approximately 88%, Fig. 3c) compared to MNIST (approximately 98%, Fig. 3a), and requires significantly more training epochs, ranging from 20–90 epochs (Fig. 3d) compared to MNIST's 10–60 epochs (Fig. 3b), which confirms the increased difficulty of the fashion item classification task.

It is noteworthy that the starting subset sizes differ across datasets. For CIFAR-10, experiments begin at 10% of the data because models trained on smaller subsets (e.g., 1%–5%) yield low accuracy, which makes the results less representative for practical analysis. In contrast, MNIST and Fashion-MNIST achieve satisfactory generalization even when trained on only 1% of the data. Therefore, starting from 1% for these datasets and from 10% for CIFAR-10 ensures that each case study remains both meaningful and informative, while maintaining fairness and relevance in cross-dataset comparisons.

Comparative Analysis of Training Dynamics To further investigate the training dynamics, Fig. 4a and Fig. 4b display the validation accuracy as a function of the mean number of training epochs for various subset sizes for CIFAR-10, MNIST and Fashion-MNIST datasets. It is important to distinguish this mean number of epochs from the one presented in Fig. 2b : while Fig. 2b shows the average number of epochs required to reach the final test accuracy, this plot displays the average number of epochs to achieve the validation accuracy. Each curve represents the average performance across multiple training runs for a given subset size. The dashed lines show the fitted sigmoid functions for each subset size. The mathematical equations for the fitted curves of CIFAR-10 dataset are given in Tab. 4 in which x is the mean number of epochs.

In contrast to CIFAR-10 (Fig. 4a), where validation accuracy increases more gradually and requires larger subset sizes to stabilize, the MNIST and Fashion-MNIST curves in Fig. 4b and Fig. 4c exhibit a much steeper rise during the first epochs across all subset sizes. This indicates that the model can quickly extract discriminative digit features even from very small subsets (as low as 1%–2.5% of the data). While CIFAR-10 benefits from larger subsets to improve gradient stability and reduce the number of training epochs, MNIST and Fashion-MNIST

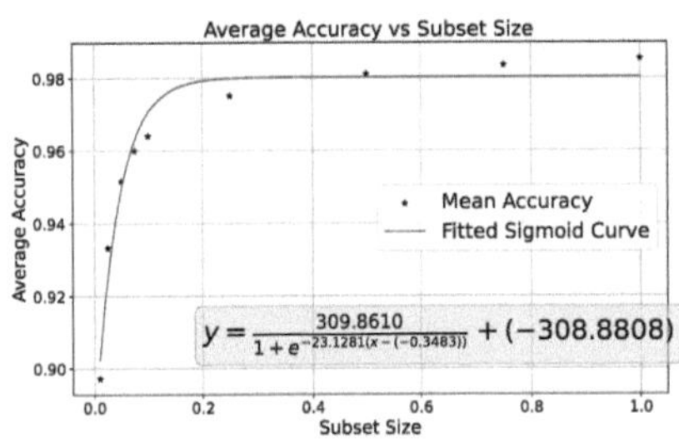

(a) MNIST: Average test accuracy.

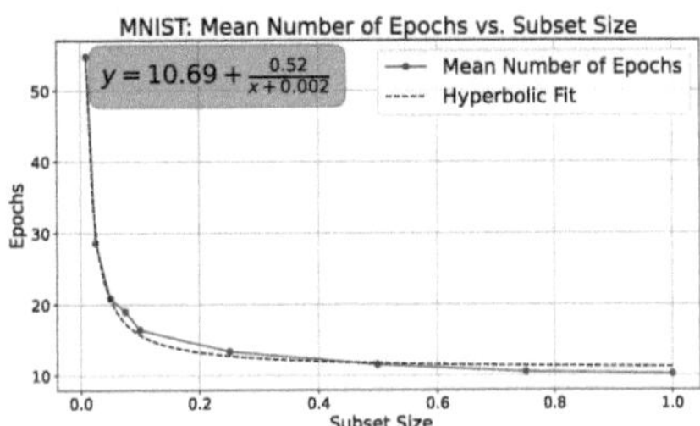

(b) MNIST: Mean epochs for convergence.

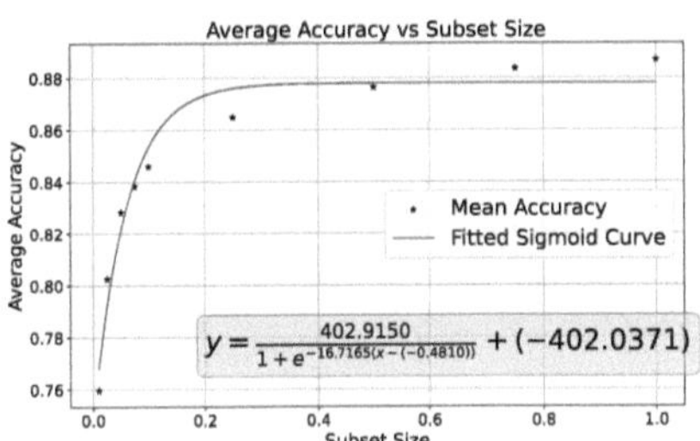

(c) Fashion-MNIST: Average test accuracy.

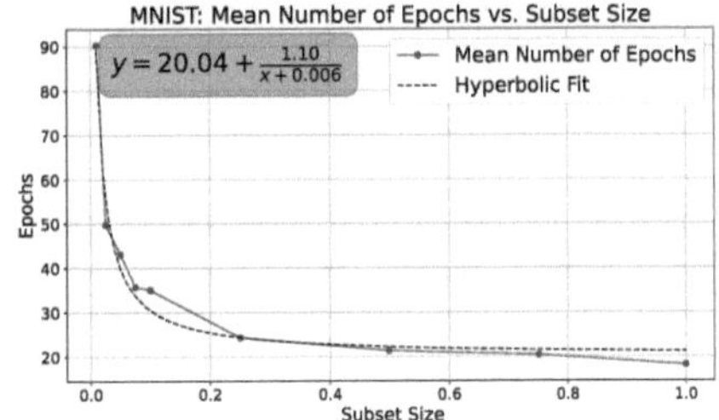

(d) Fashion-MNIST: Mean epochs for convergence.

Fig. 3. Impact of Subset Size on Model Accuracy and Training Epochs for both MNIST (Top Row) and Fashion-MNIST (Bottom Row) datasets.

Table 4. Sigmoid fit for validation accuracy for CIFAR-10.

Subset size	Sigmoid fit	Subset size	Sigmoid fit
0.1	$0.197 + \dfrac{0.620-0.197}{1+e^{-0.223(x-2.6634)}}$	0.25	$0.130 + \dfrac{0.700-0.130}{1+e^{-0.302(x-1.3366)}}$
0.5	$0.108 + \dfrac{0.760-0.108}{1+e^{-0.388(x-1.0700)}}$	0.75	$0.113 + \dfrac{0.780-0.113}{1+e^{-0.5026(x-1.009)}}$
1.0	$0.131 + \dfrac{0.780-0.131}{1+e^{-0.677(x-1.020)}}$		

achieve near-saturation accuracy with minimal data, highlighting both the lower complexity of the task and the redundancy in their dataset. This difference suggests that subset-based training is particularly effective for simpler datasets like MNIST and Fashion-MNIST, where early convergence can be achieved without sacrificing accuracy, whereas more complex datasets such as CIFAR-10 demand larger subsets to reach comparable stability.

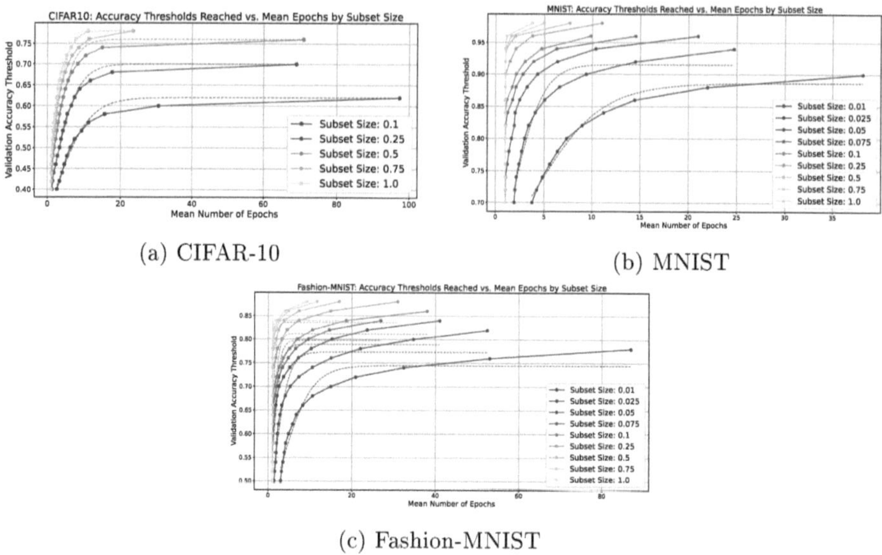

(a) CIFAR-10

(b) MNIST

(c) Fashion-MNIST

Fig. 4. Validation accuracy versus training epochs for different datasets.

6.3   Total Energy Consumption

Having established the relationship between subset size, accuracy, and epochs (both for final test and validation), we now turn our attention to the total energy consumption. Figure 5 illustrates the total energy expended during the training of SL models on CIFAR-10 and MNIST datasets. This total energy is calculated as the product of the mean number of epochs and the average energy consumed per epoch.

The CIFAR-10 plot, Fig. 5a , shows a clear and consistent increase in average energy with increasing subset size. The smoothed average curve closely follows the linear fit, demonstrating a strong linear relationship. The equation for the linear fit is given by:

$$y = 218.1639x + 286.9649 \tag{12}$$

where y represents the average energy in kilojoules (kJ) and x represents the subset size.

The MNIST and Fashion-MNIST plots (Fig. 5b, c) largely follow a linear trend. However, they show an initial dip in energy consumption for very small subset sizes (under 5%). This is due to the high number of epochs required for convergence, and the fact that the energy consumed in this range is primarily the fixed overhead, as explained in Sect. 6.1. Beyond this initial dip, at subset sizes greater than 5%, the energy consumption aligns with and proceeds along a clear linear trend. The equation for the linear fit is given by:

$$y = 10.6583x + 4.1416 \tag{13}$$

for MNIST, and

$$y = 19.6947x + 6.2646 \tag{14}$$

for Fashion-MNIST, where y represents the average energy in kilojoules (kJ) and x represents the subset size.

In summary, the results from all three datasets show that the total energy consumed for training CNN models generally follows a linear trend with respect to the subset size of the training data.

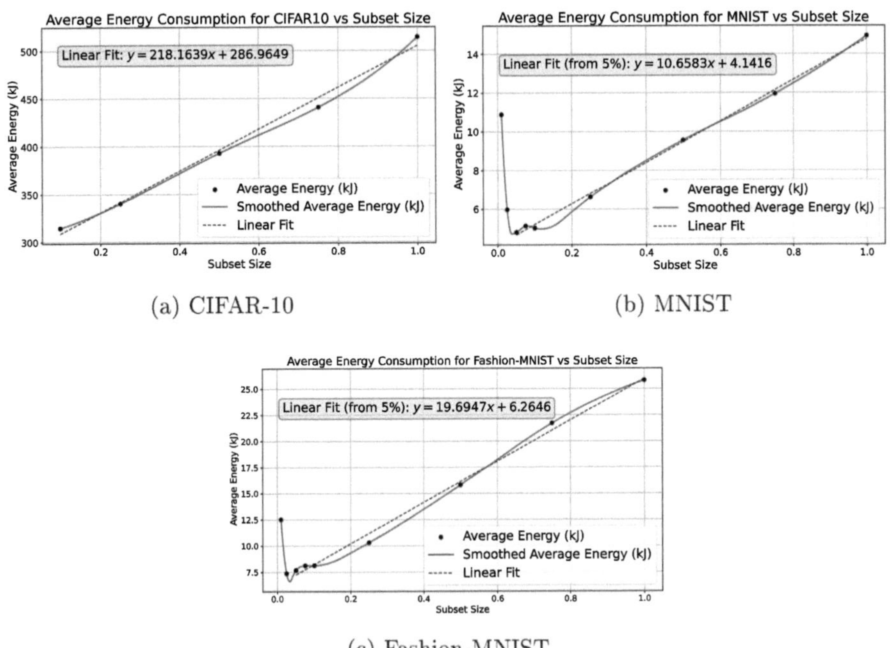

(a) CIFAR-10   (b) MNIST

(c) Fashion-MNIST

Fig. 5. Total energy curves for CIFAR-10, MNIST, and Fashion-MNIST datasets.

7 Examples of Optimization Problems

The results from the previous sections can now be applied in solving specific optimization problems of which we give two examples.

7.1 Problem 1: Maximizing Training Efficiency

The first optimization problem addresses the question: *What subset size provides the best trade-off between accuracy and energy consumption?* This corresponds to problem (1) with f taken to be the efficiency defined as the accuracy divided by the mean total energy consumption. Efficiency represents how much accuracy we gain per unit of energy invested.

For CIFAR-10, we calculate efficiency using functions (12) and (6), with the results plotted in Fig. 6. Each data point represents the ratio at a specific subset size. The analysis reveals that efficiency peaks at approximately 24% subset size (Fig. 6a), indicating that using roughly one-quarter of the training data provides the optimal accuracy-to-energy ratio. This finding suggests that for CIFAR-10, training on the complete dataset yields diminishing returns in terms of efficiency, as the additional computational cost outweighs the marginal accuracy improvements.

Similar analysis conducted for MNIST and Fashion-MNIST reveals dramatically different optimal subset sizes. Both datasets achieve peak efficiency at approximately 5% subset size (Fig. 6b, c), demonstrating that they require substantially less data to achieve optimal efficiency.

The range of efficiency is between 0.16–0.2%/KJ for CIFAR-10, 6–20%/KJ for MNIST, and 3–13%/KJ for Fashion-MNIST. This reflects that stratified random sampling is most efficient with MNIST. This observation, alongside the efficiency peaks, confirms that MNIST is less complex than Fashion-MNIST, which is less complex than CIFAR-10.

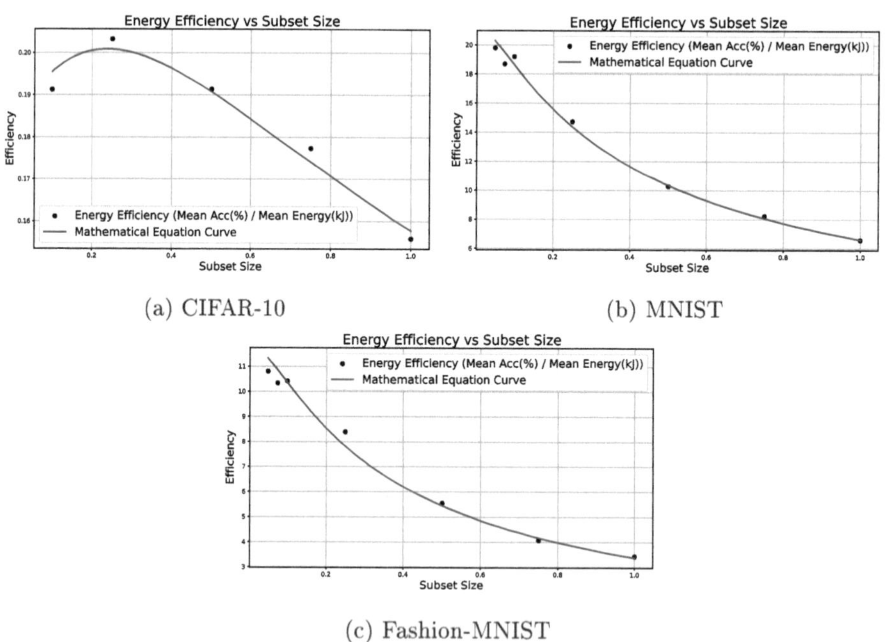

(a) CIFAR-10

(b) MNIST

(c) Fashion-MNIST

Fig. 6. Efficiency curves for CIFAR-10, MNIST, and Fashion-MNIST datasets.

7.2   Problem 2: Meeting Accuracy Targets with Minimal Energy

The second optimization problem addresses a constraint-based scenario: *What is the minimum energy required to achieve a specific accuracy target?* This corresponds to problem (3), where we have predetermined accuracy requirements and seek to minimize computational resources.

Figure 7 illustrates the energy requirements and training epochs needed to reach specific target accuracies for CIFAR-10 (75% and 64%) and MNIST (98% and 80%) using different subset sizes. Our methodology involves using the fitted validation accuracy curves (Table 4 for CIFAR-10) to determine the number of epochs each subset size requires to first achieve the target accuracy, then multiplying by the per-epoch energy consumption to calculate total energy requirements.

The CIFAR-10 analysis reveals that smaller subsets do not always reduce energy consumption. When targeting 75% accuracy (Fig. 7a), subset sizes below 50% cannot achieve this accuracy, while a 50% subset requires approximately 25.5 epochs. Remarkably, using the full dataset reaches the same accuracy in only 7 epochs, consuming 50% less energy than the 50% subset. This occurs because larger subsets provide more stable gradient estimates, leading to faster convergence despite the higher per-epoch computational cost.

However, when targeting 64% accuracy (Fig. 7b), a 50% subset achieves the goal while saving 6.3% energy compared to using the full dataset. This demonstrates that the optimal subset size depends critically on the accuracy requirements, with moderate targets allowing for meaningful energy savings through data reduction.

The MNIST dataset shows different optimization characteristics due to its lower complexity. For achieving 80% accuracy (Fig. 7c), only 7.5% of the training data is required, resulting in an impressive 82% energy saving compared to using the complete dataset. This dramatic reduction possibility stems from the high redundancy in the MNIST dataset and the relative simplicity of digit recognition compared to natural image classification.

For higher accuracy targets on MNIST, the optimization dynamics becomes more complex. As shown in Fig. 7d, for reaching 98% the energy initially increases to approximately 6.3 kJ when using a 50% subset before decreasing again for larger subsets. This non-predictable relationship illustrates why empirical analysis is essential. The optimal choice is a 25% subset which provides 14% energy savings compared to a 50% subset and 2.6% savings compared to the full dataset.

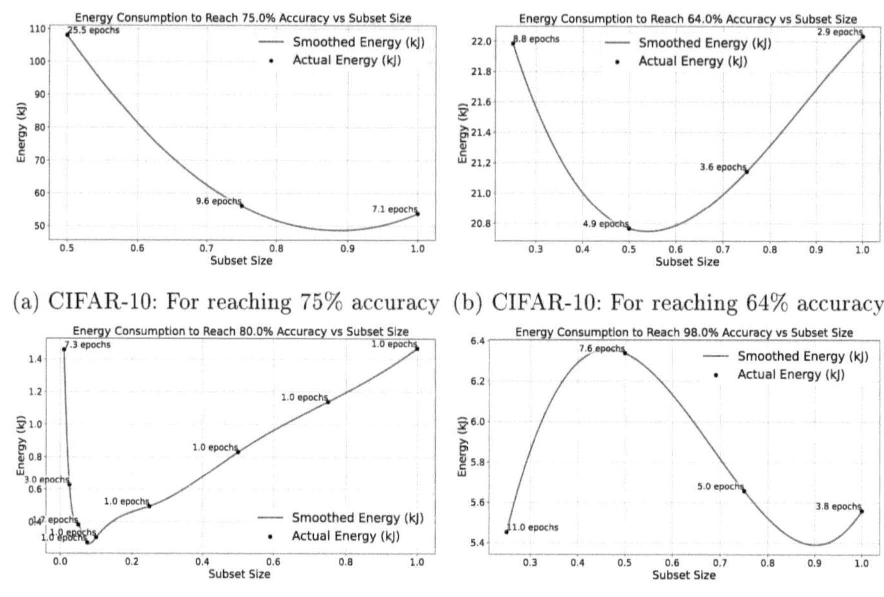

(a) CIFAR-10: For reaching 75% accuracy   (b) CIFAR-10: For reaching 64% accuracy

(c) MNIST: For reaching 80% accuracy   (d) MNIST: For reaching 98% accuracy

Fig. 7. Mean energy and number of epochs to reach target accuracies for CIFAR-10 (top row: 75% and 64%) and MNIST (bottom row: 80% and 98%).

8   Extention to Federated Learning Setup

To validate the generalizability of our findings beyond centralized training, we extend our analysis to a federated learning (FL) environment. In this setup, we distribute the training data among 20 clients under an independent and identically distributed (IID) data distribution assumption, with each client performing 5 local training epochs per communication round.

The federated learning experiments maintain consistency with our centralized approach while adapting to the distributed nature of FL. The MNIST training dataset of 60,000 samples is equally divided among 20 clients, resulting in 3,000 samples per client. To ensure fair comparison with our centralized results, we define subset sizes as percentages of each client's local data. For instance, a 20% subset corresponds to 600 samples per client, which is equivalent to 1% in the centralized setup.

The training termination criterion is adapted for the federated setting: training stops if the global model's test accuracy does not improve by at least 1% for three consecutive communication rounds, maintaining the early stopping philosophy while accounting for the federated communication structure.

Figure 8 presents the relationship between subset size and both convergence behavior and final accuracy in the federated setting. The results demonstrate patterns consistent with our centralized analysis, though with some notable adaptations to the federated environment.

The mean number of communication rounds required for convergence, shown in Fig. 8b, follows a hyperbolic relationship similar to our centralized findings. However, the federated setting requires more communication rounds due to the distributed nature of training and the need for model aggregation. The fitted curve is described by:

$$y = 2.54 + \frac{192.51 \times 3000}{100 \times s + 12.11 \times 3000} \tag{15}$$

where y represents the mean number of communication rounds and s represents the number of samples per client (ranging from 1 to 3,000).

The accuracy relationship, shown in Fig. 8a, demonstrates that the federated learning setup can achieve comparable performance to centralized training, with the fitted curve described by:

$$y = 0.93 + \frac{-0.3666 \times 3000}{100 \times s - 0.51 \times 3000} \tag{16}$$

where y represents the average test accuracy and s represents the number of samples per client.

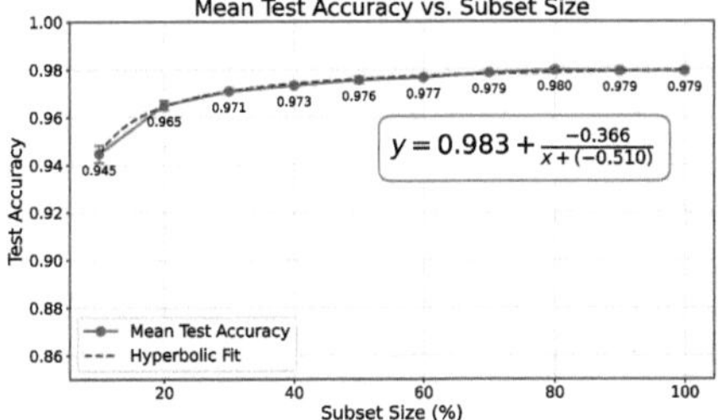

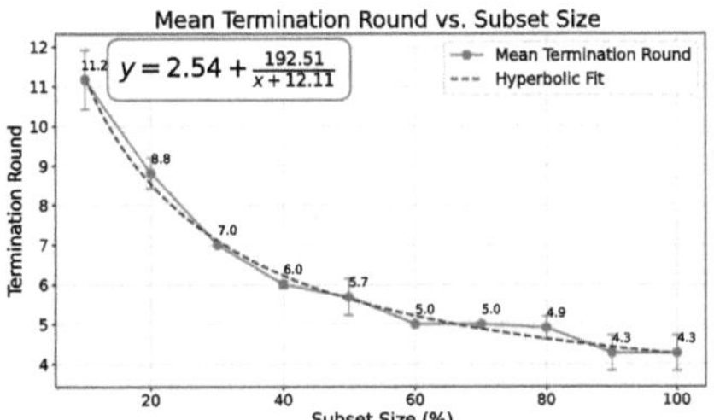

(a) The average test accuracy achieved by the model.

(b) The mean number of epochs required for convergence.

Fig. 8. Impact of Subset Size on Training Epochs and Model Accuracy for MNIST with 20 clients in federated learning with IID dataset distribution.

To calculate the total energy consumption in the federated learning setup, we consider the distributed nature of training across multiple clients. The total energy is computed as the product of the number of clients (20), the number of communication rounds, the number of local epochs per round (5), and the energy consumed per epoch. We utilize the energy per epoch values calculated in our centralized experiments (as presented in Table 3), assuming that server-side energy consumption for model aggregation is negligible compared to client-side training costs.

Figure 9 presents both the total energy consumption and efficiency curves for the federated learning setup. The total energy consumption, shown in Fig. 9a, is calculated using the energy per epoch equation from Table 3, the number of training rounds from Eq. 15, and the accuracy relationship from Eq. 16.

The results reveal that energy consumption decreases as the subset size increases, primarily because the energy consumption per epoch remains relatively stable across different sample sizes (1 to 3,000 samples per client), while the number of training rounds decreases gradually with larger subset sizes. This relationship results in the increasing efficiency pattern shown in Fig. 9b.

However, an important observation emerges from this analysis: given the relatively small size of the dataset after distribution among 20 clients (3,000 samples per client), selecting very small subset sizes becomes counterproductive. Efficiency increases with subset size, making training on the full dataset portion per client the optimal choice.

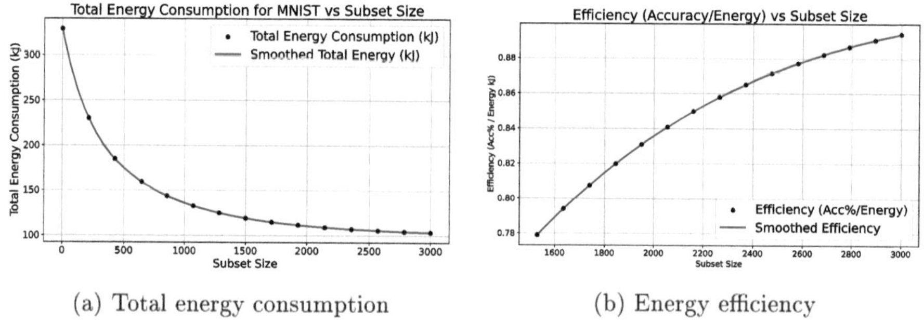

(a) Total energy consumption   (b) Energy efficiency

Fig. 9. Energy consumption and efficiency analysis for MNIST with 20 clients in federated learning with IID dataset distribution.

9   Conclusions

In this work, we provided a comprehensive empirical study of energy consumption in neural network training and introduced a practical framework for balancing accuracy and energy efficiency. Our measurements revealed linear energy scaling laws with respect to dataset size, with coefficients that vary by model complexity but remain largely independent of dataset characteristics. This finding highlights that architecture complexity is the dominant factor in energy consumption, rather than the properties of the training data.

Using these scaling laws, we developed an optimization framework to identify energy-efficient subset sizes. For instance, we showed that peak efficiency occurs at around 5% of the training data for MNIST and Fashion-MNIST and 24% for CIFAR-10, achieving significant energy savings with minimal loss in accuracy. We also demonstrated how these results can be used for practical energy budgeting strategies, such as achieving 80% accuracy on MNIST while saving more than 80% of training energy.

Finally, by extending our framework to a federated learning setup, we validated its generalizability to distributed training scenarios. This shows that our methodology can provide actionable insights for both centralized and decentralized AI training through extension to federated learning environments with 20-client configurations.

We have several important avenues warraning future investigation. Developing adaptive subset selection algorithms that dynamically adjust data usage during training without requiring pre-computed energy curves would make our approach more accessible for new datasets and one-time training scenarios. Investigating how our scaling laws apply to text-processing models such as RNNs and LSTMs. Finally, examining whether data heterogeneity affects energy scaling patterns in non-IID federated learning settings would complete our understanding of energy consumption in realistic distributed scenarios.

The energy models and optimization frameworks presented in this work provide immediate practical value for practitioners training models on CIFAR-10, MNIST, and Fashion-MNIST datasets. More broadly, our methodology establishes a template for deriving energy scaling laws for new datasets and architectures, advancing the field toward more sustainable AI development practices.

Acknowledgments. This work was partially supported by the French National Research Agency (ANR) under grant ANR-22-CE23-0024 (project DELIGHT).

References

1. Grid'5000—large-scale flexible experimental testbed. https://www.grid5000.fr. Accessed 25 Mar. 2026 19:46:46
2. MoJITOs—monitoring java infrastructure for tracing and observability solutions (2023). https://gitlab.irit.fr/sepia-pub/mojitos
3. Aquino-Brítez, S., García-Sánchez, P., Ortiz, A., Aquino-Brítez, D.: Towards an energy consumption index for deep learning models: a comparative analysis of architectures, gpus, and measurement tools. Sensors **25**(3) (2025). https://doi.org/10.3390/s25030846, https://www.mdpi.com/1424-8220/25/3/846
4. Chen, T., Moreau, T., Jiang, Z., Zheng, L., Yan, E., Shen, H., Deshpande, M., Lai, Z., Wang, J., Li, Y., et al.: Tvm: An end-to-end IR stack for deep learning systems. In: 13th USENIX Symposium on Operating Systems Design and Implementation (OSDI 18), pp. 379–394. USENIX Association (2018)
5. Chen, Y.H., Krishna, T., Emer, J., Sze, V.: Eyeriss: a spatial architecture for energy-efficient dataflows in CNNs. In: 2016 ACM/IEEE 43rd Annual International Symposium on Computer Architecture (ISCA), pp. 367–379. IEEE (2016)
6. Cheng, Y., Wang, D., Zhou, P., Zhang, T.: A survey of model compression and acceleration for deep neural networks. IEEE Signal Process. Mag. **35**(1), 126–136 (2018). https://doi.org/10.1109/MSP.2017.2765695
7. Choi, J., Liu, H., Kim, M., Oh, T., Sung, D.: Power and energy characterization of deep learning models on mobile platforms. In: 2018 IEEE 24th International Symposium on High Performance Computer Architecture (HPCA), pp. 111–122. IEEE (2018)
8. Dong, K., Zhou, C., Ruan, Y., Li, Y.: Mobilenetv2 model for image classification. In: 2020 2nd International Conference on Information Technology and Computer Application (ITCA), pp. 476–480 (2020). https://api.semanticscholar.org/CorpusID:233990160

9. Goodfellow, I., Bengio, Y., Courville, A.: Deep Learning. MIT Press (2016). http://www.deeplearningbook.org

10. Haddaji, O., Brun, O., Prabhu, B.: Optimizing energy in supervised learning with data summarization: a comparative study, accepted by 12th International Conference on Networks, Game, Control and Optimization (NetGCoop), Bilbao, Spain, 8–10 Oct. 2025

11. Hastie, T., Tibshirani, R., Friedman, J.: The Elements of Statistical Learning: Data Mining, Inference, and Prediction, 2nd ed. Springer (2009)

12. Mirzasoleiman, B., Badanidiyuru, A., Karbasi, A., Vondrák, J., Krause, A.: Lazier than lazy greedy. In: Proceedings of the 29th AAAI Conference on Artificial Intelligence (AAAI '15), pp. 1812–1818 (2015). https://doi.org/10.1145/2783258.2783262, https://www.aaai.org/ocs/index.php/AAAI/AAAI15/paper/view/10014, proposes the Approximate Lazy Greedy algorithm with theoretical guarantees

13. Mishra, R., Gupta, H., Dutta, T.: A survey on deep neural network compression: challenges, overview, and solutions, Oct. 2020. https://doi.org/10.48550/arXiv.2010.03954

14. Rodriguez, C., Degioanni, L., Kameni, L., Vidal, R., Neglia, G.: Evaluating the energy consumption of machine learning: systematic literature review and experiments (2024). zrXiv:abs/2408.15128, https://api.semanticscholar.org/CorpusID:271963423

15. Sze, V., Chen, Y.H., Yang, T.J., Emer, J.S.: Efficient processing of deep neural networks: a tutorial and survey. Proc. IEEE **105**(12), 2295–2329 (Dec2017)

16. Tan, M., Le, Q.: EfficientNet: Rethinking model scaling for convolutional neural networks. In: Chaudhuri, K., Salakhutdinov, R. (eds.) Proceedings of the 36th International Conference on Machine Learning. Proceedings of Machine Learning Research, vol. 97, pp. 6105–6114. PMLR. 09–15 June 2019. https://proceedings.mlr.press/v97/tan19a.html

17. Tripp, C.E., Perr-Sauer, J., Gafur, J., Nag, A., Purkayastha, A., Zisman, S., Bensen, E.A.: Measuring the energy consumption and efficiency of deep neural networks: An empirical analysis and design recommendations (2024). arxiv: abs/2403.08151. http://dblp.uni-trier.de/db/journals/corr/corr2403.html#abs-2403-08151

18. Wei, K., Iyer, R., Bilmes, J.: Fast multi-stage submodular maximization. In: Xing, E.P., Jebara, T. (eds.) Proceedings of the 31st International Conference on Machine Learning. Proceedings of Machine Learning Research, vol. 32, pp. 1494–1502. PMLR, Bejing, China, 22–24 June 2014. https://proceedings.mlr.press/v32/wei14.html

19. Yang, T.J., Chen, Y.H., Sze, V.: Designing energy-efficient convolutional neural networks using energy-aware pruning . In: 2017 IEEE Conference on Computer Vision and Pattern Recognition (CVPR), pp. 6071–6079. IEEE Computer Society, Los Alamitos, CA, USA, July 2017. https://doi.org/10.1109/CVPR.2017.643, https://doi.ieeecomputersociety.org/10.1109/CVPR.2017.643

20. Yang, T.J., Chen, Y.H., Sze, V., Emer, J.S.: Efficient processing of deep neural networks: a tutorial and survey. Proc. IEEE **105**(12), 2295–2329 (2017)

Multi-Objective IoT Service Placement in Cloud-Fog-Edge Environments Using Deep Reinforcement Learning

Mohamed Bouaziz[1,2], Hassan Hassan[1(✉)],
Abdel Kader Chabi Sika Boni[1], and Khalil Drira[1]

[1] LAAS-CNRS, Université de Toulouse, CNRS, UPS, Toulouse, France
`hassan.hassan@laas.fr`
[2] Ecole Polytechnique de Tunisie, Carthage, Tunisia

Abstract. The rapid proliferation of Internet of Things devices introduces significant challenges in determining optimal service placement across heterogeneous computing layers, spanning from centralized cloud servers to decentralized fog and edge nodes. Effective placement is essential to minimize latency, reduce energy consumption, and control costs, all while adhering to resource constraints such as limited memory and processing capacity. In this paper, we investigate several strategies for solving the IoT service placement problem. To overcome the limited adaptability of traditional optimization approaches, we introduce dynamic resource management in the simulation environment *YAFS* and propose a Deep Reinforcement Learning–based approach utilizing a Double Deep Q-Network (DDQN) architecture. The DRL agent autonomously learns placement policies through continuous interaction with the environment, optimizing a weighted multi-objective reward that balances execution time, energy efficiency, and cost. Experimental evaluations were conducted under two scenarios: memory-only constraints and combined memory plus CPU constraints. Results demonstrate that the DRL-based strategy consistently outperforms baseline approaches, including three meta-heuristic optimization methods—Genetic Algorithm, Simulated Annealing, and Tabu Search—as well as the cloud-only strategy, across all performance metrics.

Keywords: Deep reinforcement learning · IoT Service Placement · Cloud-fog-edge environment

1 Introduction

The growth of interconnected devices within Internet of Things (IoT) networks continues to accelerate exponentially. These devices find applications across diverse domains including intelligent urban systems, medical services, manufacturing sectors, and mobility solutions. They generate and transmit substantial data volumes while frequently requiring immediate or near-instantaneous

S. Boumerdassi et al. (Eds.): MLN 2025, LNCS 16424, pp. 173–191, 2026.
https://doi.org/10.1007/978-3-032-18494-8_12

processing responses. Nevertheless, the majority of IoT endpoints possess constrained form factors with restricted energy resources, memory capacity, and computational power. Consequently, these devices cannot independently execute sophisticated operations and must delegate computational workloads to external infrastructure.

Typically, this computational delegation targets cloud platforms, which deliver robust processing capabilities and extensive storage resources. Although this approach proves effective across numerous scenarios, exclusive cloud dependency can introduce **response delay challenges**, particularly when cloud facilities are positioned at considerable geographical distances. This limitation becomes especially problematic for time-critical applications such as self-driving vehicles or automated manufacturing systems.

To mitigate these constraints, the **Cloud-Fog-Edge** environment positions computational resources nearer to data generation points, thereby minimizing delays and enhancing system responsiveness. Nevertheless, deciding the optimal service deployment location (whether at edge, fog, or cloud tiers) presents significant complexity and importance. Suboptimal deployment decisions can elevate response latencies, energy consumption, and operational expenses.

To address this challenge, we employ the **YAFS** (Yet Another Fog Simulator) [13] framework, an open-source simulation environment specifically designed for modeling IoT and fog computing scenarios. YAFS provides flexible topology management, dynamic workload generation, and customizable performance metrics, making it particularly suitable for evaluating distributed resource allocation strategies.

Building upon this environment, we propose a novel approach based on a Deep Reinforcement Learning (DRL) agent. Simulation results using this method are promising, as the proposed agent not only performs competitively with traditional meta-heuristic algorithms widely used in the literature but also demonstrates the ability to adapt to environmental dynamics representative of real IoT infrastructures.

The contributions of this work are as follows:

- We introduce a Deep Reinforcement Learning IoT service placement approach in Cloud-Fog-Edge Environments.
- We extend the YAFS simulator in order to make changes in the resources dynamic allowing the DRL agent to learn by experience.
- We evaluate the performance of our agent against three metaheuristic agents: Simulated Anealing, Tabu Search and Genetic Algorithm.

The rest of this paper is organized as follows. In Sect. 2, we reviewed previous works that have also addressed the problem of placing IoT services in IoT environments. The IoT serivce placement problem is formally defined in Sect. 3. Our proposed DRL agent is presented in Sect. 4, and its performance is compared to three metaheuristic agents in Sect. 5. Finally, we conclude the paper in Sect. 6 and outline possible directions for future extensions of this work.

2   Related Work

The complexity of IoT service placement has led researchers to explore various optimization approaches, ranging from traditional meta-heuristic algorithms to advanced machine learning techniques. A significant portion of existing research has employed meta-heuristic optimization algorithms to address the multi-objective nature of service placement problems [5,11]. These algorithms have proven effective in handling the complex constraints and trade-offs inherent in fog computing environments while providing near-optimal solutions within reasonable computational time. Recent studies have also explored nature-inspired algorithms and quantum-inspired optimization techniques for addressing the growing complexity of IoT service placement in distributed environments [3,19].

Hybrid meta-heuristic approaches have gained considerable attention due to their ability to leverage the strengths of multiple optimization techniques. Research has demonstrated that combining different meta-heuristic algorithms can achieve superior performance compared to individual approaches [2]. For instance, studies have shown that integrating Genetic Algorithms with Simulated Annealing can provide better trade-offs among multiple objectives such as makespan, energy consumption, and cost, while achieving faster convergence rates. Similarly, the combination of evolutionary algorithms with stochastic sampling methods has proven effective in dynamic fog environments, where Monte Carlo simulations are used for initial solution space exploration followed by Genetic Algorithm refinement to evolve QoS-aware placement configurations [12]. Recent research has also investigated whale optimization algorithms for cost-efficient service placement, demonstrating the effectiveness of bio-inspired algorithms in determining optimal placement plans across distributed fog nodes [15]. Furthermore, deadline-aware multi-objective optimization approaches using parallel genetic algorithms have been proposed to address time-sensitive IoT applications, combining First Fit Decreasing heuristics with evolutionary optimization to improve placement efficiency [1].

Machine learning and artificial intelligence approaches have emerged as promising alternatives to traditional optimization methods, particularly for handling dynamic environments and learning from historical data. Classification-based approaches have been employed to model task offloading decisions, where machine learning algorithms determine optimal placement strategies based on various system parameters including task characteristics, resource availability, network conditions, and energy consumption patterns [7]. These data-driven methods have shown improved accuracy and efficiency compared to heuristic-based approaches, particularly in mobile fog computing scenarios.

Deep reinforcement learning techniques have been applied to address long-term optimization challenges in multi-service placement across heterogeneous computing layers [14]. These approaches model the placement problem as utility maximization tasks, where intelligent agents learn to balance multiple objectives such as latency minimization and cost optimization through continuous interaction with the environment. The ability of deep learning models to capture complex relationships between system parameters and adapt to changing conditions makes them particularly suitable for dynamic fog computing environments. Advanced reinforcement learning approaches, including double deep Q-networks (DDQN) [9] with prioritized experience replay, have been proposed to better capture temporal patterns of service resource demand and improve placement decisions over time [4]. Additionally, QoS-aware placement mechanisms based on open-source development models have been investigated to enhance service placement effectiveness in distributed IoT environments [6].

Mathematical programming approaches have also been explored, particularly for problems that can be formulated as integer programming or non-linear programming tasks [18]. These methods often focus on specific optimization objectives, such as minimizing service delay for latency-sensitive applications. Hybrid approaches combining mathematical programming with meta-heuristic techniques have shown promising results, where the precision of mathematical models is enhanced by the exploration capabilities of evolutionary algorithms. Such combinations have achieved significant improvements in service delay reduction and delay violation rates when evaluated using real network traffic traces. Multi-objective fault-tolerant optimization algorithms have been developed to address the deployment challenges of IoT applications on fog computing infrastructure, focusing on minimizing bandwidth wastage, resource consumption, and power usage while ensuring system reliability [16]. Recent studies have also investigated GA-PSO hybrid algorithms for multi-objective task scheduling in fog computing environments, specifically targeting big data applications where both latency reduction and energy efficiency are critical [10].

Although many studies have explored IoT service placement using heuristic and meta-heuristic methods, there are still several challenges that have not been fully addressed. Most existing solutions focus on optimizing a single objective, such as latency or energy, without considering the trade-offs between multiple goals. In addition, many simulators used in previous work, like iFogSim [8] or EdgeCloudSim [17], are limited in flexibility and do not support real-time or dynamic changes in the system. While Deep Reinforcement Learning (DRL) has recently been used to improve placement decisions, these approaches often lack a suitable simulation environment that can provide rich and realistic observations. Current simulators are not always designed to support the specific needs of DRL agents, such as dynamic topologies or detailed environment feedback. As a result, it becomes difficult to train and evaluate DRL models effectively.

3   Problem Statement

The IoT service placement problem in CloudFogEdge environments represents a multi-objective, constrained optimization challenge. It involves determining the optimal deployment of application modules across a hierarchical three-layer architecture. The primary goal is to make placement decisions that minimize execution time, energy consumption, and operational cost, while satisfying system constraints such as resource availability and application deadlines. Additionally, these decisions must be robust under dynamic and realistic operational conditions, such as network variability, node mobility, and workload fluctuations. This optimization problem becomes especially complex due to the conflicting nature of its objectives and the large number of possible service-to-device mappings. Advanced algorithmic techniques are required to navigate this space effectively and produce placement solutions that are both feasible and efficient.

3.1   Optimization Objectives

The goal of the optimization process is to identify a placement strategy that balances three key objectives:

Execution Time: This is the total time required to complete a service request - from generation to final response. It includes:

- **Processing Delay:** Time consumed by module execution on the hosting device, depending on the device's IPT and load.
- **Network Transmission Delay:** Includes propagation delay, queuing delay, and bandwidth-related delays during message transmission.

Cost: Reflects the monetary impact of executing services across the infrastructure. It includes:

- **Resource Cost:** Fees associated with the use of computing power, storage, and bandwidth resources.
- **Data Transmission Cost:** Charges incurred when transferring data across layers, especially to remote cloud servers.

Energy Consumption: Critical for energy-constrained devices. It includes:

- **Computational Energy:** Energy required to process tasks on a node.
- **Communication Energy:** Energy used for data transmission over the network.
- **Idle Energy:** Power consumed when a device is powered on but not actively executing a task.

The optimization problem is mathematically expressed as follows:

$$\min_{x_{ij}} \sum_{s \in S} \sum_{d \in D} x_{ij} \left(\alpha f_m(s,d) + \beta f_e(s,d) + \gamma f_c(s,d) \right)$$

Notation

- x_{ij}: Binary decision variable (1 if module i is placed on device j, 0 otherwise)
- $f_m(s,d)$: Execution Time function for placing service s on device d
- $f_e(s,d)$: Energy consumption function
- $f_c(s,d)$: Cost function
- α, β, γ: Weight coefficients for latency, energy, and cost, respectively
- S: Set of service modules
- D: Set of candidate devices (Edge, Fog, Cloud)

Decision Variables: The binary decision variable $x_{ij} \in \{0,1\}$ indicates whether module i is placed on device j. The goal is to compute a valid assignment of x_{ij} values that minimizes the combined weighted objective function, while adhering to system constraints such as memory capacity, device availability, and application-specific QoS requirements.

3.2   Constraints and Challenges

System Constraints The IoT service placement problem must respect several critical system constraints to ensure that service deployments are feasible and executable within the available infrastructure:

- **Memory Constraint:** Each module must be deployed on a device with sufficient available memory. This is expressed as:

$$RAM_{module} \leq RAM_{device}$$

  This ensures that modules are not placed on under-provisioned nodes, which could lead to simulation failure or unrealistic configurations.
- **CPU Constraint:** Each module also requires a certain amount of processing power. The selected node must have enough available CPU resources to satisfy this requirement:

$$CPU_{module} < CPU_{device}$$

  This constraint prevents deployment on overloaded nodes and ensures accurate simulation of computational limitations.

Optimization Challenges
In addition to satisfying hard system constraints, the optimization process faces several major challenges that stem from the nature of distributed IoT environments and the complexity of the placement task:

- **Dynamic Scenarios**: Real-world IoT systems are dynamic - devices may fail, move, or experience load fluctuations. Supporting these behaviors requires extending the simulator (YAFS) to handle time-dependent events and reactive behavior.
- **Multi-Objective Trade-offs**: Placement decisions must simultaneously optimize for execution time, cost, and energy - often conflicting objectives. Improving one metric (e.g., execution time) may degrade another (e.g., energy efficiency), necessitating intelligent trade-offs.
- **Scalability**: The placement algorithm must scale to large and complex topologies with many modules and devices. Exact methods are computationally infeasible; thus, this work employs meta-heuristics and Deep Reinforcement Learning (DRL) to find near-optimal solutions efficiently.
- **Simulator Enhancements**: To handle dynamic and intelligent behavior, YAFS was extended to support adaptive simulation features, such as dynamic topology updates, real-time resource checks, and feedback-driven placement decisions.

3.3   Performance Metrics

To evaluate and compare the effectiveness of different placement strategies, this work uses a multi-dimensional performance evaluation framework. It includes the following core metrics:

- **Execution Time**: Measures end-to-end delay for service completion.
- **Cost**: Summarizes resource usage, transmission expenses, and operational overhead.
- **Energy Consumption**: Includes energy used for processing, communication, and idle time.

Each algorithm or strategy tested is assessed based on how well it balances these three metrics. The goal is to identify placement solutions that optimize system performance while ensuring sustainability and economic efficiency.

4 DRL Agent

This section presents a DRL-based approach for solving the IoT service placement problem in a dynamic CloudFogEdge architecture. The DRL agent learns to make placement decisions by interacting with the environment and receiving feedback in the form of rewards based on system performance.

4.1 Environment Design

The placement problem is modeled, where:

- The environment represents the IoT infrastructure and all its characteristics,
- The agent is responsible for selecting where to place each service module,
- The state is the current view of the system (e.g., available resources),
- The action is the selection of a device (node) for deploying a module,
- The reward reflects how good the placement is in terms of latency, energy, and cost.

Modules are placed sequentially, one at a time, across cloud, fog, and edge nodes. For each module, the agent observes the current state and selects the node ID where it should be deployed. The environment then returns the next state and a reward based on the quality of that decision.

4.2 State Representation

The state at each step contains all the relevant information needed to make a placement decision. This includes the characteristics of:

- All nodes (e.g., IPT(Instructions Per Time), RAM, cost, energy),
- The module to be placed (e.g., RAM requirements,CPU requirements),
- The message that will be processed (e.g., data size, number of instructions).

The state is represented as:

$$\text{Observation} = [\underbrace{\text{IPT}_1, \text{RAM}_1, \text{Cost}_1, \text{Energy}_1, \text{IPT}_2, \text{RAM}_2, \text{Cost}_2, \text{Energy}_2, \ldots]}_{\text{Node Characteristics}},$$

$$\underbrace{[\text{RAM}, \text{CPU}, \ldots]}_{\text{Module Characteristics}}, \underbrace{[\text{bytes}_1, \text{instructions}_1, \ldots]}_{\text{Message Characteristics}}$$

This observation vector allows the DRL agent to reason about the suitability of each node for the current module, taking into account both performance and resource constraints.

4.3 Application Generator for DRL Training

In order to ensure the DRL agent learns a placement policy that can generalize across diverse application scenarios, we developed a custom application and message generator. This generator creates varied application graphs at each training episode by:

- Randomly choosing the number of applications and modules,
- Assigning random RAM and CPU requirements to modules,
- Defining dynamic message characteristics such as size and computational workload.

This diversity introduces stochasticity and variability into the training environment, exposing the agent to a wide range of possible placements and constraints.

4.4 Action Space Definition

The action space is discrete and corresponds to the indices of all available nodes in the topology. Each action represents the selection of a specific node (edge, fog, or cloud) for placing the current module.

At every decision step:

- The agent chooses an action a, which corresponds to a node ID,
- The environment checks whether the selected node is valid (has enough RAM and CPU),
- If valid, the module is deployed, and the environment transitions to the next state,
- If invalid, the action is rejected, and a penalty reward is given.

This approach allows the agent to learn placement strategies that balance execution efficiency with resource feasibility.

4.5 Reward Function

The reward function plays a key role in guiding the agent to learn optimal placement policies. It is defined as the negative weighted sum of three key metrics:

- Execution Time: Time taken to complete the service request.
- Energy: Energy consumed during module execution.
- Cost: Financial cost of computation and communication.

$$Reward\ Function = -(w_1 \times Execution\ Time + w_2 \times Energy + w_3 \times Cost) \quad (1)$$

where w_1, w_2, and w_3 are weights used to balance the importance of each factor based on the specific optimization priorities.

The reward is negative because the agents goal is to minimize time, energy, and cost. A poor placement receives a higher penalty, while an efficient placement results in a less negative reward.

Additionally, if the agent tries to place a module on a node with insufficient RAM or CPU, a penalty of -1 is immediately returned, and the action is rejected. This encourages the agent to avoid invalid decisions during training.

4.6 Training Methodology

The agent was trained using a standard Deep Reinforcement Learning (DRL) loop, where experience is gathered through repeated interaction with a simulated environment and later used to optimize the agents decision-making policy.

Each training episode begins by generating a new application scenario using the custom Application Generator. This ensures that the agent is exposed to diverse service graphs with varying numbers of modules, RAM and CPU requirements, and communication patterns. For each generated module, the agent receives the current system state, which includes the topologys node characteristics, the modules resource demands, and the network conditions.

Using this observation, the agent selects an action - that is, a specific node ID where the module will be placed - according to an epsilon-greedy policy. This approach introduces a balance between exploration (random action selection) and exploitation (choosing the best-known action based on Q-values). In early episodes, the agent explores frequently to discover new strategies; as training progresses, epsilon decays, and the agent relies more on what it has learned.

Upon taking an action, the extended YAFS simulator evaluates the result of the placement. If the node has sufficient resources, the module is deployed, and the simulator returns a reward based on execution time, energy consumption, and cost. If the action is invalid (e.g., insufficient RAM or CPU), the placement is rejected, and a penalty reward is issued. The resulting (state, action, reward, next_state) tuple is stored in an experience replay buffer.

At regular intervals, the agent samples a mini-batch of past experiences from the buffer to train its online Q-network. This technique reduces correlation between training samples and improves generalization. Meanwhile, a separate target network is used to compute stable Q-value targets, and it is periodically synchronized with the online network to ensure learning stability.

This training loop is repeated across thousands of episodes, with new applications and modules generated in each cycle. The result is a DRL agent capable of learning general, resource-aware placement strategies that adapt to varying workloads in a dynamic CloudFogEdge system.

4.7 Implementation Details

The DRL-based service placement framework was implemented in Python, using a modular design that integrates deep learning, fog simulation, and adaptive decision-making components.

The DDQN agent was built using the PyTorch framework, which facilitated the design and training of the underlying neural network models. To simplify and structure the reinforcement learning workflow, in this work we use PFRL, a PyTorch-compatible library that supports experience replay, epsilon scheduling, and target network updates.

The simulation engine was based on YAFS , which was extended extensively to support:

- Real-time resource management, including the ability to check and update available RAM and CPU during module deployment,
- Reward integration, enabling the environment to return immediate feedback based on the validity and efficiency of each placement.

The agents decisions were embedded directly into YAFSs event loop. When a placement action is selected, the simulator either accepts it - updating node states and computing the corresponding reward - or rejects it if the action violates resource constraints, triggering a penalty signal.

To create rich and variable training scenarios, a custom Application and Message Generator was implemented. This generator dynamically constructs new applications for each episode by:

- Randomly defining the number of applications and their internal modules,
- Assigning randomized RAM and CPU requirements to each module,
- Generating message flows with variable data sizes and computational loads between modules.

This mechanism ensures the agent is exposed to a wide range of application topologies, workloads, and constraints, which enhances the generalization capacity of the learned policy.

Together, these components form a complete and adaptive DRL training environment capable of learning robust and intelligent placement strategies in dynamic, real-world-inspired CloudFogEdge infrastructures.

5 Experimental Evaluation

This section presents the experimental setup and results used to evaluate the effectiveness of the Double DQN-based placement strategy in a dynamic CloudFogEdge environment. The evaluation was conducted through multiple training experiments, each using different hyperparameter configurations, to study the impact of training dynamics on performance.

5.1   Environment Configurations

The simulation environment was implemented using the extended version of the YAFS simulator, configured to model a moderately sized distributed infrastructure. The base topology included:

- 5 Fog nodes, each connected to the central proxy server and interconnected with one another,
- 1 Edge node per Fog node, forming a hierarchical Cloud-Fog-Edge structure,
- Simulation time set to 20,000 time units.

To increase the training challenge and ensure that the DRL agent learns effective resource-aware policies, the total Resource assigned to generated modules was calibrated to consume approximately 50% of the total available Resource in the topology. This forces the agent to make trade-offs and learn valid placements under constrained resource conditions.

Additionally, to promote generalization and diverse behavior, the Application and Message Generator was used to generate dynamic workloads at every training episode. The configuration was as follows:

Application Generator:

- Randomly selects 1 to 3 applications per episode,
- Each application consists of 3 to 5 modules,
- For each module, assign a random RAM value between 10 and 50.
- For each module, assign a random CPU value between 10×10^6 and 300×10^6.

Message Generator:

- Randomly select the message size in bytes from the list: [500, 1000, 1500, 2000],
- Randomly assign the number of instructions between 100×10^6 and 5000×10^6.

Three independent experiments were conducted (Table 1), each using a different training configuration to compare convergence behavior and cumulative rewards.

5.2   Training Parameters

The agent architecture used in all experiments consisted of a fully connected neural network with two hidden layers. The base structure was kept consistent across experiments, but various hyperparameters were tuned to study their effect.

All experiments were trained using the Prioritized Experience Replay Buffer and epsilon-greedy exploration strategy with linear decay, as implemented in the PFRL framework.

Key Parameters:

- Network: Two hidden layers with ReLU activation,
- Replay Buffer: `PrioritizedReplayBuffer` with configurable capacity and priority decay,
- Exploration: Epsilon-greedy with decaying epsilon from 1.0 to a final value,
- Training loop: Maximum 3001 episodes, using evaluation every 5 episodes.

Table 1. Comparison of Hyperparameters Across Three Experiments

Parameter	Experiment 1	Experiment 2	Experiment 3
Learning rate	1×10^{-4}	1×10^{-3}	5×10^{-4}
End epsilon	0.35	0.2	0.2
Replay buffer capacity	1,000,000	1,000,000	500,000
Decay steps	30,000	15,000	50,000
Minibatch size	216	64	256
Target update interval	15,000	5,000	10,000
Discount factor (γ)	0.99	0.95	0.95
Num steps	1	5	3

5.3   Performance Analysis

To assess the learning performance of the DRL agent, we monitored the cumulative reward convergence across training episodes for each of the three experiments (Fig. 1).

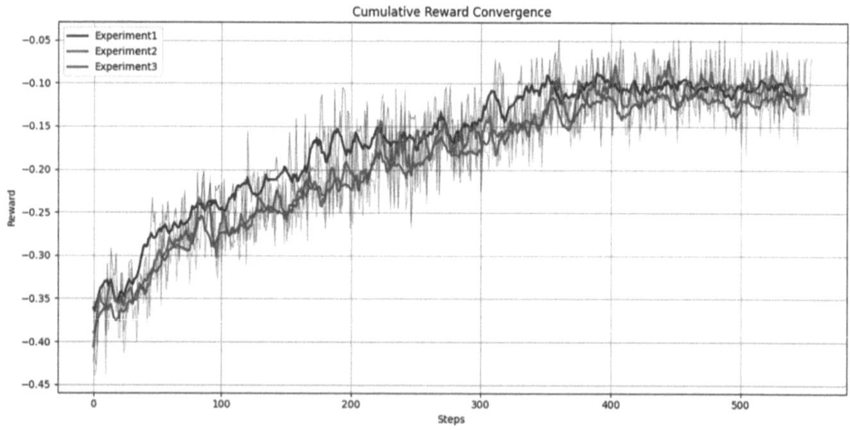

Fig. 1. Cumulative Reward Convergence

The graph illustrates the cumulative reward curves for all three configurations:

Key observations:

- All experiments demonstrate progressive reward improvement, confirming that the agent successfully learned effective placement strategies.
- Experiment 1 achieved the most stable and highest reward convergence, indicating well-balanced exploration and learning stability.
- Experiment 2 showed faster early improvement due to aggressive learning and faster decay but plateaued slightly earlier.
- Experiment 3 achieved comparable results with smoother training dynamics and a larger replay buffer, indicating better sample diversity.

Overall, the results validate the importance of hyperparameter tuning in DRL training for resource-constrained IoT service placement. The trained agents were able to learn generalizable strategies across dynamic applications and topologies, confirming the robustness of the proposed DRL-based framework.

5.4   Results Interpretation

Results Under RAM Constrained

In this experiment, the simulation topology was dynamically updated to reflect RAM consumption after each module deployment. Specifically, once a module is placed on a node, the nodes available RAM is decreased by the modules RAM requirement, ensuring that subsequent placement decisions are influenced by the nodes current resource availability. The evaluated topology consists of **1 Cloud Node, 1 Proxy Node, 5 Fog Nodes** (all interconnected), and **5 Edge Nodes**, where each Fog node is connected to one Edge node. The total simulation time in YAFS is set to **20,000 time units**.

This evaluation compares the performance of the Deep Reinforcement Learning algorithm against three meta-heuristic algorithms—Genetic Algorithm, Simulated Annealing, and Tabu Search—as well as a baseline strategy where all IoT service modules are deployed in the cloud. A consistent set of five applications was used across all experiments, with their modules configured to consume approximately 50% of the total available RAM in the topology. The application and network parameters (e.g., RAM, CPU capacities, bandwidth, and latency) were derived from realistic IoT configurations reported in previous studies using the *YAFS* and *iFogSim* simulators, ensuring that the evaluation reflects practical deployment conditions rather than random values. The performance of each algorithm was assessed based on three core metrics: *Execution Time, Energy Consumption*, and *Cost*, with the following weights applied to compute the weighted reward function: $w_1 = 0.6$ for execution time, $w_2 = 0.2$ for energy consumption, and $w_3 = 0.2$ for cost. These weights were selected to reflect the priorities of latency-sensitive IoT applications, where execution time is the most critical objective for ensuring real-time responsiveness, while still maintaining reasonable energy efficiency and cost control. All algorithms were tested under identical simulation settings, and the best-performing configuration for each was selected after training and multiple experiments. The results presented here highlight algorithm performance under RAM-only constraints.

Interpretation of X-Axis-Application Repetition: The x-axis in all the comparative plots represents the number of application repetitions during the simulation period. This value increases proportionally with simulation time and reflects how often the same application is executed across the network. As application repetitions increase, resource contention on the nodes also rises. This causes application modules to wait for previously deployed tasks to finish execution, leading to increased execution time, energy usage, and operational cost. Therefore, it is expected that all three metrics rise with the number of repetitions, reflecting realistic load dynamics in the network (Fig. 2).

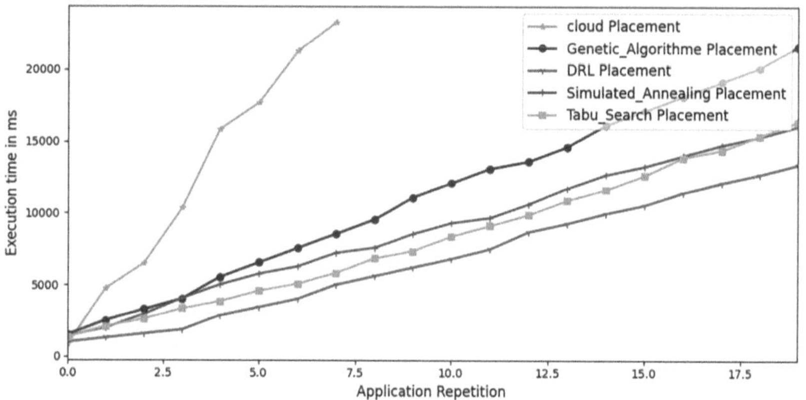

Fig. 2. Execution Time versus Application Repetition

Interpretation: DRL shows the best performance with the lowest execution time, followed by Simulated Annealing and Tabu Search. Genetic Algorithm performs moderately, while Cloud Placement exhibits the worst performance due to latency from centralized processing. This confirms that local decision-making enables faster task execution (Fig. 3).

Interpretation: DRL Placement consistently achieves the lowest energy consumption, reflecting efficient use of nearby nodes and intelligent load distribution. Simulated Annealing and Tabu Search also perform well, reducing energy use compared to the cloud strategy. Genetic Algorithm is less energy-efficient than the other heuristics. The Cloud Placement baseline consumes the highest energy due to its reliance on distant centralized infrastructure (Fig. 4).

Interpretation: DRL achieves the lowest cost among all approaches, leveraging cost-effective edge/fog nodes. Simulated Annealing and Tabu Search strategies remain economically efficient. The Genetic Algorithm incurs more cost than these two, while Cloud Placement shows a sharp increase in cost with repetition due to heavy reliance on expensive centralized computing.

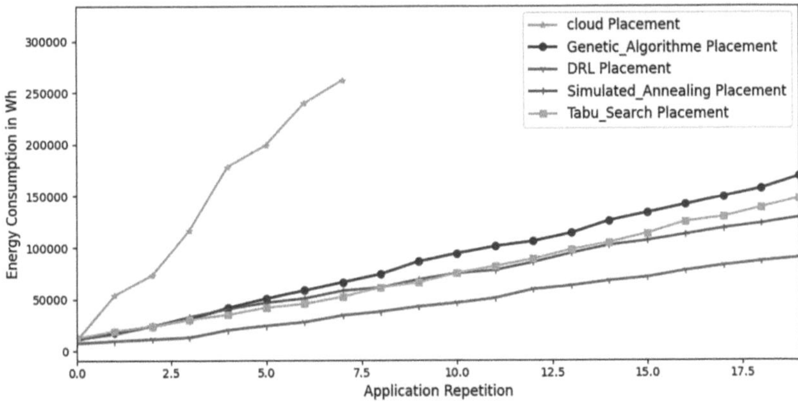

Fig. 3. Energy Consumption versus Application Repetition

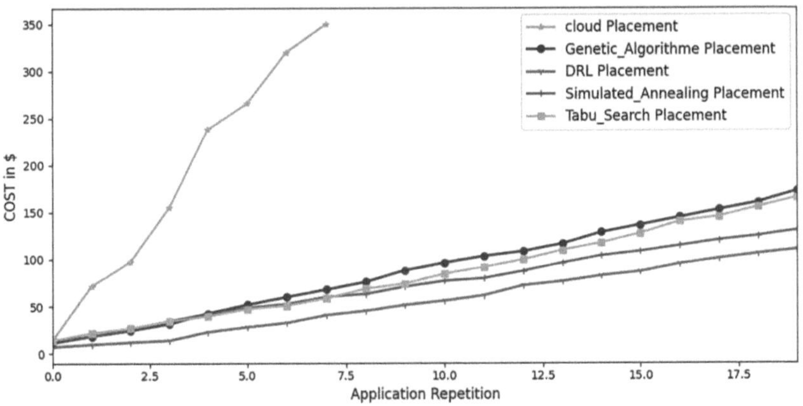

Fig. 4. Cost versus Application Repetition

DRL placement is the most effective across all metrics—energy, execution time, and cost—demonstrating strong adaptability and learning capability. Simulated Annealing and Tabu Search offer a good balance between performance and simplicity. The Genetic Algorithm lags slightly behind but outperforms the cloud baseline. Cloud-only placement remains the least optimal in dynamic and resource-constrained environments.

Results Under RAM + CPU Constraints

This experiment extends the RAM-only scenario by introducing an additional **CPU constraint**. In this setup, after deploying a module on a node, both the node's available **RAM and CPU resources** are dynamically decreased according to the module's requirements. This enhancement ensures that subsequent placement decisions consider the real-time availability of both memory and processing capacity, leading to a more realistic simulation of constrained IoT environments.

The overall simulation topology, number of applications, and experimental settings remain the same as described in the RAM-only evaluation. The main difference here is that both RAM and CPU are dynamically updated after each deployment (Fig. 5).

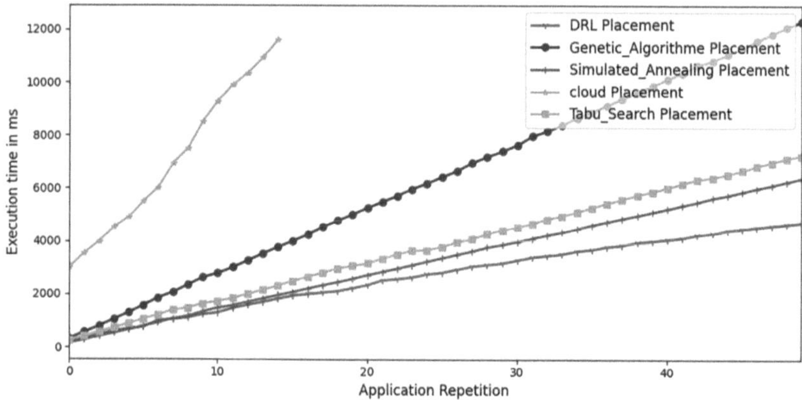

Fig. 5. Execution Time versus Application Repetition under RAM + CPU Constraints

Interpretation: With both RAM and CPU limitations, the DRL algorithm continues to achieve the lowest execution time, showing its capability to manage multiple resource constraints effectively. Simulated Annealing and Tabu Search also maintain strong performance, while the Genetic Algorithm lags slightly behind. Cloud Placement again suffers from the highest latency due to centralized processing (Fig. 6).

Interpretation: DRL continues to provide the most energy-efficient placements, balancing memory and CPU resource usage effectively. Simulated Annealing and Tabu Search follow closely, while the Genetic Algorithm consumes slightly more energy. As in the RAM-only case, the Cloud Placement baseline consumes the most energy due to longer communication paths and centralized computation (Fig. 7).

Interpretation: DRL achieves the lowest cost by efficiently utilizing both RAM and CPU resources across edge and fog nodes. Simulated Annealing and Tabu Search remain cost-effective but slightly less optimized than DRL. The Genetic Algorithm again incurs higher costs than these two heuristics. The Cloud-only placement shows the highest cost due to reliance on expensive centralized resources.

To provide a clearer quantitative comparison, we summarize in Table 2 the percentage improvements achieved by DRL over competing strategies across the three key performance metrics: execution time, energy consumption, and cost.

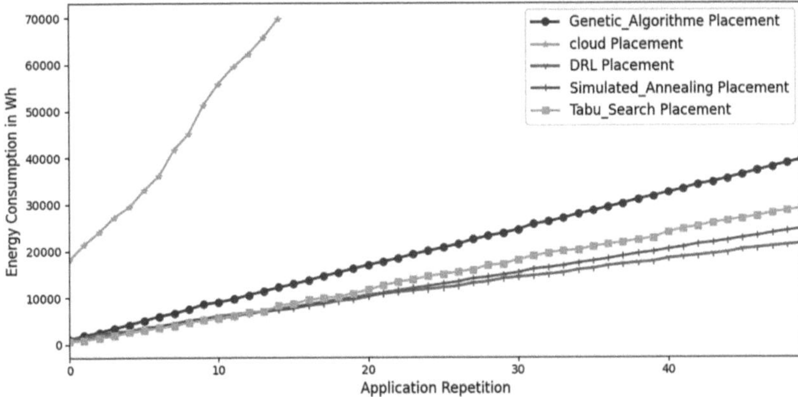

Fig. 6. Energy Consumption versus Application Repetition under RAM + CPU Constraints

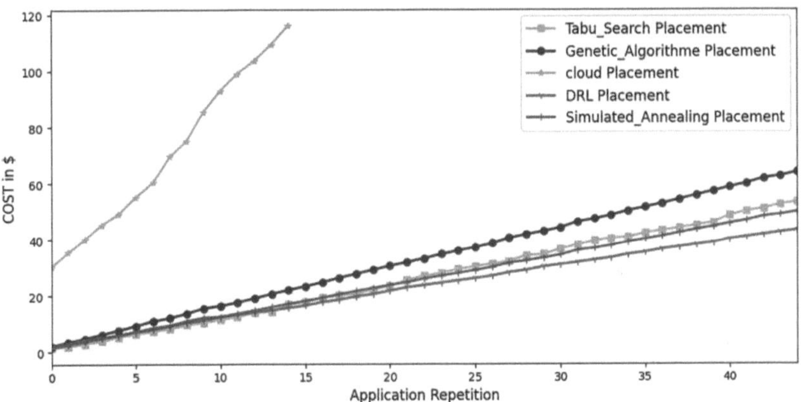

Fig. 7. Cost versus Application Repetition under RAM + CPU Constraints

As shown, DRL consistently achieves the highest gains, particularly against Cloud Placement, where improvements exceed 80% across all metrics. Even when compared to advanced metaheuristic approaches such as Tabu Search and Simulated Annealing, DRL delivers additional reductions in execution time, energy, and cost, confirming its ability to efficiently manage multi-resource constraints in IoT environments.

Overall, incorporating CPU constraints does not change the overall ranking of algorithms. **DRL maintains its superiority**, demonstrating its ability to adapt to complex, multi-resource limitations. Simulated Annealing and Tabu Search remain competitive alternatives, while the Genetic Algorithm continues to perform moderately better than the cloud baseline but lags behind the other intelligent strategies.

Table 2. Percentage improvements of DRL compared to other approaches

Criterion	vs Cloud (%)	vs Genetic Alg. (%)	vs SA/TS (%)
Execution time	82	64	40
Energy consumption	84	38	16
Cost	83	31	10

6   Conclusion

In this work, we addressed the critical challenge of optimizing IoT service placement across CloudFogEdge environments by proposing and evaluating intelligent decision-making approaches under constrained computing resources. Through the development and testing of both meta-heuristic algorithms and a Deep Reinforcement Learning (DRL) framework, results show that DRL consistently outperforms meta-heuristic and cloud-only strategies across all metrics. Simulated Annealing and Tabu Search offer good alternatives with lower complexity, while the Genetic Algorithm achieves moderate results. Overall, DRL proves to be a robust and efficient solution for IoT service placement in distributed infrastructures.

However, certain limitations remain. The current DRL design relies on a fixed action space, which limits its adaptability to dynamic or variable network topologies where the number of nodes changes over time. Additionally, all experiments were conducted in a simulated environment; thus, real-world validation on physical IoT testbeds is still required to assess deployment feasibility and practical challenges.

In future work, we plan to explore scalable reinforcement learning models capable of handling variable network structures, such as Graph Neural Network-based or hierarchical RL approaches. We also aim to extend this study toward real IoT deployments, integrating additional practical constraints (e.g., bandwidth, latency deadlines) to further validate the applicability and robustness of the proposed framework.

Acknowledgments. This work was supported by the ANR under the France 2030 program, grant "NF-NAI: ANR-22-PEFT-0003".

References

1. Ali, A., Aslam, N., Khan, Z.: Deadline-aware multi-objective optimization using parallel genetic algorithms for iot service placement. J. Parallel Distrib. Comput **145**, 136–148 (2020)
2. Apat, H.K., Sahoo, B., Goswami, V., Barik, R.K.: A hybrid meta-heuristic algorithm for multi-objective iot service placement in fog computing environments. Dec. Anal. J. **10**, 100379 (2024)

3. Baccour, R., Kaddachi, M., Saidane, L.: Nature-inspired computing techniques for service placement in fog computing: a survey. IEEE Access **9**, 131409–131429 (2021)
4. Duan, Y., Zhao, Y., Zheng, Y.: Deep reinforcement learning-based iot service placement for latency and cost optimization in fog computing. IEEE Trans. Industr. Inf. **18**(3), 1907–1916 (2022)
5. Fiaz, U., Aziz, M.A., Nasir, A.: Metaheuristic algorithms for the optimization of fog computing environments: a survey. Comput. Electr. Eng. **93**, 107247 (2021)
6. Goudarzi, H., Hassan, M.A., Buyya, R.: Qos-aware fog service placement using open-source tools: Challenges and a reference model. Softw.: Pract. Exp. **52**(4), 805–823 (2022)
7. Goudarzi, H., Xiang, Y., Yu, S., Hosseinzadeh, M.: Task offloading in mobile fog computing by classification and regression tree. Futur. Gener. Comput. Syst. **89**, 57–68 (2018)
8. Gupta, H., Dastjerdi, A.V., Ghosh, S.K., Buyya, R.: ifogsim: a toolkit for modeling and simulation of resource management techniques in internet of things, edge and fog computing environments. Softw.: Pract. Exp. **47**(9), 1275–1296 (2017)
9. van Hasselt, H., Guez, A., Silver, D.: Deep reinforcement learning with double q-learning (2015). https://arxiv.org/abs/1509.06461
10. Jia, X., Guo, Z., Wang, Y.: Hybrid ga-pso algorithm for multi-objective task scheduling in fog computing. Comput. Commun. **174**, 48–59 (2021)
11. Kaur, G., Kaur, P.: A survey on metaheuristic-based optimization approaches for fog computing. J. Netw. Comput. Appl. **182**, 103059 (2021)
12. Khalajzadeh, H., Dastjerdi, A.V., Buyya, R.: Meet genetic algorithms in monte carlo: Optimised placement of multi-service applications in the fog. Simul. Model. Pract. Theory **114**, 102384 (2021)
13. Lera, I., Guerrero, C., Juiz, C.: YAFS: A simulator for IoT scenarios in fog computing. IEEE Access **7**, 91745–91758 (2019). https://doi.org/10.1109/ACCESS.2019.2927895
14. Naha, R.K., Garg, S., Sakellariou, R., Battula, V., Georgakopoulos, D., Jayaraman, P.K.: Context-aware distribution of fog applications using deep reinforcement learning. IEEE Trans. Cloud Comput. **11**(2), 1098–1112 (2023)
15. Sharma, A., Sahu, A., Saini, R.: Cost-efficient iot service placement using whale optimization algorithm in fog computing. J. Supercomput. **77**(5), 4726–4748 (2021)
16. Sharma, P., Saini, H., Rana, N.: Multi-objective fault-tolerant fog service placement for iot applications. Futur. Gener. Comput. Syst. **110**, 173–190 (2020)
17. Sonmez, C., Ozgovde, A., Ersoy, C.: Edgecloudsim: an environment for performance evaluation of edge computing systems. Simul. Model. Pract. Theory **62**, 32–50 (2016)
18. Yousefpour, A., Fung, C., Nguyen, T., Kwon, T., Jalali, F., Jue, J., Kim, M.S.: Optimal service provisioning in iot fog-based environment for qos-aware delay-sensitive applications. Futur. Gener. Comput. Syst. **87**, 200–210 (2018)
19. Zhou, R., Chen, X., Sun, L.: Quantum-inspired algorithms in fog computing environments: a review. Futur. Gener. Comput. Syst. **127**, 78–89 (2022)

Predicting Intents: LSTM-Based Modeling

Nagham Hachem[(✉)], Manh Cuong Nguyen, and Éric Renault

LIGM, Univ. Gustave Eiffel, CNRS, ESIEE Paris, 93162 Marne-la-Vallee, France
`nagham.hachem@esiee.fr`

Abstract. By converting high-level user objectives into workable configurations, intent-based networking, or IBN, seeks to automate network administration. Predicting future intentions to facilitate proactive resource management is a major difficulty in IBN. The use of Long Short-Term Memory (LSTM) networks for network intent prediction is examined in this research. Using the Network Intent Language (NILE), we create a synthetic dataset of 8,353 intents and assess how well the LSTM model performs across a range of temporal window sizes. Our findings show that an LSTM model with a medium window size (e.g., 12) may successfully strike a compromise between stability and responsiveness, which makes it appropriate for real-world intent forecasting tasks like resource allocation in 5G networks and proactive service orchestration.

1 Introduction

Manual management techniques are no longer relevant due to the increasing complexity of contemporary networks, which is being fueled by technologies like 5G and IoT. This has led to the emergence of Intent-Based Networking (IBN) as a paradigm-shifting approach that promises to automate network operations by replacing low-level configuration with high-level business goals. The intent is a crucial idea that makes this change possible. The deployment of closed-loop systems capable of confirming and preserving the network state in accordance with these declared goals—from reactive correction to, eventually, proactive assurance—is a fundamental promise of IBN. The ability to predict future network requirements and user objectives before they are formally announced, which allows for fully predictive resource management and service orchestration, is the next step in this progression. In order to tackle this forecasting problem, this study investigates the use of Long Short-Term Memory (LSTM) neural networks. In order to offer useful insights for creating more autonomous networks, we assess the model's performance on a synthetic dataset of network intents, paying particular attention to the effect of the temporal window size.

S. Boumerdassi et al. (Eds.): MLN 2025, LNCS 16424, pp. 192–199, 2026.
https://doi.org/10.1007/978-3-032-18494-8_13

2   What Is Intent?

In the context of networking, intent is the high-level statement of user goals. It outlines the desired result without outlining the operational procedures required to get there [14]. The key to automating contemporary infrastructures is this division between "what" and "how."

Intent can be communicated in a variety of ways. `<domain, attribute, operation>` is an example of a structured primitive that offers formal representations. Non-technical users can express goals using natural language inputs, and policy templates provide reusable definitions of desired behavior. These goals must be translated into executable configurations by intent engines regardless of the input [13,14].

Closed-loop verification is one of this paradigm's key components. The system automatically corrects operations when misalignments arise, continually checks telemetry, and compares the observed state with the stated objectives [14,17]. This feature improves flexibility and decreases manual interventions. Typical applications include cross-domain IoT orchestration, where complex service chains are deployed and maintained automatically [17], and 5G network slicing, where intents define slice-specific QoS needs [13].

Different standards bodies have different interpretations of purpose. While ETSI views intent as a set of expectations guiding orchestration and management, GSMA stresses outcome-oriented statements backed by AI/ML approaches [3] [4]. While the TM Forum concentrates on business-driven objectives independent of technological implementation, the IETF emphasizes declarative objectives that allow for scalable automation [2]. Last but not least, 3GPP defines intent as high-level specifications and limitations that can be honed into specific management guidelines [1].

3   Intent Forecasting

Before they are formally stated, intent forecasting makes predictions about future user goals and network requirements. This makes proactive decision-making and dynamic resource management possible in intent-based networking.

To find trends in network behavior and user needs, the procedure uses historical, operational, and real-time data analysis [12,14]. For example, QoS requirements in 5G slices [1,3] or the coordination of services across IoT domains [17] are examples of developments that forecasting helps networks anticipate.

Forecasting works with closed-loop verification systems by keeping high-level goals and implementation specifics apart. This reduces manual involvement and increases flexibility by ensuring that expected intents convert into automated and dependable actions [14].

Standards organizations like as GSMA and ETSI point out that although predictive techniques have great promise, integration into formal intent frameworks is still ongoing [3,4].

4   The Long Short-Term Memory (LSTM) Model

A significant development in Recurrent Neural Networks (RNNs), Long Short-Term Memory (LSTM) networks are designed to address the vanishing gradient issue that restricts the ability of conventional RNNs to learn long-term dependencies [5,9]. The memory cell, which combines a self-recurrent link and a number of gating units to dynamically control information flow across time steps, is the main novelty of the architecture [7].

The input gate, forget gate, and output gate are the three adaptive gates that control the LSTM cell. To regulate the amount of information that is retained, updated, and output, these gates use sigmoid activation functions. The following is the definition of the forward pass for a single LSTM cell at time t:

- **Input Gate:**

$$i_t = \sigma(W_i \cdot [h_{t-1}, x_t] + b_i) \tag{1}$$

  The percentage of fresh data that should be stored in the cell state is decided by this gate.
- **Forget Gate:**

$$f_t = \sigma(W_f \cdot [h_{t-1}, x_t] + b_f) \tag{2}$$

  It regulates the degree to which data from the prior cell state is lost.
- **Cell State Update:**

$$\tilde{C}_t = \tanh(W_C \cdot [h_{t-1}, x_t] + b_C) \tag{3}$$

$$C_t = f_t \odot C_{t-1} + i_t \odot \tilde{C}_t \tag{4}$$

  The selectively remembered new candidate values and the selectively forgotten prior state are combined to update the cell state C_t.
- **Output Gate:**

$$o_t = \sigma(W_o \cdot [h_{t-1}, x_t] + b_o) \tag{5}$$

$$h_t = o_t \odot \tanh(C_t) \tag{6}$$

  This gate creates the output hidden state h_t by filtering the cell state.

The input vector in these equations is represented by x_t, the prior hidden state by h_{t-1}, the logistic sigmoid function by σ, the hyperbolic tangent function by tanh, element-wise multiplication by $\odot$, and learnable parameters by W and b.

Learning on continuous, non-segmented sequences is made easier by the forget gate, a subsequent improvement on the original LSTM that allows the network to independently reset its state [8,15]. The forget gate and output activation function are the most crucial elements of this "vanilla" LSTM, according to extensive empirical studies that have validated it as a reliable baseline [6].

Current studies are confirming and expanding the use of LSTM in many fields [6]. Additionally, LSTM cells continue to be essential parts of cutting-edge architectures, like encoder-decoder models with attention mechanisms, where they facilitate efficient representation learning and sequential feature extraction [16].

5   Data Preparation

For LSTM-based intent prediction, we created a synthetic dataset of 8,353 network intents using the Network Intent Language (NILE) standard [10,11]. A methodical procedure that converts operational metrics into temporal sequences appropriate for sequence learning was used to create the dataset.

5.1   Dataset Generation

Operational metrics were gathered via service traces and workload analysis, including:

- CPU and memory utilization patterns
- measures of traffic flow
- Security event logs
- Service performance metrics

Using preset rules that link network management operations with operational states, these measurements were translated to NILE intents.

5.2   Nile

NILE [10,11] is an intent language that links executable network settings with human-readable service requirements. It was created to make it easier for operators to explain goals like service chaining, security enforcement, and bandwidth guarantees without requiring them to manage intricate device setups. In contrast to conventional methods, NILE applies grammatical norms that ensure syntactic and semantic correctness, guaranteeing that every aim can be reliably verified and carried out. Its compilation process generates infrastructure-ready instructions that are compatible with various platforms, and its expressiveness encompasses a broad range of networking requirements, such as QoS parameters, policy-based routing, and middlebox placement.

6   Experiment and Result

One kind of recurrent neural network called long short-term memory (LSTM) was created especially to identify long-term dependencies in sequential input. Its utilization of memory cells and gating mechanisms, which gradually retain or erase information selectively, is its main breakthrough. Because of its architecture, LSTM is especially good at capturing intricate temporal trends and patterns that more straightforward models might overlook. LSTM offers a substantial benefit for forecasting jobs like as CPU quota use, where both short-term volatility and long-term trends are crucial.

To find the setup that best forecasts future CPU usage, we tested the LSTM model using various historical window sizes. Table 1 provides a summary of the

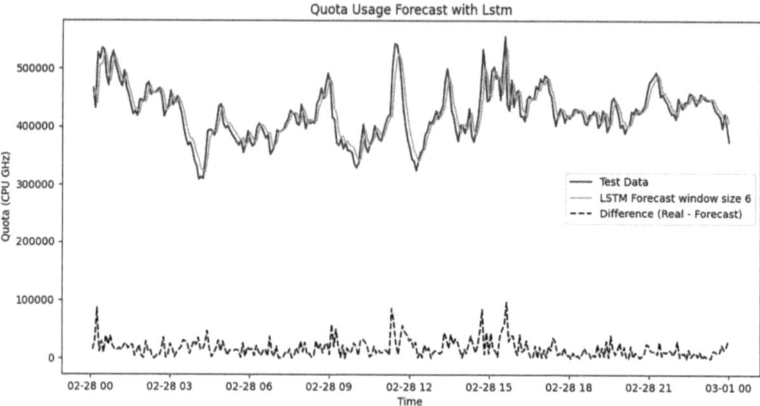

Fig. 1. LSTM forecast (window = 6).

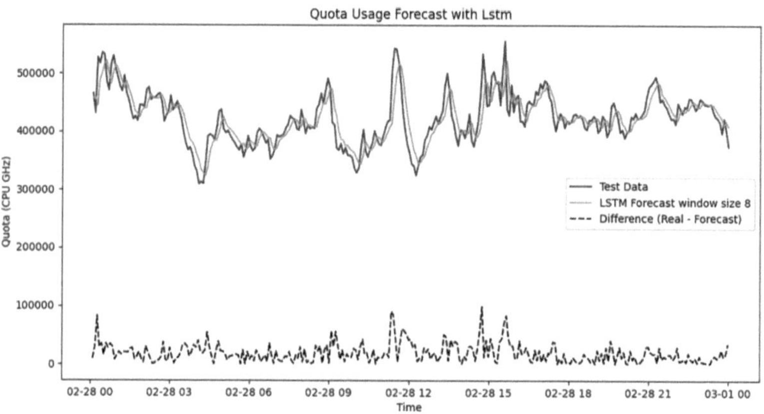

Fig. 2. LSTM forecast (window = 8).

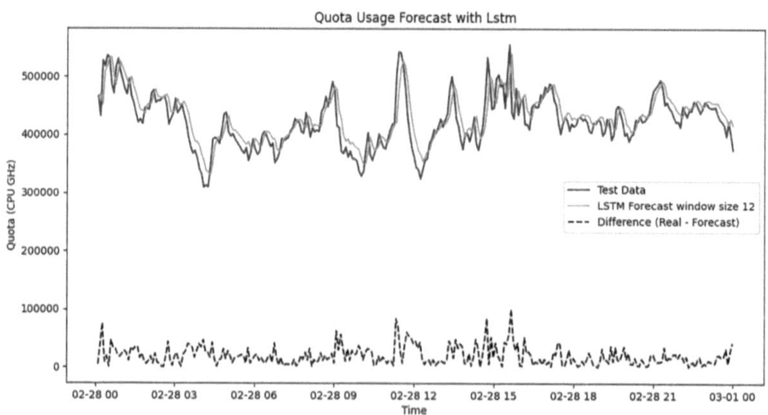

Fig. 3. LSTM forecast (window = 12).

Table 1. LSTM Performance Comparison.

Window size	MAE (GHz)	RMSE (GHz)	MAPE (%)	Time (s)	Memory (MB)
6	17173.22	23076.45	4.05	18.23	48.88
8	18523.66	24615.28	4.34	18.50	49.21
12	22460.50	29248.54	5.14	22.74	49.69
18	17282.87	23287.83	4.06	33.12	51.34
24	17351.28	23356.17	4.07	32.33	53.27

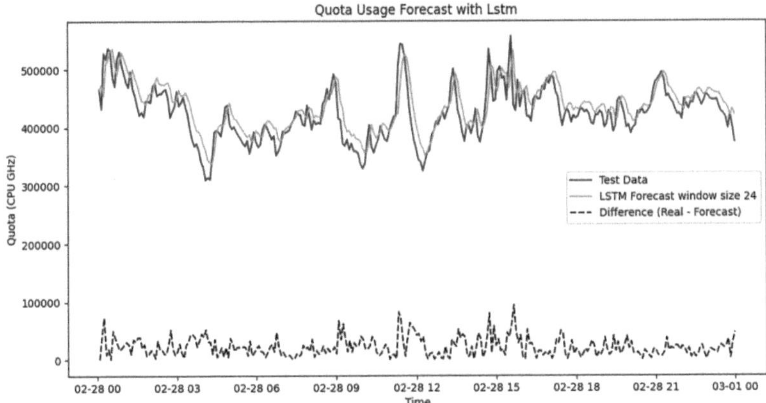

Fig. 4. LSTM forecast (window = 24).

performance parameters, such as prediction accuracy and computing efficiency for each window size.

The experiment's findings show that the tested setups have a distinct performance hierarchy. With the lowest values for each of the three main error metrics—Mean Absolute Error (MAE), Root Mean Square Error (RMSE), and Mean Absolute Percentage Error (MAPE)—the LSTM model with a window size of six exhibits the highest predictive accuracy. Figure 1 illustrates how its predictions closely mirror the real test data, skillfully capturing both abrupt rises and falls in usage. This suggests that it has a great ability to quickly adjust to sudden changes, which makes it ideal for anomaly identification and real-time monitoring. Though a positive, this great sensitivity can also be a drawback because it can sometimes mistake small noise for a large variation, which could result in unstable forecasts in situations where volatility is too high.

The performance profile of the model with a window size of 8 is extremely similar to that of size 6. Even though its error metrics are marginally higher (as seen in Table 1), as illustrated in Fig. 2, it is still a very accurate and responsive model. It can be seen as a strong substitute that, by removing some of the highest-frequency noise, might produce forecasts that are a little smoother than window size 6 while still being incredibly responsive to actual changes in demand.

This makes it an excellent choice for dynamic resource allocation where stability and reactivity must be perfectly balanced.

A window size of 12 is a compromise that sacrifices some responsiveness in favor of more smoothness. Figure 3 displays the forecasts, which are notably smoother than those produced by the smaller windows. By avoiding the extremes of great sensitivity and large delay, this arrangement produces a more uniform error distribution. Applications like intent-based resource allocation in 5G networks, where knowing the overall trend is more important than responding to every small variation, are a good fit for this approach since they demand steady and accurate forecasts for proactive planning.

The model puts long-term trend capture ahead of short-term responsiveness for the biggest tested window size of 24. The model's predictions are smooth, as shown in Fig. 4, but they frequently don't respond fast enough to abrupt peaks and troughs, which causes highs to be underestimated and lows to be overestimated. This smoothing characteristic is confirmed by the rise in residual errors that occurs after abrupt changes. For high-level, long-term capacity planning, when a consistent and comprehensive picture of resource requirements is more important than the ability to monitor volatility in real time, this setup works best.

In summary, our experiment's findings show a definite trade-off that is controlled by window size. For real-time operational duties, smaller windows (6 and 8) offer better precision. Of these, window size 6 is the best option for attaining the best predictive accuracy, and window size 8 is a great substitute for situations requiring the ideal balance of smoothness and reactivity. Size 12 and other medium windows provide a well-balanced solution for proactive orchestration. The ideal use of the larger windows (18 and 24) is for long-term strategic planning, when stability is crucial.

7   Conclusion

This study provides a clear demonstration of the efficacy of LSTM networks for intent forecasting in network management. The substantial influence of temporal window size on forecasting performance is demonstrated by our experimental findings. According to the analysis, window size 6 offers the best prediction accuracy, which makes it perfect for anomaly detection and real-time monitoring when accuracy is crucial. In contrast, window size 8 strikes a nice balance by providing almost the same precision and possibly more stability. Larger windows (size 24) offer smooth forecasts that are appropriate for long-term planning, but they are not sensitive to abrupt changes. Sizes 6 and 8 are both ideal options for real-world use in dynamic settings such as 5G networks; size 6 is advised for optimum accuracy, while size 8 is suggested for situations that call for the ideal balance between stability and responsiveness in proactive resource allocation.

The outcomes validate the potential of LSTM to identify intricate temporal patterns in network data, propelling intent-based networking in the direction of proactive automation. It worked well to convert operational metrics into dependable patterns by using NILE for intent representation. In order to get closer to the goal of self-driving networks, this work offers helpful advice for integrating forecasting into autonomous network management systems.

Acknowledgments. This work is supported by French government funding within the France 2030 framework through the INFLUENCE project.

References

1. 3gpp. https://www.3gpp.org/
2. ietf. https://www.ietf.org/
3. Intelligence brief: Does intent matter in network automation? https://www.gsmaintelligence.com/media-coverage/intelligence-brief-does-intent-matter-in-network-automation/
4. Zero-touch network and service management (zsm); reference architecture (2019). www.chrome-extension://efaidnbmnnnibpcajpcglclefindmkaj/, https://www.etsi.org/deliver/etsi_gs/ZSM/001_099/002/01.01.01_60/gs_ZSM002v010101p.pdf
5. Bengio, Y., Simard, P., Frasconi, P.: Learning long-term dependencies with gradient descent is difficult. IEEE Trans. Neural Netw. **5**(2), 157–166 (1994)
6. Chandra, R., Goyal, S., Gupta, R.: Evaluation of deep learning models for multi-step ahead time series prediction. IEEE Access **9**, 83105–83123 (2021)
7. Gers, F.L., Schmidhuber, J., Cummins, F.: Learning to forget: continual prediction with lstm. Neural Comput. **12**(10), 2451–2471 (2000)
8. Greff, K., Srivastava, R.P., Koutník, J., Steunebrink, B.R., Schmidhuber, J.: Lstm: a search space odyssey. IEEE Trans. Neural Netw. Learn. Syst. **28**(10), 2222–2232 (2016)
9. Hochreiter, S., Schmidhuber, J.: Long short-term memory. Neural Comput. **9**(8), 1735–1780 (1997)
10. Jacobs, A.S., Pfitscher, R.J., Ribeiro, R.H., Ferreira, R.A., Granville, L.Z., Willinger, W., Rao, S.G.: Hey, lumi! using natural language for $\{intent-based\}$ network management. In: 2021 USENIX Annual Technical Conference (USENIX ATC 21), pp. 625–639 (2021)
11. Jacobs, A.S., Pfitscher, R.J., Ribeiro, R.H., Ferreira, R.A., Granville, L.Z., Willinger, W., Rao, S.G.: Hey, lumi! using natural language for intent-based network management. In: 2021 USENIX Annual Technical Conference (USENIX ATC 21), p. –639. USENIX Association (2021)
12. Kim, J., Kim, H., Kim, H., Lee, D., Yoon, S.: A comprehensive survey of time series forecasting: Architectural diversity and open challenges (2024). arXiv:2411.05793
13. Leivadeas, A., Falkner, M.: A survey on intent-based networking. IEEE Commun. Surv. Tutor. **25**(1), 625–655 (2022)
14. Pang, L., Yang, C., Chen, D., Song, Y., Guizani, M.: A survey on intent-driven networks. IEEE Access **8**, 22862–22873 (2020)
15. Sherstinsky, A.: Fundamentals of recurrent neural network (rnn) and long short-term memory (lstm) network. Physica D **404**, 132306 (2020)
16. Wen, X., Li, W.: Time series prediction based on lstm-attention-lstm model. IEEE Access **11**, 48322–48331 (2023)
17. Zeydan, E., Turk, Y.: Recent advances in intent-based networking: A survey. In: 2020 IEEE 91st Vehicular Technology Conference (VTC2020-Spring), pp. 1–5. IEEE (2020)

Multi-objective Deep RLL Based RAT Selection for V2X Communication

Solomon Orduen Yese[(✉)], Sara Berri, and Arsenia Chorti

ETIS, UMR 8051 CY Cergy Paris Université, ENSEA, CNRS, Paris, France
`solomon.yese@ensea.fr`

Abstract. The proliferation of vehicle-to-everything (V2X) communication systems with diverse quality of service (QoS) requirements has created an increasingly complex heterogeneous wireless environment where vehicles must intelligently select among multiple radio access technologies (RATs) to meet these diverse and stringent QoS requirements. In this paper, we address the critical challenge of optimal RAT selection in multi-RAT vehicle to infrastructure (V2I) communication. We propose an intelligent adaptive RAT selection algorithm that combines reinforcement learning with predictive mobility modeling to enable real-time decision making under uncertainty and incomplete information scenarios with a view to simultaneously optimizing latency and reliability while reducing the number of handovers under rapidly changing vehicular network conditions. To validate our approach, we conduct extensive network simulations and the results demonstrate significant improvements compared to state-of-the-art RAT selection method: up to 63.0% reduction in number of handovers, 1.8 and 2.7% improvement in overall vehicle reliability, 12.1 and 6.2% reduction in delay experience by vehicles at low and high number of vehicles, respectively.

Keywords: V2X · RAT · ITS · Delay · Reliability · DSRC · DRL · Multi-RAT · Handover · Co-existence

1 Introduction

The rapid evolution of vehicular communication systems has greatly transformed the landscape of intelligent transportation systems (ITS). As vehicular networks mature, the complexity of communication requirements has grown exponentially, with diverse and stringent QoS requirements. This heterogeneous nature of V2X applications, coupled with the dynamic and highly mobile environment in which vehicles operate, has necessitated the development of multi-RAT communication frameworks to meet these requirements [1].

Contemporary V2X ecosystems encompasses multiple RATs with distinct characteristics in terms of coverage, latency, throughput, reliability, and energy consumption, including dedicated short range communications (DSRC), cellular V2X (C-V2X), fifth generation (5G) new radio (NR), WiFi, and emerging satellite communication systems. However, the coexistence of multiple RATs presents unprecedented challenges in terms of coordination between the multiple technologies, optimal RAT selection, resource allocation, and seamless handover management. The RAT selection problem in multi-RAT V2X networks is inherently complex due to several interdependent factors such as dynamic channel conditions and network topologies, heterogeneous QoS requirements, limited and variable availability of radio resources across different RATs [2].

While existing traditional approaches to RAT selection have provided foundational insights, they fail to capture the multi-dimensional nature of the RAT selection problem in modern V2X environments. Recent advances in machine learning, particularly reinforcement learning and deep neural networks, have opened new avenues for intelligent RAT selection. However, the integration of learning-based approaches with real-time V2X requirements, the handling of incomplete information scenarios, and the provision of performance guarantees remain significant research challenges.

This paper addresses the critical gap in multi-RAT V2X communication by proposing a comprehensive framework for intelligent RAT selection that simultaneously considers multiple QoS requirements while minimizing the number of handovers with the following key contributions:

• We formulate the multi-RAT V2X selection problem as a multi-objective optimization problem to jointly minimize vehicle delay and number of handovers while maximizing reliability.

• We propose a novel adaptive learning algorithm that employs reinforcement learning to enable real-time RAT selection decisions under uncertainty.

• We evaluate the performance of the proposed scheme against a state-of-the-art solution in terms of vehicle delay, reliability and number of successful handovers.

The rest of the paper is organized as follows. Section 2 presents the related works and Sect. 3, presents the network model and problem formulation. Section 4 introduces the proposed algorithm while Sect. 5 presents the performance evaluation of the proposed algorithm against the state-of-the-art. Finally, Sect. 6 concludes the paper.

2   Related Works

This section presents a review of some key related works on RAT selection.

In [3], an intelligent rule-based algorithm for hybrid V2X communication is proposed. The proposed solution first scans the environment after which it performs adaptive technology selection. It also employs short-range RATs for only low throughput data transfer of certain C-ITS messages and long-range Uu link for high throughput connections. The scheme optimizes CAM transmission latency, packet delivery ratio (PDR), and reliability.

A service-oriented joint long short-term memory (LSTM) multi-criteria RAT selection scheme is proposed in [4] to maximize overall network throughput. It employs an LSTM prediction technique as a network filter process to reject the worst channel quality RATs before initial RAT selection scheme is used for RAT selection. The scheme maximizes average throughput and packet delivery rate.

A deep reinforcement learning (DRL) solution for RAT selection is proposed in [5] for ITS-G5/LTE-V2X hybrid networks. It employs a double deep Q-learning algorithm that optimizes communication modes and uses a reward function that balances reception success, QoS satisfaction, and link quality improvements, enabling adaptive decision-making in highly mobile scenarios. The scheme increased packet reception rate (PRR) and resource utilization in platooning scenarios.

In [6], a context-aware task offloading mechanism (CAVTOMEC) is proposed to improve QoS. The CAVTOMEC combines dedicated short range communications (DSRC) and LTE-V2X with multi-access edge computing (MEC). It also employs priority system for task offloading and proposes two heuristic algorithms: one for real-time offloading and another for future resource estimation. The scheme reduces offloading delay for high-priority tasks and increases success rates for high priority tasks.

An adaptive network selection framework is proposed in [7] that prioritizes low-latency connections for safety applications and high-bandwidth networks for infotainment services based on application requirements, subject to bandwidth, power, and signal to interference plus noise ratio (SINR) thresholds constraints. It reduces the delay for safety applications and increases throughput for infotainment services.

In [8], a decentralized context-aware algorithm is proposed for heterogeneous vehicle-to-vehicle (V2V) communications that dynamically selects the optimal RAT based on throughput, latency and real-time channel conditions, leveraging periodic context-sharing packets to balance load across RATs. It increases PDR and lowers latency while minimizing computational overhead and communication costs.

The work in [9] presents a QoS-aware RAT selection algorithm for hybrid vehicular networks. It dynamically selects RAT based on QoS requirements and network load, dynamically switching between the RATs. It employs a distributed radio resource management system that monitors network conditions and dynamically adjusts beaconing frequencies via a beaconing frequency adaptation to reduce network load and unnecessary handovers. The scheme achieves fewer handovers, higher PDRs, lower latency, and better throughput.

In [10], a mobility and location-aware network selection solution is proposed to improve handover performance for V2I communication in heterogeneous networks. This solution selects the best candidate access point from a shortlist of those located in the vehicle's movement direction. It uses a fuzzy logic system to evaluate candidates based on the distance between the AP and the vehicle's trajectory and the vehicle's speed, with a view to maximizing the potential dwelling time within the candidate's coverage. It minimizes handover delay and ping-pong effects by enabling early, vehicle-controlled network selection. However, it primarily considers geographical and mobility factors and may not fully account for dynamic network conditions like real-time load or application-specific QoS requirements, which could limit performance for services with stringent delay or reliability needs.

A service aware RAT selection solution is proposed in [11] to improve reliability for traffic-efficiency service vehicles, delay for safety-critical service vehicles and throughput for infotainment service vehicles. This solution selects the DSRC RAT for safety-critical services, C-V2X for infotainment and chooses the RAT that offers the highest reliability for traffic-efficiency services. It minimizes delay, throughput and reliability for safety-critical, infotainment and traffic-efficiency services vehicles respectively. However, It may increase number of handovers as it will have to change RATs each time a vehicle's service changes.

Most of the existing solutions tend to select potential RATs based on the closest distance, SINR or predetermined RATs base on vehicle service type in a bid to minimize the delay of vehicles and/or maximize throughput with others focusing on reliability. While these solutions tend to minimize delay, increase throughput or reliability for vehicles, they largely do not consider the challenge of frequent handovers and the attending effect it has on the QoS of the vehicles.

3   Network Model and Problem Formulation

In this section, we describe the system model and formulate the RAT selection problem as a multi-objective optimization problem.

3.1   System Model

We consider a geographical area with vehicular communication infrastructure operating in the $5.9\,\mathrm{GHz}$ ITS band. The area is represented with coordinates (x, y) and operates over a time horizon divided into discrete time slots $\mathcal{T} = \{1, 2, \ldots, T\}$, where each slot $t \in \mathcal{T}$ has duration Δt (ms).

The communication infrastructure consists of two RATs: $\mathcal{J} = \{\mathrm{DSRC}, \mathrm{C\text{-}V2X}\}$, whose coverage area is noted as $C_j, \forall j \in \mathcal{J}$. DSRC is deployed through multiple road side units (RSUs) distributed across the geographical area and C-V2X is deployed through a single 5G next generation node B (gNodeB) providing area-wide coverage.

Let $\mathcal{R} = \{1, 2, \ldots, R\}$ denote the set of DSRC RSUs distributed across the area, where each RSU $r \in \mathcal{R}$ is positioned at coordinates (x_r, y_r) with coverage radius C_r (m). The C-V2X BS is positioned at coordinates $(x_{\mathrm{BS}}, y_{\mathrm{BS}})$ with coverage radius $C_{\mathrm{C\text{-}V2X}}$ (m).

Each RAT $j \in \mathcal{J}$ is characterized by its bandwidth capacity B_j (Hz), maximum number of supported connections N_j and transmission power Q_j^{tx} (dBm). For DSRC, the total number of connections is $N_{\mathrm{DSRC}} = \sum_{r \in \mathcal{R}} N_r$, where N_r is maximum connections that can be supported by RSU r. Let $\mathcal{V} = \{1, 2, \ldots, V\}$ denote the set of all vehicles in the considered area such that each vehicle $i \in \mathcal{V}$ is characterized by time-varying and time-invariant parameters. The time-invariant characteristics include the vehicle class $\kappa_i \in \mathcal{K} = \{\mathrm{emergency}, \mathrm{public\ transport}, \mathrm{commercial}, \mathrm{private}\}$. The time-varying characteristics at each time slot $t \in \mathcal{T}$ include the current position/coordinates $(x_i(t), y_i(t))$, speed $v_i(t)$ (m/s), direction vector $\boldsymbol{d}_i(t) = (d_x(t), d_y(t))$ and active service type $\tau_i(t) \in \mathcal{S} = \{\text{safety-critical}, \text{traffic-efficiency}, \text{infotainment}\}$. The dynamic priority level $p_i(t) \in \{1, 2, \ldots, P\}$ (where 1 represents the highest priority) is determined as a function of both the vehicle class and the active service type.

Each vehicle's QoS requirements are service-dependent and vary with time slots based on the active service type. These requirements are defined in terms of maximum tolerable latency $D_i^{max}(t)$ (ms), minimum reliability $\lambda_i^{\min}(t)$ and minimum data rate $\nu_i^{\min}(t)$ (bps). Similarly, $D_{i,j}(t)$ and $\lambda_{i,j}(t)$ and $\nu_{i,j}(t)$, are the delay, reliability and data rate for vehicle i when connected to RAT j at time slot t, respectively. We define the estimated reliability for vehicle i on RAT j at time slot t as:

$$\lambda_{i,j}(t) = \lambda_j^{\text{base}} \cdot \left(1 - \xi_j \cdot \frac{N_j(t)}{N_j}\right), \quad \forall i \in \mathcal{V}, \forall j \in \mathcal{J}, \forall t \in \mathcal{T}, \tag{1}$$

where: ξ_j and λ_j^{base} are the degradation factor of RAT j with respect to its load and the RAT's base reliability while $N_j(t)$ and N_j are the current number of vehicles connected to RAT j at time slot t and the maximum possible connections for RAT j, respectively.

Similarly, we define the estimated delay for vehicle i on RAT j at time slot t as:

$$D_{i,j}(t) = \frac{\text{distance}_{i,j}(t)}{c} + D_{j,\text{proc}}^{\text{base}} + \left(\frac{N_j(t)}{N_j}\right) \times Q_j, \tag{2}$$

where: the first, second and third term on the right hand side account for the propagation, processing and queuing delays respectively. Similarly, $\text{distance}_{i,j}(t)$, c, and $D_{j,\text{proc}}^{\text{base}}$ denote the euclidean distance between vehicle i and serving node of RAT j at time t, speed of light and base processing delay of RAT j, respectively, while $N_j(t)$, N_j and Q_j are the current number of vehicles connected to RAT j at time t, the maximum possible connections for RAT j and the queuing sensitivity coefficient of RAT j, respectively.

The data rate $\nu_{i,j}(t)$ for vehicle $i \in \mathcal{V}$ connected to RAT $j \in \mathcal{J} = \{\text{DSRC}, \text{C-V2X}\}$ at time slot $t \in \mathcal{T}$ is given by:

$$\nu_{i,j}(t) = B_j \cdot \max\left(0, 1 - \frac{\text{distance}_{i,j}(t)}{C_j}\right) \cdot \max\left(0, 1 - \frac{N_j(t)}{N_j}\right), \tag{3}$$

where: B_j, $\text{distance}_{i,j}(t)$ and C_j denote the bandwidth capacity of RAT j, euclidean distance between vehicle i and serving node of RAT j at time t and coverage radius of RAT j, respectively; while $N_j(t)$ and N_j are the current number of vehicles connected to RAT j at time t and the maximum possible connections for RAT j, respectively.

Furthermore, we assume that in every time slot, each vehicle initiates the RAT switching procedure by sending a message containing its current profile to the selection orchestrator. The orchestrator then sends the profile information of all the available RATs that the vehicle is within coverage. A high level diagram of the scenario is captured in Fig. 1.

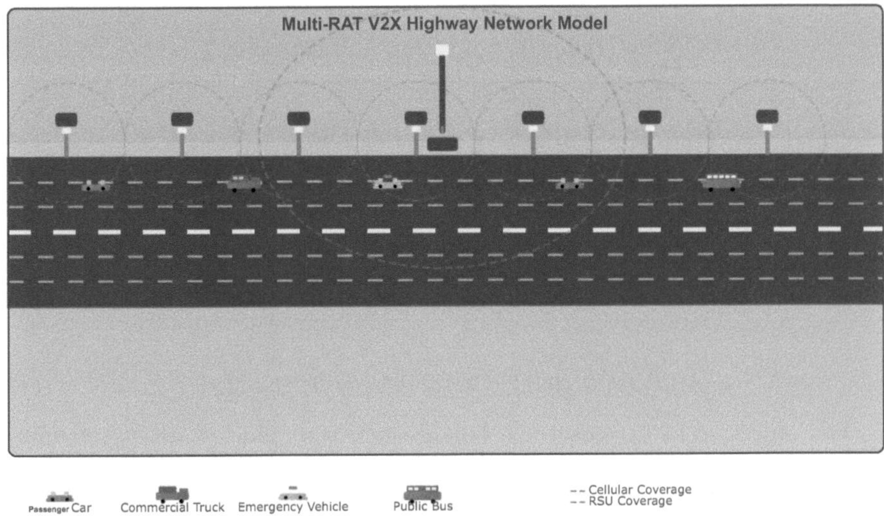

Fig. 1. System Model

3.2 Problem Formulation

In this section, we formulate the RAT selection problem as an optimization problem for the two-RAT scenario with DSRC and C-V2X.

Let $s_{i,j}(t) \in \{0,1\}$ denote the binary decision variable indicating whether vehicle i is assigned to RAT $j \in \mathcal{J}$ at time slot t. Let $h_i(t) \in \{0,1\}$ denote the binary variable indicating whether vehicle i undergoes a handover at time slot t. Next, we formulate our multi-objective function that seeks to minimize the delay and handovers and maximize reliability.

$$\min \sum_{t \in \mathcal{T}} \sum_{i \in \mathcal{V}} \left(\alpha \sum_{j \in \mathcal{J}} s_{i,j}(t) D_{i,j}(t) - \beta \sum_{j \in \mathcal{J}} s_{i,j}(t) \lambda_{i,j}(t) + \gamma h_i(t) \right) \tag{4}$$

Subject to:

$$\sum_{j \in \mathcal{J}} s_{i,j}(t) = 1, \quad \forall i \in \mathcal{V}, \forall t \in \mathcal{T} \tag{5}$$

$$\sum_{i \in \mathcal{V}} s_{i,j}(t) \leq N_j, \quad \forall t \in \mathcal{T}, \forall j \in \mathcal{J} \tag{6}$$

$$\sum_{j \in \mathcal{J}} s_{i,j}(t) D_{i,j}(t) \leq D_i^{\max}(t), \quad \forall i \in \mathcal{V}, \forall t \in \mathcal{T} \tag{7}$$

$$\sum_{j \in \mathcal{J}} s_{i,j}(t) \lambda_{i,j}(t) \geq \lambda_i^{\min}(t), \quad \forall i \in \mathcal{V}, \forall t \in \mathcal{T} \tag{8}$$

$$\sum_{j \in \mathcal{J}} s_{i,j}(t)\nu_{i,j}(t) \geq \nu_i^{\min}(t), \quad \forall i \in \mathcal{V}, \forall t \in \mathcal{T} \tag{9}$$

$$s_{i,j}(t) \leq \mathbf{1}((x_i(t), y_i(t)) \in \mathcal{C}_j), \quad \forall i \in \mathcal{V}, \forall t \in \mathcal{T}, \forall j \in \mathcal{J} \tag{10}$$

$$h_i(t) \geq \sum_{j \in J} \left(s_{i,j}(t-1) \cdot (1 - s_{i,j}(t)) \right), \quad \forall i \in \mathcal{V}, \forall t \in \mathcal{T}, t \geq 2 \tag{11}$$

$$h_i(1) = 0, \quad \forall i \in \mathcal{V} \tag{12}$$

$$s_{i,j}(t), h_i(t) \in \{0,1\}, \quad \forall i \in \mathcal{V}, \forall j \in \mathcal{J}, \forall t \in \mathcal{T}, t \geq 2 \tag{13}$$

The objective in (4) ensures a balance between vehicles' delay, reliability, and the number of handovers, where α, β, and γ are the delay, reliability, and handover weights, respectively. The constraints in (5) ensure that each vehicle is assigned to exactly one RAT, (6) ensure that the number of vehicles assigned to each RAT cannot exceed its maximum number of connections. Constraints (7), (8), and (9) are the QoS (delay, reliability, and data rate) constraints that ensure that the assigned RAT must meet the vehicle's QoS requirements. Similarly, (10) are the coverage constraints that ensure that a vehicle i is only assigned to a RAT if it is within its coverage area. Constraints (11) are the handover constraint that track handovers. Constraints (12) ensure that there is no handover in the first time slot. Constraints (13) define the binary decision variables for RAT assignment.

4   Proposed Algorithm

In this section, we introduce a DRL based solution to address the multi-objective optimization problem of RAT selection in vehicular networks, leveraging the learning capabilities of DRL to automatically discover optimal RAT assignment policies that adapt to the dynamic and complex nature of vehicular communication environments while simultaneously minimizing delay, maximizing reliability and reducing handovers.

The core of our proposed solution is formulated as a Markov decision process (MDP) where an intelligent infrastructure agent learns to make optimal vehicle-RAT association decisions through continuous interaction with the vehicular network environment. Our DRL-based solution automatically adapts to varying network conditions and traffic patterns by learning from experience. We define in the following the set of possible states, actions and the reward.

States: the state in our approach encompasses comprehensive information about both individual vehicle characteristics and the overall network condition. That is, for each decision-making instance, the state vector captures vehicle-specific features including normalized (ratio of the parameter to its maximum possible value) position $(x_i^{\mathrm{norm}}(t), y_i^{\mathrm{norm}}(t))$, speed

$(v_i^{\mathrm{norm}}(t))$, vehicle service type $(\tau_i^{\mathrm{norm}}(t))$, priority level $(p_i^{\mathrm{norm}}(t))$, direction $(\boldsymbol{d}_i^{\mathrm{norm}}(t))$ and QoS requirements such as maximum tolerable latency $(D_i^{max,\mathrm{norm}}(t))$, minimum data rate $(\nu_i^{min,\mathrm{norm}}(t))$ and minimum reliability $(\lambda_i^{min,\mathrm{norm}}(t))$ threshold requirements. Additionally, the state incorporates network-wide information including current RAT load ratios for DSRC $(N_{\mathrm{DSRC}}^{\mathrm{norm}}(t))$ and C-V2X $(N_{\mathrm{C\text{-}V2X}}^{\mathrm{norm}}(t))$ technologies, estimated network delays for DSRC $(D_{i,\mathrm{DSRC}}^{\mathrm{norm}}(t))$ and C-V2X $(D_{i,\mathrm{C\text{-}V2X}}^{\mathrm{norm}}(t))$ technologies, reliability for DSRC $(\lambda_{i,\mathrm{DSRC}}^{\mathrm{norm}}(t))$ and C-V2X $(\lambda_{i,\mathrm{C\text{-}V2X}}^{\mathrm{norm}}(t))$ technologies and data rates for both DSRC $(\nu_{i,\mathrm{DSRC}}^{\mathrm{norm}}(t))$ and C-V2X $(\nu_{i,\mathrm{C\text{-}V2X}}^{\mathrm{norm}}(t))$ technologies. The state vector

$$s_i(t) = [x_i^{\mathrm{norm}}(t), v_i^{\mathrm{norm}}(t), \tau_i^{\mathrm{norm}}(t), p_i^{\mathrm{norm}}(t), \boldsymbol{d}_i^{\mathrm{norm}}(t), D_i^{max,\mathrm{norm}}(t), \nu_i^{min,\mathrm{norm}}(t),$$
$$\lambda_i^{min,\mathrm{norm}}(t), N_{\mathrm{DSRC}}^{\mathrm{norm}}(t), N_{\mathrm{C\text{-}V2X}}^{\mathrm{norm}}(t), D_{i,\mathrm{DSRC}}^{\mathrm{norm}}(t), D_{i,\mathrm{C\text{-}V2X}}^{\mathrm{norm}}(t), \lambda_{i,\mathrm{DSRC}}^{\mathrm{norm}}(t), \lambda_{i,\mathrm{C\text{-}V2X}}^{\mathrm{norm}}(t),$$
$$\nu_{i,\mathrm{DSRC}}^{\mathrm{norm}}(t), \nu_{i,\mathrm{C\text{-}V2X}}^{\mathrm{norm}}(t)].$$

Actions: The action for vehicle i at time slot t is represented as $a_i(t) \in \mathcal{A} = \{0, 1\}$, where $a_i(t) = 0$ denotes assignment to DSRC and $a_i(t) = 1$ denotes assignment to C-V2X. The collective action vector for all vehicles at time t is given by $\mathbf{a}(t) = [a_1(t), a_2(t), \ldots, a_V(t)]^T \in \mathcal{A}^V$. To ensure feasibility, action masking is applied such that the valid action space for vehicle i is defined as $\mathcal{A}_i^{\mathrm{valid}}(t) = \{a \in \mathcal{A} : (x_i(t), y_i(t)) \in \mathcal{C}_j, N_j(t) < N_j\}$, where j corresponds to the RAT selected by action a.

Reward *($r_i(t)$):* The reward function for vehicle i at time slot t is derived from the objective function in (4) which is aimed at jointly minimizing delay, maximizing reliability and minimizing handovers. We achieve this reward by negating the objective to convert the minimization problem into a reward maximization problem suitable for reinforcement learning. It is formulated as:

$$r_i(t) = -\alpha \sum_{j \in \mathcal{J}} s_{i,j}(t) D_{i,j}(t) + \beta \sum_{j \in \mathcal{J}} s_{i,j}(t) \lambda_{i,j}(t) - \gamma h_i(t) \qquad (14)$$

where α, β and γ are weighting coefficients for delay minimization, reliability maximization and handover minimization respectively. The assignment variable $s_{i,j}(t) \in \{0, 1\}$ indicates whether vehicle i is assigned to RAT j at time t based on the agent's action $a_i(t)$ while $h_i(t) \in \{0, 1\}$ indicates whether a handover occurred as a result of the action differing from the previous assignment. The total system reward at time t is given by $R(t) = \sum_{i=1}^{V} r_i(t)$.

The proposed approach employs a priority-based sequential decision-making strategy that processes vehicles in order of their priority levels, with highest-priority vehicles making RAT selections first to ensures that critical vehicular services such as emergency and safety applications are prioritized compared to global optimization methods that attempt to solve for all vehicles simultaneously.

The DRL architecture utilizes a deep Q-network (DQN) enhanced with experience replay and target networks to handle the temporal correlations and high-dimensional nature of the vehicular network environment. The experience replay mechanism stores past decisions and their outcomes, enabling the agent to learn from historical patterns and break temporal correlations that could lead to unstable learning. Training incorporates an exploration-exploitation strategy that balances learning new policies with utilizing existing knowledge.

The algorithm workflow, as depicted in Algorithm 1, follows a systematic approach for each time slot. First, vehicles are sorted by priority (line 5). For each vehicle, the algorithm computes the comprehensive state vector incorporating both vehicle characteristics and current network conditions (line 8). The set of valid actions is determined based on coverage and capacity constraints (lines 9–14). If the set of valid actions is empty, no RAT selection is performed for that vehicle and it continues execution (lines 15–17). The action selection mechanism employs an epsilon-greedy policy that balances exploration and exploitation (lines 18–27), where the agent either explores random valid actions or selects the action with the highest predicted Q-value based on current policy.

After action execution and RAT assignment (lines 28–35), the algorithm evaluates the decision quality by computing individual rewards based on QoS satisfaction and handover occurrence using (4) (line 38). The experience tuple consisting of state, action, reward and next state is stored in the replay buffer for future learning (line 39). Model updates occur periodically when sufficient experiences are available, using mini-batch training to update the neural network parameters (lines 40–46). The target network is updated through soft updates to maintain training stability (lines 48–51).

The proposed DRL solution demonstrates superior adaptability compared to traditional approaches by continuously learning from network dynamics and automatically adjusting decision-making strategies based on observed outcomes. The infrastructure-centric design enables global optimization while the priority-based processing ensures that critical vehicular communications receive appropriate resource allocation, making it particularly suitable for realistic V2X communication scenarios.

5   Performance Evaluation

In this section, we present an evaluation of the performance of the proposed solution against a service-aware state-of-the-art algorithm. First, we describe the simulation setup in Sect. 5.1, and present some results in Sect. 5.2.

5.1   Simulation Settings

The simulation scenario consists of one C-V2X base station with a capacity of 100 MHz bandwidth and 500 maximum connections as well as 3 RSUs of 10MHz bandwidth and 200 maximum number of connections each. The RSUs are positioned at coordinates $(250, 0)$, $(500, 0)$ and $(750, 0)$ meters along a straight highway segment of length 1000 m, while the C-V2X station is centrally located at $(500, 0)$. The coverage radius of each DSRC mounted on a RSU is set to 400m while that of the 5G gNodeB (C-V2X) is 1000m/1km. Similarly, transmit power is set to $Q_{\text{DSRC}}^{\text{tx}} = 23$ dBm for DSRC and $Q_{\text{C-V2X}}^{\text{tx}} = 46$ dBm for C-V2X while the reliability degradation factors are $\xi_{\text{DSRC}} = 0.15$ and $\xi_{\text{C-V2X}} = 0.08$, with base reliability values $\lambda_{\text{DSRC}}^{\text{base}} = 0.99$ and $\lambda_{\text{C-V2X}}^{\text{base}} = 0.95$ while the base processing delay values are set to $D_{\text{DSRC,proc}}^{\text{base}} = 2\text{ms}$ and $D_{\text{C-V2X,proc}}^{\text{base}} = 1\text{ms}$.

Algorithm 1: Deep Reinforcement Learning based RAT Selection Algorithm for P5.

Input: $\mathcal{V}$, $\mathcal{J}$, $Q(s, a; \theta)$, $Q(s, a; \theta^-)$, ϵ, α, γ, N_j
Output: $s_{i,j}(t)$, $h_i(t)$, $\forall i \in \mathcal{V}, j \in \mathcal{J}$

1   Init θ randomly, $\theta^- = \theta$, $\mathcal{D} = \emptyset$, $handovers = 0$
2   **for** $episode\ e = 1\ to\ E$ **do**
3   Init network state and vehicle positions
4   **for** $time\ slot\ t = 1\ to\ T$ **do**
5         $\mathcal{V}_{sorted} = \text{sort}(\mathcal{V}, \text{key} = p_i)$, $handovers = 0$
6   **for** $i \in \mathcal{V}_{sorted}$ **do**
7           $prev\_assign = s_{i,j}(t - 1)$
8   Compute state $s_i(t) =$
$$[(x_i^{\text{norm}}(t), y_i^{\text{norm}}(t)), v_i^{\text{norm}}(t), \tau_i^{\text{norm}}(t), p_i^{\text{norm}}(t), d_i^{\text{norm}}(t), D_i^{\text{max,norm}}(t), \nu_i^{\text{min,norm}}(t),$$
$$\lambda_i^{\text{min,norm}}(t), N_{\text{DSRC}}^{\text{norm}}(t), N_{\text{C-V2X}}^{\text{norm}}(t), d_i^{\text{norm}}(t) D_{i,\text{DSRC}}^{\text{norm}}(t),$$
$$D_{i,\text{C-V2X}}^{\text{norm}}(t), \lambda_{i,\text{DSRC}}^{\text{norm}}(t), \lambda_{i,\text{C-V2X}}^{\text{norm}}(t), \nu_{i,\text{DSRC}}^{\text{norm}}(t), \nu_{i,\text{C-V2X}}^{\text{norm}}(t)]$$

9           $\mathcal{A}_i^{\text{valid}} = \emptyset$
10   **for** $j \in \mathcal{J}$ **do**
11   **if** $(x_i(t), y_i(t)) \in C_j \wedge N_j(t) < N_j$ **then**
12             $\mathcal{A}_i^{\text{valid}} = \mathcal{A}_i^{\text{valid}} \cup \{j\}$
13   **end**
14   **end**
15   **if** $\mathcal{A}_i^{valid} = \emptyset$ **then**
16           $s_{i,j}(t) = 0, \forall j \in \mathcal{J}$; **continue**
17   **end**
18   **if** $random() < \epsilon$ **then**
19           $a_i(t) = \text{random\_choice}(\mathcal{A}_i^{valid})$
20   **else**
21           $q\_vals = Q(s_i(t); \theta)$, $masked\_q = -\infty \cdot \mathbf{1}$ // otherwise selects optimal action based on Q-values for state $s_i(t)$ with policy θ. The mask ensures infeasible RATs (e.g., beyond C_j) are excluded
23   **for** $a \in \mathcal{A}_i^{valid}$ **do**
24            $masked\_q[a] = q\_vals[a]$
25   **end**
26           $a_i(t) = \arg\max masked\_q$
27   **end**
28          $j^* = a_i(t) + 1$
29          $s_{i,j^*}(t) = 1$, $s_{i,k}(t) = 0, \forall k \neq j^*$
30   **if** $prev\_assign \neq NULL \wedge prev\_assign \neq j^*$ **then**
31           $h_i(t) = 1$, $handovers = handovers + 1$
32   **else**
33           $h_i(t) = 0$
34   **end**
35          $N_{j^*}(t) = N_{j^*}(t) + 1$
36   Compute $D_{i,j^*}(t)$, $\lambda_{i,j^*}(t)$, $\nu_{i,j^*}(t)$, check against (7), (8) and (9)   // where $D_{i,j^*}(t)$, $\lambda_{i,j^*}(t)$ and $\nu_{i,j^*}(t)$ are defined as (2), (1) and (3)

38   Compute the reward ($r_i(t)$) based on (4)
39   Compute $s_i(t + 1)$; Store $(s_i(t), a_i(t), r_i(t), s_i(t + 1), done) \rightarrow \mathcal{D}$
40   **if** $|\mathcal{D}| \geq batch\_size \wedge steps\_done \bmod update\_every = 0$ **then**
41   Sample mini-batch from $\mathcal{D}$
42           $m = r + \Gamma \max_{a'} Q(s', a'; \theta^-)$
43   Minimize $L = \text{MSE}(Q(s, a; \theta), y)$ and update θ
44   Apply gradient clipping with max norm 1.0
45   **end**
46          $\epsilon = \max(\epsilon_{min}, \epsilon \times \epsilon_{decay})$
47   **end**
48   **if** $steps\_done \bmod target\_update = 0$ **then**
49          $\theta^- \leftarrow \tau\theta + (1 - \tau)\theta^-$
50   **end**
51         $steps\_done = steps\_done + 1$
52   **end**
53   **end**

Similarly, we consider $V \in 100, 200, 300, 400, 500$ vehicles of types emergency, public transport, commercial and private comprising 5%, 10%, 20% and 65% respectively, moving bidirectionally along the highway with velocities $v \in [60, 120]$ km/h and random velocity perturbations ($\pm 5\%$ each time slot).

These vehicles request services of type safety-critical, traffic-efficiency and infotainment with diverse quality of service requirements. The latency requirements for the safety traffic efficiency and infotainment services is set to 100, 200 and 300 ms, respectively, while their reliability 0.99, 0.95 and 0.90 and their data rate to 1, 2 and 5Mbps, respectively. Furthermore, we set the priorities for the different types of vehicles to $1, 2, 3, 4$ and that of the services (safety-critical, traffic-efficiency, infotainment) to $1, 2, 3$ in that order. Thus at time slot t, the priority of the vehicle i $(p_i(t))$ is set to the sum of its type and service class priorities.

The simulation runs for $T = 40$ time slots with duration $\Delta t = 100$ ms each. RAT selection is triggered every $\Delta d = 25$ m (25 m) of vehicle movement. The objective function weights are set to $\alpha = 0.5$ for delay, $\beta = 0.3$ for reliability and $\gamma = 0.2$ for handover. The DQN was implemented using the PyTorch framework. The network architecture is a multi-layer perceptron (MLP) consisting of two hidden layers with 256 and 128 neurons, respectively, with rectified linear unit (ReLU) activation functions and dropout layers ($\Psi = 0.2$) for regularization. The agent was trained online using an experience replay buffer and the Adam optimizer. The simulation settings used are similar to those in $[3, 4, 7]$ are summarized in Table 1 (Table 2).

5.2   Comparison to State-of-the-Art (SoA)

In this subsection, we evaluate the performance of the proposed solution against the state-of-the-art (SoA) solution [11]. The SoA solution selects the DSRC RAT for safety-critical services, C-V2X for infotainment and chooses the RAT that offers the highest reliability for traffic-efficiency services. In addition to the proposed DRL solution we refer to as DRL-DRH that aims to optimize delay, reliability and handovers, we also solve our problem including delay, reliability and handovers optimization using the Gurobi optimization solver, we denote the obtained solution by PP-EXACT. We evaluate the proposed DRL solution and its exact solution based on the objective defined in (4) against the SoA. The results presented are averages taken over 150 simulation runs.

Figure 2 shows the total end to end delay incurred by vehicles against the number of vehicles V. It shows that the proposed DRL and its exact solution outperform the SoA solution, incurring the least delay. This is likely because while the SoA selects the DSRC RAT for vehicles with traffic-efficiency services to presumably minimize their delay, it does not consider current network conditions except for traffic-efficiency services for which it determines the best RAT based on current reliability conditions. On the contrary, the proposed DRL solution jointly considers delay, reliability and number of handovers in its decision making.

The results in Fig. 3 shows the average reliability achieved by all vehicles. It can be observed that the proposed solution and its exact solution achieve higher reliability compared to the SoA solution. This improved performance by the proposed solution is due to their attempt to jointly minimize delay and number

Table 1. Simulation Parameters

Parameter	Value(s)
Highway length	1000 m
Number of RSUs	3
RSU coverage radius	400 m
C-V2X coverage radius	1000 m
C-V2X position	Center (500m, 0)
RSU positions	((250m, 500m, 750m), 0)
Max DSRC connections per RSU	200
Max C-V2X connections	500
DSRC bandwidth	10 MHz
C-V2X bandwidth	100 MHz
DSRC transmit power	23 dBm
C-V2X transmit power	46 dBm
DSRC degradation factor	0.15
C-V2X degradation factor	0.08
Base DSRC reliability	0.99
Base C-V2X reliability	0.95
Vehicle speed range	60–120 km/h
Time slots	40
Time slot duration	100 ms
Trigger distance	25 m
Number of vehicles tested	50, 75, 100, 125, 150
Delay weight (α)	0.5
Reliability weight (β)	0.3
Handover weight (γ)	0.2
Safety-critical latency requirement	100 ms
Traffic-efficiency latency requirement	200 ms
Infotainment latency requirement	500 ms
Safety-critical reliability requirement	0.99
Traffic-efficiency reliability requirement	0.95
Infotainment reliability requirement	0.90
Safety-critical data rate requirement	1 Mbps
Traffic-efficiency data rate requirement	2 Mbps
Infotainment data rate requirement	5 Mbps
$D_{\text{DSRC,proc}}^{\text{base}}$	2 ms
$D_{\text{C-V2X,proc}}^{\text{base}}$	1 ms

Table 2. DRL specific Parameters.

Parameter	Value(s)
DRL hidden layer Size	128
DRL learning rate (η)	0.001
DRL batch size	32
DRL buffer size	10,000
DRL discount factor (Γ)	0.99
Final exploration rate (ϵ_{end})	0.05
ϵ_{decay}	0.98
ϵ_{min}	0.005
Target network update (τ)	0.005
Training update frequency	Every 4 steps

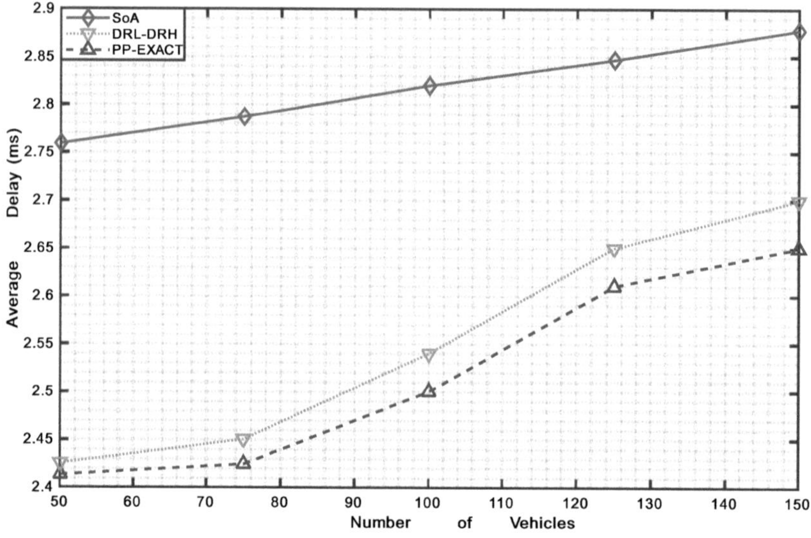

Fig. 2. Total vehicle delay.

of handovers while maximizing reliability as opposed to the SoA solution that only considers the reliability of one type of service in its decision making.

Figure 4 captures the total number of handovers performed by all vehicles. The result shows that the SoA incurs the highest number of handovers which is due to the proposed solutions jointly optimizing handover, delay and reliability consideration as opposed to the SoA solution that associates vehicles based on service class, increasing the chances of handovers from one decision point to another due to the changing service class of vehicles.

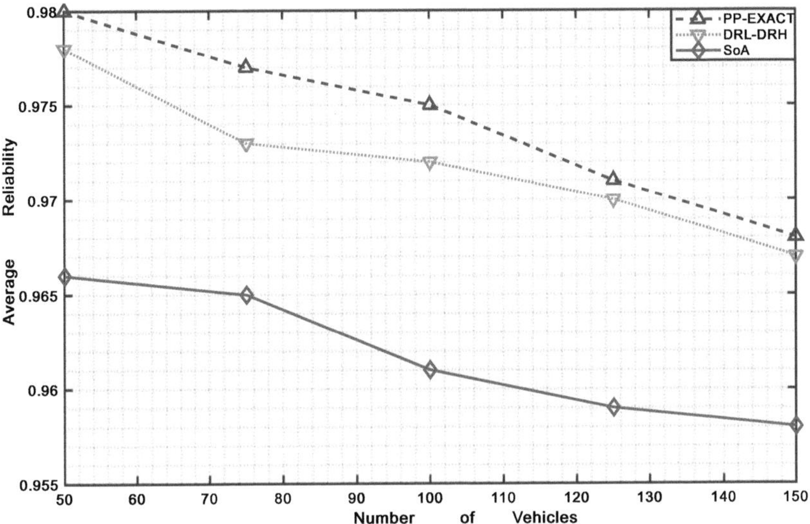

Fig. 3. Achieved reliability.

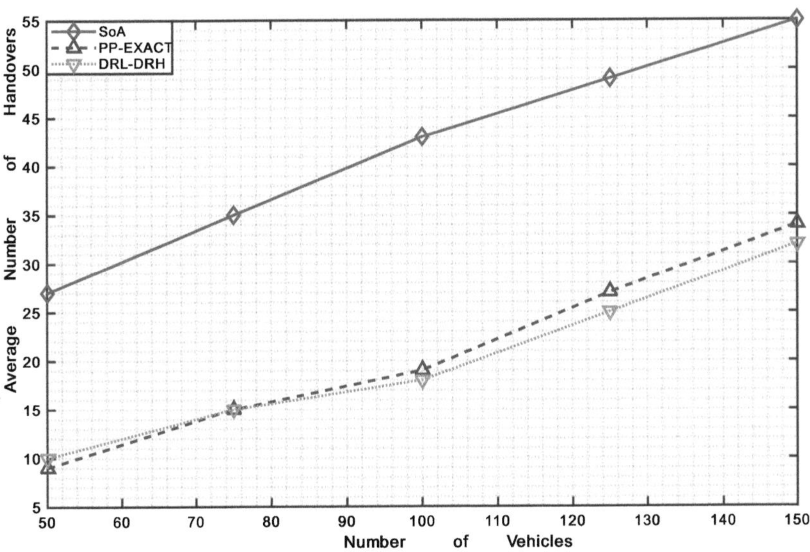

Fig. 4. Comparison in terms of number of handovers.

5.3   Impact of Reward Function Weighting

In this subsection, we evaluate the performance of the proposed solution by solving our problem using three DRL variants of the proposed DRL-DRH solution. The first variant DRL-DR unlike the DRL-DRH, considers only the delay and reliability by setting the delay, reliability and handover weights to 0.5, 0.5 and

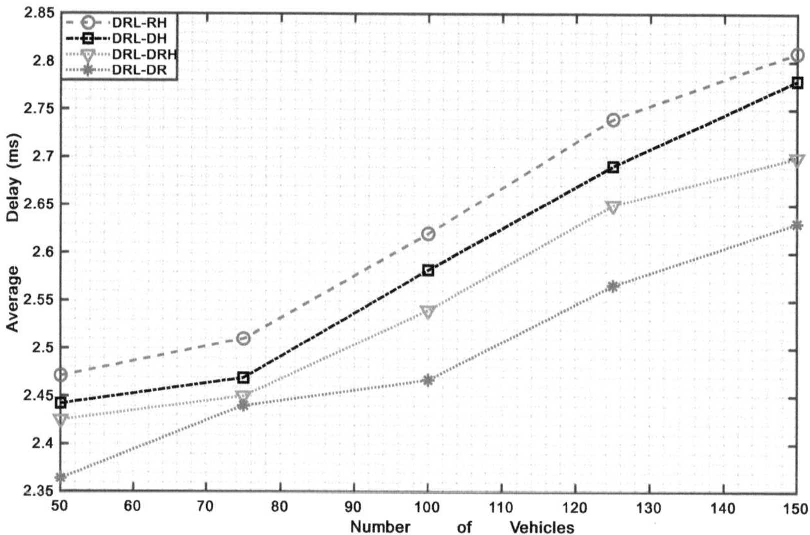

Fig. 5. Total vehicle delay.

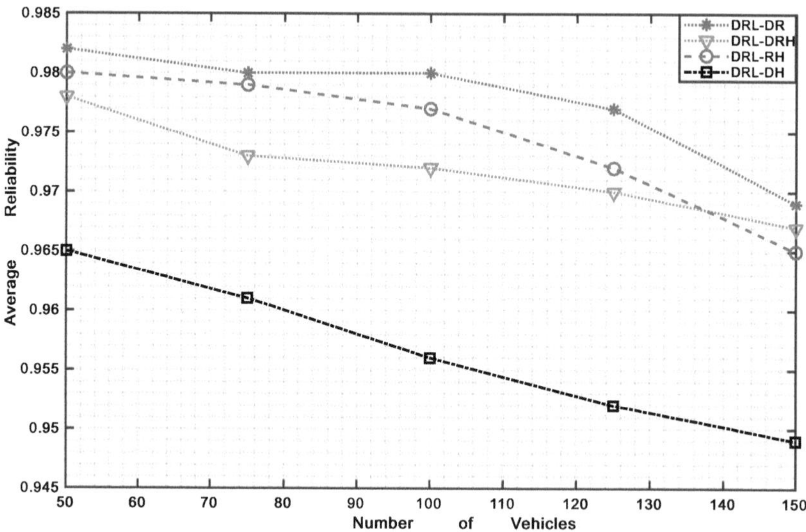

Fig. 6. Achieved reliability.

0 respectively. The second variant DRL-DH, considers only the delay and handovers by setting the delay, reliability and handover weights to 0.5, 0 and 0.5 respectively, while the third variant DRL-RH considers only the reliability and handovers by setting the delay, reliability and handover weights to 0, 0.5 and 0.5 respectively. Thus, we evaluate the proposed DRL solution based on the objec-

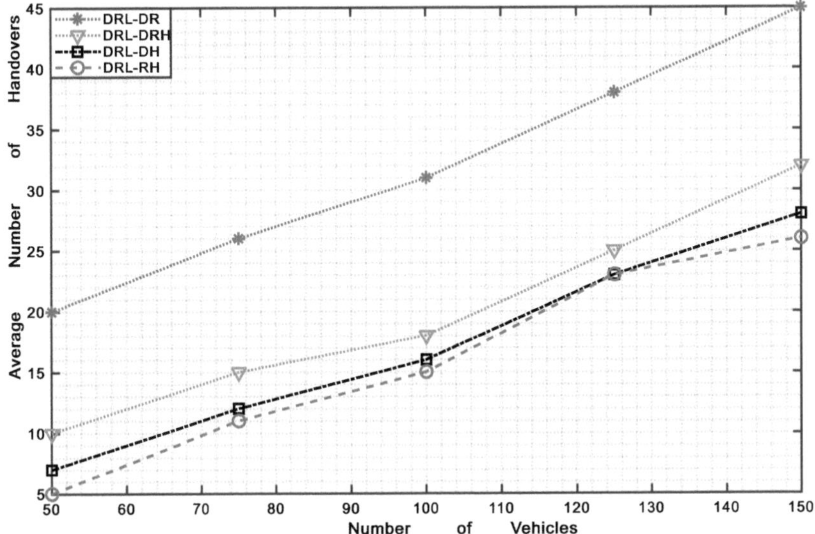

Fig. 7. Comparison in terms of number of handovers.

tive defined in (4) and its three variants. We present the average of the results obtained over 150 simulation runs.

Figure 5 shows the total end-to-end delay incurred by vehicles against the number of vehicles V. We can observe that the variant of the proposed DRL solution (DRL-DR) achieves the minimum delay closely followed by the DRL-DH variants. This is due to the DRL-DR solution intelligently selecting RATs based on delay and reliability considerations unlike the proposed DRL-DRH solution that attempts to jointly optimize all three objectives. The DRL-RH variant incurs the highest delay among the proposed solutions, followed by the DRL-DH. This is because while it is also an intelligent solution, it assigns a weight of 0 to the delay component of the objective as opposed to the other variants that assign non zero weights to the delay component.

The results in Fig. 6 shows the average reliability achieved by all vehicles. It can be observed that the DRL-DR variant achieves the highest reliability with the DRL-DH variant that selects RATs based on delay and handover consideration without accounting for reliability achieving the lowest reliability among the compared variants. This performance by the DRL variant (DRL-DR) is because by considering only two of the three aspects of the objective, it is able to assign higher weights to the reliability component thereby leading to improved reliability performance.

Figure 7 captures the total number of handovers performed by all vehicles. It can be observed that the DRL-DR variant incurs the highest number of handovers with the DRL-RH incurring the least number of handovers followed by the DRL-DH. This performance by the DRL variants (DRL-RH and DRL-DH) is because by considering only two of the three aspects of the objective, they are able to assign higher weights to the handover component thereby leading to improved performance in this regard. In comparison, the DRL-DR and DRL-DRH that assign 0 and 0.2 weights to the handover components of the objective, respectively.

6 Conclusion

In this work, we proposed a DRL-based RAT selection algorithm to jointly minimize delay and number of handovers while improving reliability. Our solution addresses the critical challenge of optimal radio access technology selection in multi-RAT vehicle-to-infrastructure communication networks, presenting a comprehensive framework that significantly advances the state-of-the-art in vehicular network optimization. We solved the problem using two distinct approaches: an exact optimization method, and a deep reinforcement learning solution. Each of these approach consistently outperforms existing state-of-the-art method in terms of delay, reliability and number of handovers. In the future, we will consider other types of vehicular communications and perform more extensive simulations.

Acknowledgment. This work is funded by the Petroleum Technology Development Fund (PTDF), Nigeria, the EU HORIZON MSCA-SE TRACE-V2X project (Grant No. 101131204) and the CY Initiative (grant "Investissements d'Avenir" ANR-16-IDEX-0008).

References

1. Jacob, R., Franchi, N., Fettweis, G.: Hybrid V2X communications: multi-RAT as enabler for connected autonomous driving. In: IEEE 29th Annual International Symposium on Personal, Indoor and Mobile Radio Communications (PIMRC). Bologna, Italy, vol. 2018, pp. 1370–1376 (2018). https://doi.org/10.1109/PIMRC.2018.8580953
2. Caso, G., Alay, Ö., Ferrante, G.C., Nardis, L.D., Benedetto, M.-G.D., Brunstrom, A.: User-centric radio access technology selection: a survey of game theory models and multi-agent learning algorithms. IEEE Access **9**, 84417–84464 (2021). https://doi.org/10.1109/ACCESS.2021.3087410
3. Khalid, I., Maglogiannis, V., Naudts, D., Shahid, A., Moerman, I.: Optimizing hybrid V2X communication: an intelligent technology selection algorithm using 5G, CV2X PC5 and DSRC. Future Internet. **16**, 107 (2024). https://doi.org/10.3390/fi16040107
4. Altahrawi, M., Abdullah, N.F., Nordin, R.: Service-oriented LSTM multi-criteria RAT selection scheme for vehicle-to-infrastructure communication. IEEE Access **10**, 110261–110284 (2022). https://doi.org/10.1109/ACCESS.2022.3214852
5. Yacheur, B.Y., Ahmed, T., Mosbah, M.: DRL-Based RAT selection in a hybrid vehicular communication network. In: IEEE 97th Vehicular Technology Conference (VTC2023-Spring). Florence, Italy, vol. 2023, pp. 1–5 (2023). https://doi.org/10.1109/VTC2023-Spring57618.2023.10199400

6. Bréhon–Grataloup, L., Kacimi, R., Beylot, A.-L.: Multi-RAT-enabled edge computing for vehicle-to-everything architectures. Ad Hoc Networks, vol. 154 (2024)
7. Waqas, K., Nadia, N.Q., Omer, C., Sadiq, A., Heejung, Y., Muhammad, Z.U.H.: Adaptive network selection for enhanced connectivity in vehicular-to-everything (v2x) communications. SSRN (2024). https://doi.org/10.2139/ssrn.5123284
8. Sepulcre, M., Gozalvez, J.: Heterogeneous V2V communications in multi-link and multi-RAT vehicular networks. IEEE Trans. Mobile Comput. **20**(1), 162–173 (2021). https://doi.org/10.1109/TMC.2019.2939803
9. Mir, Z.H., Toutouh, J., Filali, F., Alba, E.: QoS-Aware Radio Access Technology (RAT) Selection in Hybrid Vehicular Networks. In: Kassab, M., Berbineau, M., Vinel, A., Jonsson, M., Garcia, F., Soler, J. (eds.) Communication Technologies for Vehicles. Nets4Cars/Nets4Trains/Nets4Aircraft 2015. Lecture Notes in Computer Science(), vol 9066. Springer, Cham (2015)
10. Ndashimye, E., Sarkar, N.I., Ray, S.K.: A novel network selection mechanism for vehicle-to-infrastructure communication. In: IEEE 14th International Conference on Dependable, Autonomic and Secure Computing, 14th International Conference on Pervasive Intelligence and Computing, 2nd International Conference on Big Data Intelligence and Computing and Cyber Science and Technology Congress(DASC/PiCom/DataCom/CyberSciTech). Auckland, New Zealand, vol. 2016, pp. 483–488 (2016). https://doi.org/10.1109/DASC-PICom-DataCom-CyberSciTec.2016.94
11. Shen, X., Li, J., Chen, L., Chen, J., He, S.: Heterogeneous LTE/dsrc approach to support real-time vehicular communications. In: 2018 10th International Conference on Advanced Infocomm Technology (ICAIT), Stockholm, Sweden, pp. 122–127 (2018). https://doi.org/10.1109/ICAIT.2018.8686612

Author Index